UNCROWNED EMPEROR

ALSO BY GORDON BROOK-SHEPHERD

Russia's Danubian Empire

The Austrian Odyssey

Where the Lion Trod (India)

The Anschluss

Dollfuss

Eagle and Unicorn

The Last Habsburg

Between Two Flags

Uncle of Europe (Edward VII)

The Storm Petrels (Soviet pre-war defectors)

November 1918

Victims at Sarajevo

Royal Sunset

The Storm Birds (Soviet post-war defectors)

The Last Empress

The Austrians

Iron Maze (Secret Service and the Bolsheviks)

Uncrowned Emperor

The Life and Times of Otto von Habsburg

Gordon Brook-Shepherd

Hambledon and London

London and New York

Hambledon and London

102 Gloucester Avenue
London, NW1 8HX

175 Fifth Avenue
New York 10010

First Published 2003

ISBN 1 85285 439 1

A description of this book is available from the
British Library and from the Library of Congress.

Typeset by Carnegie Publishing Ltd, Lancaster
and printed in Great Britain by The Bath Press.

Distributed in the United States and Canada exclusively
by Palgrave Macmillan, a division of St Martin's Press.

Contents

Illustrations

Introduction

The life of Otto von Habsburg has encompassed all the dramas of twentieth-century European history. At its beginning was the collapse of the Austro-Hungarian Empire, which his family had reigned over for more than six hundred years and of which he was the last Crown Prince. The old continental order disintegrated around him, a process that he witnessed as a perceptive young child. Then, after the peacemakers of Versailles had cobbled together composite states out of the eleven nations of the former Habsburg Monarchy, these fragile structures were swept away into two new empires, both of tyranny: first, that of Hitler, followed by that of Stalin. At last, towards the end of the century, came the implosion of Soviet Communism – and the emergence of new democracies throughout Central Europe and their gradual fusion within the European Union. The Danube linked East and West again, as it had done in his childhood.

Otto von Habsburg has played a unique role in all this. A political animal by instinct, and a great persuader by nature, he always stood in the wings of great events. Sometimes – as in the long struggle in exile to save his Austrian homeland from Hitler's clutches – he occupied centre stage. Finally, after his return to post-war Europe, he was able to serve for twenty years on a platform which seemed predestined for him: the child who had started life as the heir to a multinational European empire ended it as the senior member of a multinational European Parliament. He became its only deputy to have been born before the First World War.

A personal note needs to be injected here, since it is integral to the whole of this book. I have known Archduke Otto for more than forty years and a close friendship has developed between us. This was largely based on common endeavour. Throughout the Cold War (and the Second World War which preceded it) we pursued, in different spheres and in different ways, the same broad aims. He had often told me that he would never write his own account of this. When, however, three years ago, his public political life came to en end with the laying down of his parliamentary mandate, the moment had clearly arrived for someone to tell the story of his life and times. He gladly agreed that I should take this on and promised full help from his own reminiscences, plus whatever could be extracted from his family archives – which, he warned, were in 'a very disorderly state'.

That promise has been amply fulfilled. When I returned for one last time to that world of double- and single-headed Austrian eagles, I imagined that I would find little that was unfamiliar. Seven of my seventeen books had already been devoted to them, prompting one leading critic to declare, rather to my alarm, that I 'knew more about Austria and the Austrians than any living Englishman'. I soon realised, from the help my subject was giving me, that I had much more to learn.

Otto von Habsburg has a memory that is as remarkable as the long life it records. He is not given to exaggeration (though others have exaggerated on his behalf) and it was only occasionally, on checking over and amplifying his written reminiscences, that queries emerged. These were easily put right from the mass of other related material I had at my disposal. The end result was that the familiar tale of Europe's fate down the twentieth century could be told with many new insights and from a fresh perspective.

In his case, we are talking about almost the whole of that century. Grained and jerky newsreel pictures of a procession through the streets of Vienna on 30 November 1916 preserve his public debut on the stage. It was at the funeral cortège of that dynastic demigod, the Emperor Franz Josef. Otto, four years and ten days old, walks – a tiny figure in a white tunic – directly behind the huge black hearse, the new Crown Prince of the Habsburg Empire. He is flanked by his young parents, the Bourbon princess Zita, and Karl, the ill-fated last ruler of the Dual Monarchy.

Otto has dim recollections of that numbing day. His recollections are much sharper of the day, a month later, when he attended his father's sumptuous coronation in Budapest as Hungary's king. They are sharper still of the autumn of 1918 when, in the aftermath of military defeat, the Habsburg Empire dissolved into fragments around them. He and his siblings were rescued from the short-lived revolution in Budapest barely in time to join their parents in a night-time flight from their abandoned Vienna palace of Schönbrunn.

He has vivid, if incongruously pleasant, memories of the first stage of their exile: four months spent at his father's shooting lodge in Eckartsau, still on Austrian soil. Here they were eventually threatened again by revolutionary marauders – this time Austrians – and were only rescued and whisked off into Switzerland by a British officer, Lieutenant-Colonel Edward Lisle Strutt, who remained, then and afterwards, a heroic figure in the child's memory. (The Englishman had been dispatched on one of the most extraordinary missions of those post-war months: as personal envoy of King George V, he had been charged with securing the safety of an ex-enemy ruler and his family as a gesture of solidarity between fellow monarchs.)

The years of childhood exile abroad were marked for him above all by the premature death of his father at their second refuge, the Portuguese island of Madeira. On that unforgettable 1 April 1922, Otto became 'His Majesty' to the tiny and impoverished court in exile and to what remained of its royalist followers back in the homelands. He recalls what amounted to the dead man's political testament, which had been passed on to his son on their walks around the island. He was to follow its central theme of reconciliation throughout his life.

It was at the somewhat gloomy moated castle of Hams in Belgium – their fourth country of asylum – that Otto, now aged eighteen, took over the formal headship of the dynasty. The Nazis were soon to seize power in Germany and the following years can be truly described in terms of Habsburg versus Hitler as regards the fate of his homeland. Inevitably, Otto became a key player in the struggle. His efforts to mobilise resistance culminated in an offer to fly to Vienna, while there still seemed to be some Austrian backbone left to stiffen. He proposed to take over the reins of government from the nerveless hands of its last Chancellor, the professed monarchist Kurt Schuschnigg. (The offer was turned down, perhaps just as well for the young Pretender: only a month later, Hitler was to walk in unopposed.)

Family archives have been drawn upon for this Anschluss crisis, but Otto's own vivid reminiscences are the main source of fresh material. This also applies to the events that followed: the family's adventurous flight to the south after the German invasion of Belgium (with Otto now already high on the Gestapo's wanted list). There were hazardous stopovers at Bordeaux and Lisbon until, finally, thanks to the powerful hand of President Roosevelt, they were whisked off in flying-boats to the safe heaven of America. It was here that Otto, together with three of his four brothers, spent most of the war. A remarkable personal friendship that developed with the President enabled him not only to keep in secret touch with anti-Hitler elements in Central Europe but also to attempt a last-ditch bid to drag Hungary away from Hitler's grip.

He returned to a post-war Europe where that German grip along the Danube Basin had been replaced by a Russian one. Hungary was now unreachable, and was to remain so until the implosion of the Soviet Empire. Austria, however, had re-emerged from the Third Reich, felicitously cate-gorised among the liberated nations, albeit under four-power Allied control. This phoenix of a Second Republic, however, had reaffirmed all the anti-Habsburg decrees of the First, so when Otto embarked on a highly political foray into the French-occupied Tyrol, the Allies had no choice but to expel him.

Now came the first really low point in his life. He had no legal passport, no job, no funds, no home and no powerful protector. The next five years changed all that. He buckled down to an exhausting career as author, newspaper columnist and lecturer. This brought in so much money, particularly through his American tours, that, by 1950, he had paid off, to the last cent, all his wartime debts and had a solid enough income to think about starting a family of his own. A chance meeting in a Munich care centre for Hungarian refugees with a German princess – herself a refugee – provided the ideal partner in terms of looks, age, lineage and temperament. The marriage, which produced five daughters (all in succession!) and, finally, two sons, was to celebrate a radiant golden anniversary in the next millennium.

Otto's election to the Strasbourg Parliament came about also partly by lucky chance, however predestined this appeared. The Parliament's splendid archive service meant that I was able to study any item I chose among the hundreds of the speeches, written questions, motions and special reports he had made down the years. They displayed an enormous variety of interests; proved, in some cases, prophetic (such as warnings about the catastrophe potential of international terrorism); were usually succinct and to the point; and, despite his underlying short fuse, were almost always conducted in the most courteous of parliamentary styles. (An exception came when that Protestant fireball from Northern Ireland, Dr Ian Paisley, brandished some anti-Catholic paper to the House. That was too much for the son of an Apostolic Majesty and Otto rushed over to force down the doctor's arm.)

He took a leading role in the promotion of a European passport. More prosaically he launched a dogged campaign to persuade members to work the five-day week for which they were paid, instead of melting away on Thursday evenings. But his greatest achievement was in the early years when he successfully fought what he called the Yalta Syndrome of accepting as a *fait accompli* the division of Europe into East and West. The interests of his Central European homelands were always uppermost in his mind.

Valuable though all this official documentation has been, it would have remained lifeless without his own commentaries and recollections. I had had many discussions with him over the years: in Strasbourg, Vienna, Brussels, London and, above all, in the Kaiservilla at Pöcking, his Bavarian home for nearly half a century, where I saw his children grow up and go their separate ways. For the present work, he has added to all this background more than 20,000 words of detailed replies to my scores of questions, ranging from his childhood down to today.

He is, by his own cheerful admission, a political workaholic, and seems

contented that politics has absorbed his whole life. There has been a price
to pay. In family terms, his ceaseless travels meant that he had less time as
a father to devote to his young children (his wife Regina doing a heroic
job of running the home in his absence). In personal terms, it has meant
that he has been unable to steep himself enough in that European culture
which he regards as the continent's greatest treasure. He regrets in particular
missing out on the study and enjoyment of great music.

Of necessity, it has been a life that comes up distinctly short on hobbies
or sports. (Shooting is an exception: one wall of his large first-floor study
is lined with roedeer and chamois heads, some of them prize specimens).
Nor is he a wine connoisseur or a gourmet. None of this has left him
colourless, let alone charmless; quite the reverse. It has simply left him with
fewer things, outside the absorbing realm of world affairs, about which he
can readily communicate. Even his sense of humour is politically aligned.
One of his best *bon mots*, for example, was to ask for a 'Kir Republican'
when offered a 'Kir Royale'. I have never heard him tell an ordinary joke,
just for the fun of it. He has a keen wit but it tends to be pointed, rather
than genial.

What follows is, therefore, the story of that rare animal, a completely
political royal more interested in the contemporary international stage than
in his own ancient lineage (though the latter inevitably comes into play).
Obviously, his own massive contribution to the story has far overshadowed
other help. Much of that has come from his youngest daughter, Walburga.
She not only tackled those 'very disorderly' family papers on my behalf,
but also provided a wealth of information on related matters such as the
Pan-European Movement. She has long been the guiding administrative
force of this infinitely active body, of which her father has served as the
equally active President for nearly thirty years.

My special thanks are due to an old Austrian friend, the very knowled-
geable Martin Pfunder. He has devilled away with speed and energy at any
odd query I threw at him. These have ranged from obscure questions about
genealogy and the number of motor vehicles in Franz Josef's Vienna to the
down-to-earth problems of contemporary Austrian politics. He has saved
me from at least one major chronological error.

In London, my special thanks go to Adam Ferguson, a close colleague
of Otto von Habsburg as a fellow right-wing MEP at Strasbourg. He has
offered many perceptive thoughts about our mutual friend – both as a
person and as a politician. I am also grateful to Avis Furness, Librarian of
the European Union's UK office, who retrieved and placed at my disposal
everything on 'Dr Habsburg's' record. I must also thank an old family
friend, Count Mark Pejacesevic, for translating for me useful material from

Hungarian, the only language in the very varied research material which totally defeats me.

I must again express my gratitude to Susan Bunker, my long-term secretary and helper, who has transposed yet another of my increasingly illegible manuscripts into typed text for the publisher. Finally, my thanks to my editor and publisher, Martin Sheppard. He has combined constructive suggestions with a meticulous line-by-line scrutiny of the content. These are qualities which are hard to find in the present-day publishing world. No scribe could ask for better all-round support.

London SW1   Paziols, Languedoc

A Shaky Heritage

The Austro-Hungarian Empire into which Otto von Habsburg was born – and which his ill-fated father was soon to rule – sensed that its days were numbered. Yet nobody, not even the few wiser heads at court, had any idea how those numbers were to be counted. Least of all could they imagine the terrible way in which the last ones would eventually be called. So, though foreboding was there, fear could be stifled, smothered under various devices to escape from reality into illusion. Indeed, some of those intellectuals – who, as a group, had led the charge for upheaval and change – could look back on the Habsburg Monarchy in later years as a fortress of stability and peace.

A good example is Robert Musil, not only the foremost of Austrian novelists but one of the century's greatest in any language. At the beginning of the 1930s, he had started to work in Switzerland on his massive masterpiece *Der Mann ohne Eigenschaften*, directly translatable as *The Man without Qualities*. He had re-christened the vanished Monarchy 'Kakania', a play on the various ways in which the old imperial and royal initials 'K und K' (*Kaiserlich und Königlich*) could be combined or separated according to which aspect of that multinational realm was being labelled. The name may sound irreverent; but there is no lack of affection and respect in the way Musil recalls his great homeland of eleven nations which was now shrivelled up into the tiny body of an Austrian republic. Indeed, his imaginary Kakania, which amounts to a reincarnation in memory of the real empire, is presented as the model for civilised life throughout the western world:

> There was speed of course; but not too much speed ... Cars drove along its roads, but not too many cars! [1] The conquest of the air had begun here too; but not too intensively. Now and then, a ship was sent off to South America or the Far East, but not too often. Here, one was in the centre of Europe, at the focal point of the world's old axes; the words 'colony' and 'overseas' had the ring of something as yet utterly untried and remote. There was some display of luxury but it was not, of course, oversophisticated as that of the French. One went in for sport; but not in madly Anglo-Saxon fashion. One spent enormous sums on the army, but only just enough to assure one of remaining the second weakest of the great powers ...[2]

His backward glance at the Monarchy's domestic political muddle is even more acute:

> There was a Parliament which made such vigorous use of its liberty that it was usually kept shut; but there was also an emergency powers act by means of which it was possible to manage without Parliament, and every time that everyone was just beginning to rejoice in absolutism, the Crown decreed that there must now again be a return to government. Many things happened in this state, and among them those national struggles that justifiably aroused Europe's curiosity and are today completely misunderstood. They were so violent that, several times a year, they caused the machinery of state to jam and come to a dead stop. But, between whiles, in the breathing spaces between government and government, everyone got on excellently with everyone else and behaved as though nothing had ever been the matter. Nor had anything real *ever* been the matter ...[3]

Other non-polemical writers took much the same kindly view in retrospect. Stefan Zweig, the Austrian novelist who is far better known than Musil (though only reaching in stature up to his shoulder), even looked back on the early years of the twentieth century as, above all, the golden age of security, and the Monarchy as 'the foremost guarantor for this durability'. Despite the underlying queasiness, such was indeed the popular mood at that time. 'Muddling through' (the nearest one can get to rendering *fortwürsteln*) had always been an Austrian speciality. So why could not the Habsburg dynasty, which had often operated on that same principle during its six and a half centuries of rule, carry on a bit longer? Why not, indeed, for ever?

This feeling that, though time could not be conquered, one might get along for quite a while by ignoring it, was, of course, centred on the supreme sovereign, Franz Josef. At the turn of the century, he had already occupied the throne for nearly fifty-two years, longer than the average life-span of his medley of forty-nine million subjects. It was on the steps of that throne that their nationalist squabbles had to stop and be soothed by compromise or concession. When Musil maintained that, in all the mayhem, nothing real ever had mattered, he was right in this one sense: the vast majority of those squabblers sought only more status and privilege within the empire. Until its end was near, the leading malcontents, with one exception, never thought of a life outside it.[4] Even the Hungarians, who had achieved full domestic autonomy in 1867, realised that they now had the best of both worlds: home rule through their own Parliament in Budapest, combined with equal partnership in what was henceforth the Austro-Hungarian Dual Monarchy. They were thus both citizens of a great European power with all the prestige and protection which that carried, yet virtually free to run their own affairs, as though Hungary were a truly independent state.[5] Franz Josef had become the metronomic heartbeat of an empire united only through his crown. No one dared to think what would happen when that heartbeat stopped, so they pushed the idea from their mind.

Announcements which greeted the dawn of the twentieth century displayed him sharply enough in this key role. The lists of New Year appointments and honours bestowed among his subjects were typical of any monarchy. But the batch of imperial decrees (as opposed to parliamentary decisions) published on New Year's Day showed that this was an empire whose sovereign ruled as well as reigned. One stood out to demonstrate that this rule could be well-nigh absolute. As usual, the Austrian and Hungarian finance delegates had been wrangling throughout the last months of the old century as to how the budget costs of the empire as a whole should be divided between its two halves. As so often, they had failed to agree. So, on 1 January 1900, the Emperor, using his reserve powers of supreme personal authority, simply announced their decision for them: during the first six months of 1900, he decreed in an order to his Cabinet, the Austrian half would pay two-thirds of the combined budget, leaving the Hungarian kingdom to pay the remaining one-third. And that, for the time being, was that.

The New Year's Day was significant for something else: the contrast between the styles in which Franz Josef and his German counterpart, Wilhelm II, spent it. At his Hofburg Palace that morning, the Austrian Emperor first received the season's loyal good wishes from his personal staff and afterwards welcomed all the Habsburg archdukes who happened to be in Vienna for a small family luncheon. He then set off for three days' hunting accompanied by one of them, the archduke Franz Salvator. The new century had been greeted quietly and *en famille* with no public pronouncements and no elaborate receptions. In Berlin, however, the forty-year-old Wilhelm saw to it that the elite of his brash and bustling empire assembled in his palace to do him homage as the century turned. The gathering included the entire government, headed by the then Chancellor, Prince Hohenlohe; all the Knights of the Order of the Black Eagle; all the Royal Princes; and all the heads of Foreign Missions, who each brought their Military Attachés along with them. The Emperor had also summoned all his leading generals and admirals, as well as the commanders of the regiments stationed in the capital. After a midnight church service, the assembly moved to the famous White Salon of the Imperial Palace to offer their ruler New Year congratulations.

That this ruler was also their Supreme War Lord (a title in which he revelled, though time was to show that he was never up to the role) was reflected in a thunderously bombastic speech he had delivered earlier that day to the officers of his Berlin garrison. He praised the rebirth of a powerful and dedicated German army under his grandfather, Wilhelm I, and lauded the great victories it had won in the century that had just ended. He pledged that he would now carry out the same work of expansion with the German navy, to bring it level with his military forces. This would ensure that in the new century the empire 'would be able to secure for itself that place in the world which it had not yet reached'. The ending, as so often with this imperial poseur, was theatrical: 'If one wants to achieve something in this world, the pen will not do it alone unless it is backed up by the force of the sword.'[6]

The creation of a great German fleet and the extension of German power overseas was to become one of those time-bombs which eventually were to detonate all together and blow Europe apart. But it was the reference to Germany's victorious campaigns over the past century that would have caused the most discomfort in Vienna. These, after all, had included the brutally rapid defeat of the Austrians in 1866, followed by their expulsion from the German Confederation – all part of Bismarck's design to create a purely Teutonic Hohenzollern empire, free of all that Slavic dross which the Monarchy was obliged to carry along with it. The effects of this creed would be felt by the Habsburg dynasty to the end of its days, and then, even more acutely, by its German-speaking subjects afterwards.

If in 1900 the Berlin of the Hohenzollerns knew where it was heading, with the new century a firm extension of the old, the mood was much wobblier in the Vienna of the Habsburgs, where new and old tugged in opposite ways. Physically, the old had never looked stronger, more invulnerable or more imperial. The Ringstrasse, the three-mile long boulevard encircling the cramped inner city of the capital, was almost finished, after decades of construction. It was one of the grandest spectacles of urban planning to be seen anywhere in Europe and the contrasting buildings which had arisen to line its broad route were of matching splendour: the Hellenic Parliament, the neo-Gothic Town Hall; the Renaissance-style Burgtheatre and, at the main entrance to the old city, the Imperial Opera House.

It was fitting that this should crown the entire gigantic enterprise, not only because music crowned Austria's cultural life, but also because it had been the Emperor himself who had inspired the work. Back in 1857, when he had been sitting only nine years on the throne, he had personally ordered the old girdle of stone walls surrounding the heart of his capital to be torn down and the flat so-called 'glacis' of meadows outside the walls to be cleared for the new boulevard. He had been obliged to wait the best part of half a century for the final effect to be seen. But now, his Vienna really looked like a mighty metropolis, one for the peasants coming in from the countryside to gawp at and for even the most sophisticated of foreign visitors to admire. The Monarchy, whose great town palace, the Hofburg, was enclosed inside this asphalt ring, seemed more secure than at any time when it had lain within fortress walls.

The underlying political reality was of course very different, while even above the surface paradoxes had arisen. Everything which lined the Ringstrasse, whether in fluted columns or baroque frescoes, was ornamental. But a new breed of architects was now at work whose high priest, Otto Loos, had pronounced the outrageous dictum: 'Ornament is crime'. Moreover, he was to put words into action by constructing, dead opposite the elaborately-figured entrance to the imperial palace, a building of straight lines and angular corners, whose windows stared out in plain squares. The challenge was social as well as architectural.

It was not the only challenge being raised at the time; indeed, the entire spectrum of arts and literature was quivering with this struggle between devotion to the old and the quest for the new. In painting, for example, the nineteenth-century cult of Hans Makart, the embodiment of 'old German' solidity combined with elaborate decoration, now faced the derision of the famous 'Sezession' movement headed by the impressionist Gustav Klimt.[7] The movement's very name defined its objective: to secede not merely from the old canvasses of art but from the entire fabric of established society which they had depicted. The rich bourgeoisie, who were already challenging the nobility for a hand on the tiller of empire, was the main target of contempt. They had financed the Makart cult; now they were branded by it.

The philosophers continued the battering down of doors. Sigmund Freud, whose major work *The Interpretation of Dreams* came out as the century turned, gave the Austrians what one might term a formal introduction to their hidden egos (other pointers had appeared before). Ludwig Wittgenstein was redefining the meaning of language – for anyone, that is, who could understand what this complex genius was on about. As with Freud, his was not a specific assault on the house of Habsburg so much as a throwing open of the shutters, and those of all buildings around.

In this respect, the writers displayed a mixture of political mood. We have seen the affection which both Musil and Zweig felt for the empire – at any rate after it had vanished. On the other hand, Karl Krauss (another great, and greatly underestimated, figure) devoted his entire life to a caustically sarcastic tirade against the Monarchy and every facet of its existence. The attacks appeared in journalist form in the diatribes of *Der Fackel* ('The Torch'), the fortnightly periodical which he edited and ended

up by composing single-handedly. His onslaught against the Vienna of his
day was to be sublimated in his masterpiece, *Die letzten Tagen der Menschheit*
('The Last Days of Mankind'), which he equivalated with the collapse of the
Habsburg Empire. Among the others, Hugo von Hofmannstal (renowned,
in one of his many incarnations, as the librettist of Richard Strauss) founded,
in 1905, his 'Young Vienna' movement; but this was an attempt to plant
fresh seeds, without pulling up old roots. As for the playwright Arthur
Schnitzler, whom we shall meet with later, he certainly had his own insights
into the malaise of the Monarchy; but though penetrating, they cut only
with the shallow knife of irony.

The turn of the century was, of course, a period of intellectual ferment
throughout Europe as well as throughout all the lands of the Habsburg
Monarchy. But here it could not be described as a 'golden age', for that
implies the crowning ripeness to which the fruit has aspired throughout its
growth. The cultural outburst in *fin-de-siècle* Vienna resembled rather the
sudden sprouting of a mixed crop of *fleurs du mal*. The mystery is how
these vibrant new shoots could have been nourished in such dry and
exhausted earth. One answer, so far as the Austrians were concerned, is
that the native soil had little to do with it, for they themselves were a
strangely rootless nation – if indeed a nation at all. When, in 1867, Franz
Josef had been persuaded to divide the orb of his empire with Budapest,
the jubilant Magyars had an obvious and simple name for their portion:
'the lands of the Hungarian crown' (which, incidentally, had preceded the
arrival of the Habsburgs on the European scene by precisely 374 years).

But how to describe the western half? Here the Czechs, Moravians, Slovaks,
Poles, Ruthenes, Slovenes, Serbo-Croats, Italians and Rumanians far exceeded in numbers the German-speaking Austrians.[8] Both the mixture and
the balance had to be given a name. So, after some agonising, it was
christened as 'The Kingdoms and Lands Represented in the Imperial Parliament' and that indigestible mouthful remained its constitutional name
for the final half-century of the dynasty's existence.

There was a shorter description, which arose from the circumstance that
the Leitha, an undistinguished little stream which ambled on its way south
of Vienna, had been chosen by the racial cartographers as the dividing line
of the new Dual Monarchy. No Hungarian to the east of it would have
dreamt of calling himself a 'Transleithanian'. The label of 'Cisleithanian'
was more plausible for a citizen of that medley of peoples, stretching in a
huge arc from Cracow in the Galician north to Ragusa in the Adriatic south,
who lived in the western half. More plausible but hardly more palatable.
Nobody was happy to live with such a name, let alone proud enough to
die for it. So this western half continued to call itself Austria, which was

not only unconstitutional but meaningless. Viktor Adler, the leader of its Social Democrat party, once declared as much: 'We Austrians have a country, but no fatherland. There is no state of Austria'.

The contrast with the Slav peoples of the empire was stark. They fed their culture with nationalist fervour. Indeed, especially for the Czechs and Poles, culture in the nineteenth century *was* the fervour. In their music, drama and literature alike it provided a spiritual substitute for political autonomy. Austria's intellectuals had no such symbiosis. There was the one exception: that small but virulent minority of the 'Greater German' party who sought nothing less than the absorption of the Dual Monarchy into the Hohenzollern empire. These Austrians, at least, knew what they wanted and had a clear aim ahead of them: the sacrifice of their country on the Teutonic altar.

They were equally certain about their cultural heroes, who were German not Austrian. They celebrated the hundred and fiftieth anniversary of Schiller's birth, which fell in 1909, as a national holiday. In philosophy, they took their lead from another nineteenth-century German giant, Friedrich Nietzsche, with his creed of the supreme and purifying glories of war. All this would not have troubled an Austrian people secure in its own self-belief. As it was, it provided a tempting and fateful vision of where that missing fatherland of theirs might lie. The vision was one day to become an ugly reality; but that was after the Monarchy, which alone had given the Austrians an alternate faith, had been swept away.

Typically, the pan-Germans dismissed as 'decadent' (meaning divorced from the natural roots of the people) the escapism which characterised so much of contemporary Austrian life. The most powerful aspect of this flight from reality was the obsession with sex which quivered through the culture of the *avant-garde*. This was, of course, also a European phenomenon: the opera *Salome*, for example, was composed in 1905 by a German, Richard Strauss, on the text of England's *homme de scandale*, Oscar Wilde. But such, in Vienna, was the fear of officialdom about the effects this lustfully bloody work might have on a vulnerable population that their instant reaction was to ban the work as pornographic. Like most such bans, this one was also counter-productive. When the opera was eventually performed in Vienna five years later, it was greeted ecstatically as the symbol of the new age of moral licence.

The roots, and most of the branches, of Freudianism had been sexual; dreams represented the repressed fantasies of desire. This was for the intellectual to ponder. For the general public, a simpler and most compelling work of eroticism appeared the year after *The Interpretation of Dreams*, written by a lesser figure in the pantheon of *fin-de-siècle* Vienna. This was

Schnitzler's *Der Reigen*, a title smoothly translatable as *La Ronde* in French but not so easy to render in English. However, the theme of the play had the same stark impact in any language: the tale of a prostitute's mixed series of clients, ranging from aristocrat to plain soldier, linked to each other only by the quick relief each had found within the same pair of thighs. Relief, but not rescue from boredom and frustration. Unlike Freud, Schnitzler offered no explanation and no cure for the *malaise* he saw around him. He simply depicted a sick society which needed treatment. His work was also banned as pornography, but, like the opera *Salome*, flourished world-wide down the years.[9]

Der Reigen was a sort of Dance of Death on the body of a whore, before whom all were equal. If Schnitzler had any message, it was that life itself, as he saw it around him, had little value and even less meaning. This linked up with that other vent of escapism which the Austrians had carried with them from the nineteenth century into the twentieth: the obsession with death. Indeed, this had loomed large at the actual time of changeover. The phenomenon became known as 'Das Grosse Sterben', 'The Great Dying Off'. It encompassed the dozens of leaders of Austria's intellectual elite who had chosen (it seemed) not to see the new century in, departing while their memories of the old were still intact.

The list of notables who had died in the year 1899 alone (as recorded in the serious press) covered several hundred names, all grouped into categories, reflecting the vertical lines of the Monarchy's social structure. The top group, perhaps surprisingly, was of scientists and academicians; the second was devoted to state officials, doctors and lawyers; the third to poets, writers and journalists; the fourth to personalities of the theatrical and musical word;[10] the fifth to painters, sculptors and architects; and the sixth to engineers, industrialists and merchants (the last-named ranking very low, despite the fact that many of the rich *grande bourgeoisie* came from their ranks). Most of the categories were sprinkled with titled names; but these had been included for what the dead person had achieved in life, always specified after his name, not how he had been born into it. Of considerable social significance was the final group, headed simply 'Women'. It contained only nine names, three of which had been included because they were the widows or female relatives of famous men. Clearly the Monarchy was a masculine world.

This cult of death had been developing well before the turn of the century, firmly engraved in the cemeteries of the capital. Their elaborate gravestones became almost a sculptural art form and, as with the death lists in the papers, wherever the deceased or their family had filled a role – any role – in the machinery of the empire, this was hammered into the stone. Thus one worthy woman, buried in Vienna's Zentralfriedhof, was commemorated as having been the 'widow of a train driver on the Imperial and Royal Railways'.

Yet, though the aesthetics of death were already well-established, the turn of the century seemed to bring them new emphasis. Here – for once – the culture of the *avant-garde* sometimes joined hands with the popular mood, perhaps because this mood was tinged with despair. It was in 1901, for example, that Gustav Mahler started to compose his monumental *Kindertotenlieder*. Freud's death wish is clearly depicted in some of the paintings of Klimt's Sezession. Finally, in that cult opera *Salome*, Eros and Thanatos sing side by side.

The one person who was simply not allowed to die was, of course, Franz Josef himself. Indeed, one could imagine that even the angel of death himself would have coughed politely before knocking on the old sovereign's door. By now he inhabited alone a world above the highest of his nobility. He had become indispensable to his ordinary subjects precisely because he was so far removed from them as to look down on them all in equal measure. Loyalty to the crown, whether grudging or unreserved, was the only sentiment that all eleven nations of the empire could share. It was fiercest amongst those who were most vulnerable. The Jews, for example, were monarchists to a man (apart from some of those *avant-garde* rebels), because they shared the protection of common citizenship afforded to all other subjects. The Croats, part of 'Transleithania' since 1867 (and duly marginalised by the Magyars), also clung tenaciously to the Hofburg for help.

As for the Austrians of 'Cisleithania', the great majority among them who were not pan-Germans had drifted into a tacit bargain with the crown. They ran the whole gamut of public affairs and filled many of the top ministerial and court appointments, but strictly as the stewards and game-keepers of a great feudal estate. In return, they accepted having their manhood, or rather their nationalist virility, neutered. As they had no clear idea who they were anyway, this was not much of a sacrifice. It took a world war to erode that pragmatic loyalty. It took final defeat on the battlefields to crush it.

All this, however, seemed unthinkable as Franz Josef – the greatest pragmatist of them all – led his empire into the first decade of the new century. It was a serene performance. In November 1905, for example, he produced one of those abrupt transformations between absolutism and democracy which Musil was to smile about a generation later. The Emperor suddenly announced that, by his personal decree, general suffrage would be introduced throughout the Monarchy. As with that New Year's Eve pronouncement

on the budget, he had acted to cut short a prolonged debate on the subject
between Vienna and Budapest. And, once more, Hungary demurred. The
handful of magnates who still ran that country in the style of medieval
barons were in no mood to hand even the semblance of political power to
the people. They may well have congratulated themselves for their stand
once they regarded the circus-like spectacle of Vienna's new imperial Parliament which finally convened in May of 1907. This became little more than
a battleground for ethnic and nationalist wrangles, with ink-wells, as well
as insults, being hurled freely around the chamber.

The following year, 1908, the sixtieth of his reign, marked the apotheosis
of Franz Josef's reign and, with it, of the multinational concept of empire.
The event needed to be staged with especial pomp and fervour since the
celebrations planned for his fiftieth year on the throne had had to be
cancelled in the shadow of the greatest of his many family tragedies.[11] Ten
years later, the court, the nobility, the ministries, all the provincial governors,
the army command and its garrisons from even the remotest stations, the
vast bureaucratic apparatus, all combined with the artists, costume and
scenic designers and, not least, with the shopkeepers, carpenters and ordinary
workmen of the capital to unroll, along the Ringstrasse, a procession eight
miles long depicting the history of the Habsburg Monarchy and the diversity
of its peoples.

The day chosen for the pageant, 12 June, turned out to be a lovely
summer's day – *Kaiserwetter*, 'The Emperor's Weather', as it was dutifully
called whenever it displayed itself on state occasions.

Despite the heat, the old Emperor's shoulders never sagged an inch in
his field-marshal's uniform as the seemingly endless pageant marched past:
nineteen faithfully costumed groups depicting the military valour of the
past, including victories against the Turks and Napoleon. Then came the
present. Eight thousand marchers drawn from all parts of the Monarchy
filed past the imperial tribune, each wearing the distinctive costumes of
their particular province, and each greeting the Emperor in their own
tongue. It may have sounded like Babel but it felt, on that day, like concord.
Austria being Austria, the cracks showed up in all the inevitable grumbling
afterwards. The Pan-Germans, for example, criticised the multi-national
loyalist theme, which, for them, was anathema. The Slavs thought it was
not Slav enough; the pacifist Socialists deplored the martial themes. For
their part, the Hungarians dismissed it disdainfully as an irrelevance. Yet
in pageant, at any rate, the empire had displayed itself for a few hours as
one, in homage to the only person who made that semblance of unity
feasible.

However touched he may have been on that 12 June (much as he had come to dislike public pomp),[12] what would certainly have moved Franz Josef more was a private ceremony which had taken place in his summer palace five weeks before. At midday on 7 May, the ruling princes of the German empire gathered in the great pink salon of Schönbrunn to pay homage to the Habsburg monarch whom Bismarck had ejected from that nascent empire less than half a century before. They were nearly all of them there, on which ever side their sympathies or their soldiers had stood at Koniggraetz, the battle which in 1866 had sealed the Monarchy's defeat at Prussian hands.

For Franz Josef, the most welcome guest would certainly have been the oldest among his visitors, the eighty-eight-year-old Prince Regent of Bavaria, a blood relative and a faithful ally, who had actually commanded a Bavarian division on his side in the brief war against Prussia. Among the others there had come King Frederich August of Saxony; King Wilhelm II of Württemberg; the Grand Dukes of Baden, Oldenburg and Mecklenburg; the Duke of Anhalt; the Princes of Lippe and Schaumberg-Lippe; and, bringing up the rear in protocol, the frock-coated Mayor of Hamburg, Dr Buchard, representing the three cities of the Hansa League, his own, together with Bremen and Lübeck. At the head of the protocol list and at the head of proceedings stood, inevitably, Wilhelm II, King of Prussia and, since 1888, ruler of that German Empire which his grandfather, Wilhelm I, had, somewhat reluctantly, agreed to form only seventeen years before.

The Kaiser, who had been holidaying with his wife in Corfu (a suitable choice, this, for it had been the cherished summer refuge of the late Empress Elisabeth), had elected to enter the confines of the Monarchy at the great Istrian port of Pula. Here, he had inspected the Austro-Hungarian fleet and spoken some uncomfortably strident words about the importance of naval cooperation. A similar theme of alliance ran through the address which he delivered in Schönbrunn now.

It was as though Königgrätz had never happened; there was not a mention even of past differences. Instead, once the obligatory compliments had been offered to the 'august personage of your Imperial and Royal Apostolic Majesty' (revered, he claimed, throughout the world), the emphasis was all on the military treaty signed between the two German-speaking empires only thirteen years after their fratricidal war. Speaking for the three generations of German rulers grouped around him, Wilhelm rendered homage to the noble sovereign who was also their 'faithful ally and powerful force for peace', praying for God's blessing on his head.

Franz Josef's reply might have been crafted by one of those astute advisers who, at the end of the century, came to be known as 'spin doctors'. He stressed above all the importance of the doctrine of monarchy, which had ensured for him the 'loyalty and unshakeable love' of his peoples. He then pointed out that Germany, too, owed its present 'power and greatness' to this same doctrine, which had not so far been mentioned. Finally, he laid much greater emphasis on the theme of peace. The alliance between the German-speaking peoples had only peaceful aims and he hoped that 'the other powers' would strive towards the same goals. [13]

So much talk in Schönbrunn of peace; yet before this anniversary year was over, it was the Monarchy itself which, in a display of vainglorious folly, had lain one of those long and twisting fuses which were to lead to war. Ironically, it had been conceived as part of the jubilee celebrations.

On 5 October 1908, to the astonishment of both his peoples at home and his fellow monarchs abroad, Franz Josef announced that he had annexed the two southern Slav provinces of Bosnia and Herzegovina, 'which would henceforth fall under the hereditary possessions of the House of Habsburg'. It was far from an invasion. The two provinces had been 'occupied and administered' by the Monarchy for the past forty years, as part of the general European settlement agreed in Berlin in 1878 after the end of the Russo-Turkish war. After thirty years of trouble-free occupation, the Austrians had begun trailing the idea of converting it into annexation proper, and the major powers of Europe, on either side of their great divide, had tacitly accepted that, one day, the conversion might well be made. Yet the provinces remained, in law if not in fact, part of the Turkish Empire and it was therefore taken for granted that any formal transfer of sovereignty would have to be agreed by all the powers, with the Turks getting something in return. Now, with a stroke of the pen, Franz Josef had pre-empted any international settlement, while offering Turkey nothing in the way of compensation.

The psychological reason for his action was not difficult to fathom. Throughout the sixty years he had sat on the throne, the Monarchy had only shrunk in size and prominence. First Lombardy and then Venice had been surrendered in the wars of Italian unification and, to cap these losses, the leadership of the Germanic world had been surrendered to Prussia on the field of Königgrätz. The temptation actually to extend the empire's confines – even if it only concerned a wretchedly poor region populated by less than two million south Slavs – was palpable. Moreover, what better time to pick than this Jubilee year? In fact, it turned out to be one of the most disastrous moves of his reign.

Domestically, the annexation, instead of stirring patriotic hearts (as had been hoped), only fanned those nationalist flames which always threatened to become the Monarchy's funeral pyre. Its pan-Germans fumed at this extension of the empire's boundaries towards the Slavic south – both the wrong direction and the wrong ethnic choice for their doctrine. The Socialists, in high moral dudgeon, attacked the Emperor's decree as being both absolutist and against all international law. In Prague, where the Czechs were already at odds with Vienna over other issues, the annexation crisis so added to tension that martial law had to be proclaimed – on, of all days, 2 December 1908, the exact anniversary date of the Jubilee.

Even more serious for the long term was the reaction abroad. After that October decree, neither the allies nor the putative opponents of the Monarchy trusted it any longer to behave prudently in a dangerous world. England, for example, still the Continent's leading power, looked to the Habsburg Empire above all to do nothing rash and somehow sit tight and quiet on its Balkan powder-keg which was capable of blowing everyone up. Now it had done the opposite and in such peremptory fashion as to affront all the niceties of monarchist diplomacy. King Edward VII, a powerful influence over the foreign policy of his government, could not at first believe the news from Vienna.[14] Less than two months before, on 12–13 August, while on his way to his annual cure (and frolic) at Marienbad, he had paid his usual call on the Emperor at Bad Ischl and they had talked politics. The King found it inconceivable that he had not been forewarned, even as a confidence between sovereigns.[15]

Most serious for the future was the impact on the kingdom of Serbia, which had long coveted those provinces for itself as part of its dream of a 'Greater Serbian Empire'. Nor was the reaction confined to official anger. Throughout the kingdom there arose calls for war against Austria, always the great enemy. The extremist wing of pan-Slavism gained fresh impetus and fresh volunteers. Only six years later, at Sarajevo, young assassins from those ranks were to sign the death warrants of all three continental empires.

The grotesque aspect of the crisis was that it had been propelled along, and possibly even initiated by, an exercise in social climbing. Only one person was involved but that person happened to be the Foreign Minister of the empire. Freiherr Alois von Aehrenthal was reputed to have been the son of an ennobled Jewish grain merchant in Prague. The title chosen was apt (it means 'Corn Valley'). The rank of Freiherr was also lowly, as measured on the archaic aristocratic scales of the day, which only started to weigh in properly from Count upwards. That dignity could only be bestowed by a grateful sovereign. So, in order to procure that gratitude, through the summer Aehrenthal had been planning the annexation coup in close council with his Russian opposite number, Alexander Izvolski.[16] After Germany had saved the Monarchy's bacon by forcing Turkey to accept a settlement of the crisis, Aehrenthal duly got his nine-pointed coronet. Yet he had shaken the imperial crown in the process.

In the middle of it all, on 2 December 1908, came the exact anniversary of the placing of that crown on the eighteen-year-old Franz Josef's head. In every garrison town of the empire parades were held; in every officers' mess loyal toasts were drunk. The flags and bunting were out in all the villages, the church bells rang and the bonfires lit up the hills. But the most spectacular celebration was reserved for the capital – ablaze on the ground with special illuminations, while the sky above flamed with a monster firework display. On this day, too, the Emperor received the last of the seemingly endless sequence of greetings from foreign potentates and kings. The King of Sweden had come to pay his Protestant respects. The Emperor then retired, exhausted, and needing more than that extra one hour's sleep (rising at 5 a.m. instead of 4 a.m.) he had allowed himself after the departure of the German Princes in May.

The year had resounded as one long anthem of traditionalist loyalty. Or was it a requiem? The simile is apt for, less than three weeks after the fireworks had fizzled out, it was in music that the *avant-garde* sounded its most startling blast of defiance. On the evening of 21 December 1908 atonality was born. The birth was in Vienna's Bösendorfersaal where Arnold Schönberg's Second String Quartet was given its première. The Rosa Quartet and the soprano, Marie Gutheil Schoder, managed to plough through the work, though probably not much of it was heard, thanks to the storm of abuse coming from the audience. The crescendo reached its climax after the opening of the last movement when the composer abandoned even the use of a key signature to show his rejection of harmony.

This did indeed mark the end of a world. Startling new styles in painting or architecture may have excited the professionals, yet the general public remained unaffected and indifferent. Rhyme was about to be dismantled in poetry and narrative to be blotted out from the novel. But music lay at the centre of the Austrian soul, its pride as well as its nourishment in everyday life ranging from the village fire brigade band to the famous operas and concerts of the capital. Harmony had always been its essence, and though composers like Wagner and Richard Strauss had sometimes pushed at its frontiers, nobody, until now, had marched across them.

Schönberg had led the greatest of all those *fin de siècle* breakaways from tradition and therefore he, too, brought a social message. The music shrieks with disillusionment even at the one point where harmony is let in. Here, the soprano sings, against all the discord, the old Viennese street song of 'Die Liebe Augustin', with its doleful repetitive refrain: 'Alles ist hin, Alles ist hin' – 'It's all over, it's all gone'.

2

The Perfect Match

Three years after that Jubilee and all its conflicting signals, an event took place within the Habsburg family which suggested that things were far from being 'all over'; indeed, for the dynasty, new hope had been glimpsed. The occasion was the marriage, on 21 October 1911, of the Emperor's great-nephew, the Archduke Karl, to the nineteen-year-old Princess Zita of Bourbon-Parma. The ceremony, held at the bride's family castle of Schwarzau in the flat woodlands of the Steinfeld south of Vienna, was presided over by Franz Josef in person. Never before, and never again, did the aged monarch display such joviality in public. He even chuckled aloud once during the service (literally, an unheard of sound), and afterwards took it upon himself to arrange the august company for the formal wedding portrait.

There was good reason for his delight. Throughout that enormous reign of his, he had seen almost nothing in the house of Habsburg but marriages which were disastrous or disenchanted. There were two salutary examples in the bridegroom's own family. His father, Otto, as handsome and charming a man as any in Viennese society, had also turned into one of most debauched. He soon drifted away from his plain and placid bride, Princess Maria Josefa of Saxony, and slid into a vortex of self-indulgence which dragged him down to an early death when aged barely forty in 1906. The Monarchy was thus spared him as a future sovereign, just as the British Empire had had its lucky escape when the odious and perverted Duke of Clarence met his death in 1892 at the even earlier age of twenty-eight.[1]

As for Otto's younger brother, Ferdinand, his physical passions had ended by sweeping him off the family tree altogether. Nothing could dissuade him from marrying one Berta Czuber, the daughter of a Viennese university professor. For the Emperor a marriage between an Archduke and a mere Fräulein was not just unthinkable, it was unseeable. Ferdinand and his bride had to be driven out of sight. After stripping him successively of title, military rank and income, Franz Josef finally destroyed his youngest nephew's identity. In 1912 his name was erased from the tables of the imperial house and he became a Habsburg 'non-person'. Needless to add, this genealogical assassination had driven him from Vienna – as was its intention. After years of wandering with his beloved 'Milly', Ferdinand died in 1915, aged forty-seven, and was buried in Munich as 'Herr Burg'. To the end he had clung to one half of that great name.

So much for the marriage miseries of the bridegroom's relatives. But those of the Emperor and his immediate family were not much brighter. His own wedding back in 1853 to the lovely Bavarian princess Elisabeth, with whom he had fallen in love at first sight, had looked like a fairy tale romance. But the marriage had drifted slowly into the disenchantment as 'Sisi' herself started drifting around Europe, a restless and neurotic soul, seeking a peace and fulfilment she could no longer find at her husband's side in imperial Vienna.

The dark tragedy of their only son had done much to unhinge her. Archduke Rudolf possessed a lively mind, handsome royal looks, a charm of manner and a fervent belief in the Habsburg mission – all of them promising qualities in the Heir Apparent to the throne. But there was a demon of self-destruction always at work inside him. Its final triumph was the death pact of himself and his seventeen-year-old mistress, Marie Vetsera, enacted shortly before dawn on 30 January 1889 in his hunting lodge at Mayerling.

It is conceivable that the right marriage partner could have held the demon at bay and kept the husband away from the beds of his countless mistresses, a chain of lechery in which Marie had the misfortune to serve as the final link. But Rudolf, who would have needed a tigress to hold him to the bridal bed, had been landed instead – in a dynastic *mariage de convenance* – with a mouse. Princess Stephanie of Belgium, with her receding chin and scrawny frame, was the sort of wife who would positively drive a sensualist like Rudolf out of the bedchamber once the marriage had been consummated.[2]

Last, but far from least, in the Emperor's gallery of family marriage dramas was the saga of his nephew, Franz Ferdinand, who, at Rudolf's death had become second in line to the throne. Because of his lofty station, his marital problems had to be resolved on the very steps of the throne, and in the closing years of the old century the tussle had nearly ripped the dynasty apart. The Archduke was by then already in his forties and it was clearly high time for him to settle down and produce an heir of his own. Franz Ferdinand's own character did not ease the process. He was imperious, short-tempered, humourless, demanding and almost devoid of that charm which was, traditionally, the Austrians' saving grace. On the other hand, he shared Rudolf's faith in the future of the Monarchy and, unlike that tragic prince, he had the will, once his time came, to do something about ensuring that future. Though the Emperor felt no affection for his nephew, he recognised the mettle of this difficult man – the iron in him which was so badly needed to stiffen the flabbiness of the court.

Franz Ferdinand may have been hard enough to please in the first place, yet the task was made even more difficult by the dearth of suitable brides in the Europe of the day. (Queen Victoria had faced similar problems in finding the right match for the heir to her own empire, the gallivanting 'Bertie', or Prince Edward of Wales.) In Franz Ferdinand's case, it was deemed that the bride should be a Catholic Princess of ruling or former ruling stock; but trawls in those favourite waters, like Saxony, where the Habsburgs had so often netted their partners, proved unrewarding. It was not merely that most of the candidates were too plain; they were also too young. The marriageable princesses, he once famously proclaimed, 'were all children, chicks of seventeen or eighteen, and one uglier than the other'.

Then, as the century was nearing its end, there came, in quick succession, two shocks which brought the problem to an unexpected climax. The first was the extraordinary death of the man who was the immediate heir to the throne, the Emperor's younger brother and father of Franz Ferdinand. The Archduke Karl Ludwig, who, in fact, took no interest in the crown, was an exceptionally worthy and pious man and it was his piety which proved his undoing. In the spring of 1896, while on a pilgrimage to the Holy Land, he ignored the horrified protests of his doctor and drank from the River Jordan. The doctors were right. The water proved as polluted as it was sacred and by May of that year the sixty-three-year-old royal pilgrim lay dead of typhoid. Though sidelined for a while by a bout of tuberculosis which fed court intrigue against him, by 1898 Franz Ferdinand was duly confirmed as the new Heir Apparent. The following year, the secret of his romantic scandal broke, threatening to overturn the succession.

For the past four years, the Archduke had been deeply in love with the lady-in-waiting of his cousin by marriage, the Archduchess Isabella. Sophie Chotek, who had captured the heart of this difficult middle-aged bachelor, was no Milly Czuber. The Choteks of Chotkova and Wogrin were an ancient noble family: Barons of Bohemia since 1556; Counts of Bohemia since 1723 and Counts of the Empire from twenty years after that. Her father, a diplomat, had once served the Emperor as Minister to Brussels (where, ironically, he had helped to launch the dismal marriage of Princess Stephanie to Crown Prince Rudolf). Her mother was a Kinsky, highly respected inside the Monarchy as one of its most distinguished families and perhaps best known in the world outside for the fact that, in 1883, a Count Kinsky had won the famous Grand National steeplechase in England. Though no one realised it at the time, this had put the name on a roll of honour that was still to unfold in the next millennium, let alone the next century – long after the books had closed on all the continental empires.

Yet none of this could alter the fact that, though the Chotek blood was undeniably blue, it was not tinged with the necessary purple. They were, quite simply, not on the list of some twenty families (mainly 'princely houses domiciled in the Monarchy') deemed eligible for marriage with the reigning dynasty. The list was engraved on stone tablets. Nothing could be chiselled away or added on; and that was that. Or so a horrified Emperor had thought when in the late summer of 1899 his nephew not only owned up to the secret attachment but declared that he intended to marry the lady in question.

Franz Ferdinand had found what he had been searching for in vain among those 'ugly chicks' of the European courts. His 'Sopherl' was a mature young woman (probably about twenty-seven when he fell in love with her), handsome and wholesome enough with huge brown eyes set under a mass of brown hair to match. Just as appealing as her physical attraction was her temperament. She radiated a soothing calm, and that, the Archduke sensed, was what he needed in life to damp down his own explosive character. So, in the autumn of 1899, battle was joined at court. The Archduke demanded both his bride and, eventually his throne. The Emperor was determined that he must choose between them. Horns were locked for the next nine months.

Franz Ferdinand's strength lay – apart from his own fierce obstinacy – in the very gravity of the situation. He was not, like the pathetic Ferdinand, an Archduke outside the direct line of succession who could be swept away accordingly, but the Heir Apparent of the Dual Monarchy. A solution simply had to be found if the dynasty were not to shatter. Found it eventually was, though the in-born Austrian genius for compromise was taxed to the full in the search.

The saga ended on 28 June 1900 with a ceremony in the Secret Council Chamber of the Hofburg, the very room where, more than half a century before, the eighteen-year-old Franz Josef, newly crowned as Emperor, had read his own speech from the throne. This time, he spoke as head of a divided family and the words had been wrung out of him with some difficulty. His nephew, he said, had 'followed the call of his heart' in desiring to marry Countess Sophie Chotek. Consent had been given, but as the Countess was of noble but not of equal birth, the marriage could only be morganatic and neither she nor her children could be accorded any of the rights of a marriage between equals. Franz Ferdinand signified acceptance by swearing an oath of renunciation on a Bible held out for him by Cardinal Archbishop Gruscha and then signing the matching deeds drawn up in both German and Hungarian.[3]

For the first time in the history of the dynasty, the heir to the Habsburg crown had been accorded an 'unsuitable' wife. To mark the solemnity of

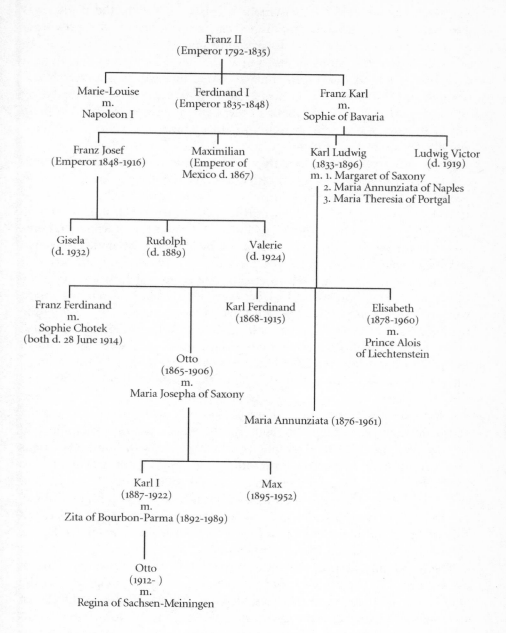

Franz II
(Emperor 1792-1835)

Marie-Louise
m.
Napoleon I

Ferdinand I
(Emperor 1835-1848)

Franz Karl
m.
Sophie of Bavaria

Franz Josef
(Emperor 1848-1916)

Maximilian
(Emperor of
Mexico d. 1867)

Karl Ludwig
(1833-1896)
m. 1. Margaret of Saxony
2. Maria Annunziata of Naples
3. Maria Theresia of Portgal

Ludwig Victor
(d. 1919)

Gisela
(d. 1932)

Rudolph
(d. 1889)

Valerie
(d. 1924)

Franz Ferdinand
m.
Sophie Chotek
(both d. 28 June 1914)

Karl Ferdinand
(1868-1915)

Elisabeth
(1878-1960)
m.
Prince Alois
of Liechtenstein

Otto
(1865-1906)
m.
Maria Josepha of Saxony

Maria Annunziata (1876-1961)

Karl I
(1887-1922)
m.
Zita of Bourbon-Parma (1892-1989)

Max
(1895-1952)

Otto
(1912-)
m.
Regina of Sachsen-Meiningen

Habsburg family tree.

the event and to bind the heir more tightly to his oath, the pledge was also witnessed by the chief ministers and court officials, the provincial governors from each province of the empire and every other adult Archduke from all lines of the family – fifteen in all. So Franz Ferdinand had secured both his bride and his throne, but his blood-line would not stretch out beyond him. To judge by the fears and doubts expressed beforehand by all sections of this audience, many of them would have wondered, on filing out of the Secret Council Chamber, whether Franz Ferdinand as Emperor would honour this final clause.

Now, eleven years later, here they were among the guests at Schwarzau, witnessing a wedding which contrasted in every way to their own. This had been held not, as was normal, at a house of the bride's family but at the sprawling castle of Reichstadt in northern Bohemia, a Habsburg property since 1824.[4] The fact that Sophie was indeed 'unequal' was reflected in every aspect of the service. It was conducted not by a bishop, let alone a cardinal, but by the aged deacon from the local town. And, whereas nobody had expected the Emperor himself to attend, one or two at least among those fifteen adult Habsburgs who had witnessed the Hofburg ceremony might well have turned up at this one. All fifteen chose to stay away, leaving the bridegroom as the only Archduke at his wedding. As the bride was orphaned, it was her guardian, Prince Loewenstein, who gave her away; and it was a Count Nostitz in the service of Franz Ferdinand who acted as best man of the Heir Apparent – though walking into the chapel well behind him and not at his side.

Schwarzau was a very different story. Not only, as we have seen, was the Emperor omnipresent and in high spirits. The wedding group he had arranged for the court photographer's benefit blazed with Bourbon-Parmas and other relatives of the bridal pair – the King of Saxony, Princes and Dukes of Liechtenstein, Württemberg, Braganza and so on. The Heir Apparent was tucked away well right of centre and in the second row with his Sophie, as ever, a step behind and not beside him.[5] The biggest contrast between this wedding and their own cannot have been far from their minds. It was, of course, that between the two brides.

There was no question that this marriage was, in every sense, a match between equals. The bride's father, Duke Robert, had only reigned over the tiny realm of Parma (and had been deposed from that during the Italian Risorgimento half a century ago); yet, as a Bourbon prince, he traced his descent back to the 'Sun King' of France, Louis XIV – a tapestry of whose coronation decorated the salon of the Villa Pianore, the ducal residence which the Parmas had been allowed to keep. Through the great Italian family of the Farneses, the bride could look even further back towards illustrious ancestors – to the sixteenth-century Pope, Paul III, for example, who had raised a family (and patronised Michelangelo) before assuming the papal throne. Then came the intermittent marriages down the centuries between the houses of Parma and the Spanish line of the Habsburgs, which meant that the wedding couple at Schwarzau shared some of the same ancestors. Moreover, as Zita's own mother had been Princess Maria Antonia of Braganza,[6] the royal family of Portugal with all its European links came into the genealogical tables.

The contrasts between the brides at Reichstadt and at Schwarzau did not stop at their ancestry. Sophie's father was far from being a wealthy man. Five of his eight children were daughters, all of them without private means. Those who had reached marriageable age without finding a husband were usually faced with one of two futures – that of becoming a nun or a lady-in-waiting, the choice which Sophie had made.

Zita, on the other hand, had felt neither the pressure of years nor of family circumstances in deciding her fate. Sophie was thirty-two when she married, an age when most women of the time would have begun to put all thoughts of wedlock behind them. Zita was a radiant nineteen year old. She was no classical beauty, but if anything all the more strikingly attractive for that with her perfect skin and large brown eyes set under a mass of dark hair. If she shared the colour of her eyes with Sophie, there was every difference in the gaze. The older woman had the demure, almost retiring look well-suited to a former lady-in-waiting. The teenage Zita already had the confident air of someone quite prepared to take on anything which the world might offer her, or throw at her. There was something in the look which suggested she would relish the challenge. This was a personality for centre stage, not for the wings.

Again, part of that confidence and zest for action stemmed from her childhood. The twenty-two offspring of her father's two marriages gave her a background from birth of cosmopolitan royalty that was unusually copious even in this age of large families.[7] Her father's great wealth and the location of his properties ensured that these contacts continued through childhood. From his uncle and guardian, the Legitimist Pretender, the Count of Chambord, Duke Robert had inherited not only the great Loire Valley castle of that name, but also estates which lay close to his own castle of Schwarzau. Indeed, Lower Austria at the turn of the century resembled a vast refuge ground where the Catholic royalty of Europe, dispossessed by revolutions, had gathered to live in safety and reassuring proximity to one another. Thus Frohsdorf, a former Chambord property, was now occupied, with his son Jaime, by Don Carlos, the leader of the Spanish Carlist faction; his near neighbour, the one-time ruler of Parma, was also his brother-in-law.

The castle of Seebenstein, again in the same area, was the residence of ex-King Miguel, head of the Braganzas, who had been driven out of Portugal in 1910. The fact that Zita's own mother was a Braganza added further to the one-family atmosphere of this gathering of exiles. Finally came the dynasty, still very much in power, which had welcomed them all in. The Habsburgs too had a property nearby, Wartholz on the Semmering Pass into Styria. It was no match in either grandeur or style for the castles of the exiles.

Wartholz was spoken of as a shooting lodge, yet described as a villa, a confusion of identities which was matched by its strange blend of architecture – three floors of massive carved Germanic stonework topped by steeply sloping roofs in the French style from which mini-turrets poked out. It somehow managed to combine plainness with pretension as though built by some mid nineteenth-century industrialist with more money than taste. Yet the extraordinary thing about this unprepossessing building was that it had always felt like home to the young bridegroom at the wedding; moreover, even when Karl eventually had a dozen or more palaces and castles to choose from, it was always to Wartholz that he returned to relax with a family of his own.

Because of the dynasty who owned it, the villa stood at the centre of that mosaic of royal residences dotted around Lower Austria. It was in this constant exchange of visits between Wartholz and Schwarzau that the bridal couple had first met as infants – he, to begin with, just out of the nursery while she was still in it. The romance which eventually linked the pair was the grandest example of boy marrying the girl next door. What he saw in her needed little explaining, for she had grown up into a fascinating young woman whose sense of fun and sparkling personality matched her striking good looks. For Zita, the attraction was a powerful blend of the dynastic and the personal. After the premature death of his father in 1906, Archduke Karl was second in line for the crown of a great empire; to be his consort would fulfil the tug of destiny which Zita had always felt inside her.

This most eligible of all the royal bachelors of Catholic Europe was also an appealing young man in himself. He was handsome enough in a cheerfully gentle way which gave an instant impression of kindness mixed with a certain softness. He had none of the pompous airs and graces with which many of his fellow Archdukes pumped themselves up and certainly none of the wildness which had destroyed his father. When, aged eighteen, he was posted to Kostelitz for his first spell of military service he had settled down happily in his two-room quarters of the barracks as though he were just another lieutenant of the Emperor's Seventh Dragoons. This unaffected popular touch was to stay with him throughout all the dramas and tragedies which lay ahead. He never strove for power or greatness, nor even desired it. Once it was clear that the burden of empire would one day be his – however distant that day might be – he felt no impatience to wear the crown but only concern to be worthy of it.

He knew that the Monarchy of Franz Josef could not survive in the same rigid form once the Titan who held the whole structure together was gone. Often, on that same balcony of Schwarzau Castle where the wedding group now posed, he had sat with the young Parma princes debating into the night how the empire could be recast in a new mould to enable it to survive the challenges of liberalism, nationalism and democracy. He was, in short, a decent and honourable man ready to face up to any responsibility, though perhaps at heart nervous that his shoulders might prove a touch too narrow for the imperial mantle.

This was where his bride was to prove the ideal partner. Unlike her husband, she was by temperament a born leader. Her favourite saying from the sportsman's field – 'You also miss by not even firing' – became her motto for life.[8] In everyday parlance, she was always ready to have a go at things; however risky it might be to act, to her it seemed preferable to just sitting still and watching. There were to be times enough ahead when that choice had to be made.

However different their four personalities were, there was an interesting parallel between the newly-wed couple at Schwarzau and those fascinated wedding guests, the Heir Apparent and his morganatic wife of 1900. In each pairing, an active element had combined with a passive one to produce the current between them. In Franz Ferdinand's case the roles were reversed, in that he was the dynamic force of the match. The result was the same: a balance which produced happiness and harmony.

The Austrians seemed to have sensed that, with this Bourbon princess now in their midst, things might change. The Vienna astronomer Dr Palisa had just discovered a new body in the heavens. He named it 'Zita', as though it were a new star on earth. There was certainly a new look about some of the daywear fashion designs which the Viennese couturiers named in her honour. Unfussy, unornamented and very businesslike, these clothes might have been conceived by that apostle of the down-to-earth and functional, the architect Emil Loos.

The couple slipped out of the limelight for most of the following year. Part of it was spent in the obscurity of a garrison posting to Kolomea, an unattractive station in the remote region of eastern Galicia, where the Habsburg Monarchy rubbed shoulders with the Russian Empire. Then, at the beginning of November, Karl, who had been convalescing after a bad fall from his horse, was given a new rank in a new regiment based in the capital itself. Moreover, it was announced that the pleasant little palace of Hetzendorff, close to Schönbrunn, had been placed at his disposal as a Vienna residence. The reason for these arrangements became clear three weeks later. On 20 November 1912, Zita gave birth at Schwarzau to their first child, a healthy son. Five days later, the baby prince was christened with a plethora of names drawn from his Habsburg, Bourbon-Parma, Braganza and Saxon ancestry: Franz Josef, Otto, Robert, Maria Antonia, Karl Maxmilian, Henry, Sixtus Xavier, Felix, René, Ludwig, Gaetus, Pius and Ignateus ...[9] This impossible roll-call was designed to satisfy dynastic sensibilities. The infant was to be known simply as Otto, and that was the name he carried throughout his life.

The old Emperor's cheerful hopes at the wedding thirteen months before had been fulfilled. He could see around him no fewer than three future successors: his difficult nephew, Franz Ferdinand; his great-nephew, the amiably modest Karl; and now this new arrival. It seemed like a three-pronged anchor to be cast ahead, securing the dynasty amidst all the slippery rocks underneath. The vision ran a long time ahead. 'The new-born child', so ran one newspaper commentary on the day the birth was announced, 'will, according to human probability, only be summoned in the last quarter of this century to guide as Emperor the destiny of this state.' [10] Hopefully, the paper added, things would then be more peaceful for him than at these turbulent times of his birth. There was a tentative note about this loyal prophesying, which was just as well. The century ahead – throughout which the baby prince lived – was to know little tranquillity.

The first shock, the assassination of Franz Ferdinand and his wife at Sarajevo on 26 June 1914, came barely eighteen months after Otto's birth. He remained blissfully unaware of the transformation not only in his own position within the dynasty but of the shattering effects on the Habsburg Monarchy and on the whole world outside. It was the plainest of domestic settings in which his parents received the news. A small wooden summer house had been erected in the gardens of the Villa Wartholz and, on fine days when they were by themselves, as on this fateful 26 June, the couple would eat their lunch there, the dishes brought out to them from the kitchens. They noticed that there was a long pause before the main course was served and, when it did arrive, a telegram came with it. Karl first glanced casually at the sender's name. 'Rumerskirch, that's strange. Why him?' The reason lay in the one sentence of the text. Baron Rumerskirch was Franz Ferdinand's aide-de-camp. He was reporting the Heir Apparent's murder that morning, alongside that of his wife the Duchess of Hohenberg.

The two lethal bullets – which went on to cause the deaths of millions more – had been fired by a Belgrade student Gavrilo Princip. He was one of a group of six fanatical Serbian youths who had sworn to kill the Archduke as the symbol of Habsburg 'tyranny'. Moreover they had been armed and trained for the task by 'The Black Hand' a terrorist secret society which contained many senior Serbian army officers among its members.

It was only through a freak series of mishaps and misunderstandings that Princip had been able to pull the trigger. The original plan of the assassins had been to blow up the Archduke's car as it entered along the riverside boulevard of Sarajevo, where all six had lined up. This failed when their bomb bounced off the roof of the Archduke's car. The convoy was duly rerouted for a fast non-stop exit (after a ceremonial lunch at the town hall) to bring the Archduke and his wife as rapidly as possible to safety. But the driver had muddled up his instructions and started off along the roundabout journey originally planned. When ordered to reverse, he backed his car into a side street where it stopped for a few seconds to change gears on the corner.

At that very spot, on the kerbside, stood Gavrilo Princip. He had simply wandered there aimlessly after abandoning his morning position along the main boulevard and now found the Archduke and his wife suddenly staring down at him at arm's length. He fired a shot at each. At that range, the target was almost impossible to miss. Bleeding profusely, the couple were driven off to the old palace of the Turkish governors of the city where medical aid was summoned. But they never regained consciousness and died, within minutes of each other, about a quarter of an hour later. It was left to Baron Rumerskirch to telegraph the shattering news, first to the Emperor and then to the new Heir Apparent.

Zita watched her husband's face go white in the sunshine. Their uncle had been not yet fifty and in the best of health. Assuming the empire itself were to survive, he could easily have ruled until the late 1930s, when their turn would come. Now, in a flash, it was they who were next in line. Moreover, it soon emerged that what they stood to inherit was an empire embroiled in war. The next six weeks saw a slowly mounting frenzy in Vienna, and in all the other capitals of Europe, as one by one the six countries of the rival power blocs ratcheted themselves, notch by notch, into the conflict – with the Habsburg Monarchy contributing its ample share of the multiple folly and miscalculations responsible.

Wartholz remained curiously isolated from all this. Throughout that critical July, Karl was not even fully informed, let alone consulted, about what was going on. It was almost as if the old Emperor – who had himself lingered far too long at his beloved shooting lodge in Bad Ischl – wanted to shield his successor from any shadow of blame. Not until 1 August, when the empire was about to march, were Karl and Zita summoned back from the mountains to do a morale-boosting tour of Hungary. By the time they got back to Vienna, the old order in Europe had already set about destroying itself. Truly could Karl say, after he assumed the throne, that he had played no part in causing a war which he was determined to end.

His succession took place in the very middle of the conflict which was to drag on for four years. In November 1916, the Emperor's strength, taxed by the enormous extra burdens of war, began to ebb. He was struck down by bronchitis and then pneumonia. For a fortnight he battled on, signing away his daily pile of documents despite a high fever, as though his pen could hold the end at bay. Karl and Zita saw him – still lucid and even cheerful – a few hours before that end. The final collapse came suddenly in the evening of 21 November. A few minutes after nine o'clock, the unimaginable but inevitable had happened: Franz Josef was dead after sixty-eight years on the throne. The new Emperor was twenty-nine, the new Empress twenty-four, the new Crown Prince exactly four, and it is from here that the infant's images of a doomed empire begin.

3

Collapse: A Child's Eye View

The child's very first public appearance was at the old Emperor's funeral procession which wound its way through the inner city on the afternoon of 27 November 1916. At the time, his images of the day were blurred and it was only later in life, after he had trod the great modern cities of the world, that those images sharpened. 'I suddenly knew what it had felt like on that day. It was like walking among sky-scrapers.'[1]

The figures who had loomed up on either side of him were his own parents. To his left walked his father, the new sovereign, wearing field-marshal's uniform, and carrying a plumed hat. On his right was his mother, a walking column of mourning, swathed from head to toe in black, with one hand slipped out of the dark curtain to hold her son's. Theirs was a familiar and comforting presence. The unfamiliar 'skyscrapers' lay around and ahead. The whole route from St Stephen's Cathedral to the burial church of the Capuchins was lined with walls of saluting soldiers in helmets while, just in front of him, marched a phalanx of dignitaries in full array.

Then there was the hearse itself on which the little Prince's eyes were glued: an immense ceremonial carriage with black plumes nodding around the heavy coffin. Though it was a mild November day with some pale early winter sunshine, his memories were all of darkness. Even in the cathedral (where he sat in the presbytery between his parents to watch the rites of committal), the blaze of electric lights was blotted out by the black drapes which smothered the doorway and swathed the stone columns inside.

In fact, Otto himself was the only exception in the entire cortège to the display of uniforms and high regalia in mourning. He recalls that it was his mother who had decided exactly what he should wear on this momentous day. Her choice turned out to be an unconscious masterstroke of show-manship. As if to set him apart from the gloom of the day, she had dressed him in a white knee-length tunic with white shoes and socks and a white fur hat to carry in his hand. A black waist sash and cravat and a thin black armband on his left sleeve did duty enough for mourning. Apart from that, his was the only splash of light in the procession, the effect heightened by blonde hair which fell almost to his shoulders.

Whether or not his mother had meant this to be a symbol of hope, that was how much of the crowd thought of it at the end of the day. Many among the tens of thousands filling the pavements, balconies and windows along the route were asking themselves whether the old Emperor's funeral carriage was not also the hearse carrying his Monarchy to its grave. There seemed no end in sight to a murderous war which, after two and a half years of conflict, was beginning to inflict serious suffering and hardship on the people. And, to the man in the street, their new sovereign, while appearing likeable and honourable enough, was an unknown quantity. Obviously, he possessed very little of the experience and semi-divine status of the ruler they were mourning. Could he ever display the iron will and statesmanship needed to steer the empire to victory or even bare survival? For those who wondered, the little figure in white, stepping out vigorously at his side, seemed to guarantee at least survival.[2]

It all felt very different a month later when the boy watched his parents being crowned King and Queen of Hungary in the cathedral of Mathias Corvinus in Budapest. Everything was indeed different. To begin with, this was a coronation, a ceremony which would not have been staged in Vienna, though that was the ancient seat of the empire. Then there was the crown itself, so unlike anything else, both in its form and in its symbolism, in the massive collection of Habsburg regalia. Its four open arches were held to have formed the original circlet sent by Pope Sylvester for the coronation of Stephen, first Christian king of Hungary, in the year 1000. The jewelled headband was thought to be almost as ancient – a gift of the Byzantine Emperor in or around 1075 to Stephen's successor, King Geza. Legend, rather than fact, had embellished this extraordinary object. The cross at the top, which was bent askew, was said to have been knocked that way by a blow sustained in battle, though such a heavy and unstable object would have been a ludicrous choice for a helmet.

No matter; legend and fact were fused together to make this battered head-piece the emblem not just of Hungarian kingship but of the Magyar nation and its history. That was why, immediately after the funeral in Vienna, Hungary's redoubtable Prime Minister, Count Stefan Tisza, had persuaded Karl to come to Budapest before the year was out for his coronation.[3] They just made the deadline: the ceremony was held on 30 December 1916.

The little Crown Prince could now register images which were much more vivid – and to prove much more lasting – than anything he had experienced at the funeral.

> In Vienna, I had been hemmed in as part of the proceedings. But in Budapest I was an observer. I travelled separately to the coronation church where I could watch everything from a loge. I remember being particularly struck by Count

Tisza for, like all Hungarian Calvinists, he was wearing a costume in black which stood out among the vivid coloured dresses of the majority of Catholic nobility present.

Then there were the unforgettable highlights of the lengthy ceremony. The first came when he saw his father take the naked state sword (allegedly wielded by King Stephen) and make nine strokes with its massive blade – three each in front and to left and right – as a pledge to ward off imaginary foes. The climax came when Cardinal-Archbishop Janos Csernoch, assisted by Count Tisza, placed the ancient crown on his father's anointed head, at which precise moment salvoes of cannon and trumpet fanfares resounded outside. The new King, who had received the crown kneeling on the topmost step of the altar, was then handed the royal orb and sceptre and led back to his seat on the double thrown to the shouts of 'Éljén a Király!' ('Long Live the King!'). It was Count Tisza who led the acclamation and the singing of the Hungarian national anthem which followed.

Finally, the boy could watch his mother's role in the proceedings. Clad in a gown of gold-embroidered white brocade, she was led back by the Cardinal-Archbishop to sit on her husband's side at the throne, but not before St Stephen's crown had been lowered, again at the altar, to touch her right shoulder. This merest of brushes with the sacred emblem turned her into the royal consort and the Hungarian Queen. A religious message came with it. 'Receive this crown of glory,' the archbishop intoned, 'so that you know you are the King's wife and are charged always to care for the people of God.'

It was a riveting spectacle for the new Crown Prince of Hungary; his only regret was that he had not been left alone to enjoy it in peace. A mentor had been allotted to sit next to him in his loge and, unhappily for him, the man his parents had chosen was his uncle by marriage, King Ferdinand of Bulgaria.[4] 'Foxy Ferdinand', as he was known, was the archetypal club bore in the royal circle of the old European order. With his huge pointed proboscis and large ears, this jewel-bedecked bisexual apparition resembled rather an elephant than a fox; he was certainly possessed of both elephantine tact and, above all, an elephantine memory. He had an unrivalled knowledge of genealogy and heraldry (a passion of many minor royals). Moreover, after the death in 1910 of King Edward VII of England (the undisputed arbiter in his day of European fashion and etiquette), Ferdinand had taken over as the self-proclaimed expert on protocol and ceremony. This was the man who now, for hour after hour, poured a stream of commentary into the ears of the four year old. As that royal child put it, with restraint, when looking back many years later: 'What I could never get over was that he tried to explain to me all sorts of philosophical things which I did not understand, and I was somewhat unhappy about it, because I would rather have concentrated on following the great event taking place below me.'

However, the greatest spectacle – for the Hungarian magnates, the crowd of onlookers and, above all, for the child himself – was still to be enacted in the open air outside, and Uncle Ferdinand was not allowed to spoil it. When the coronation ceremony was over, Otto and his mother drove by themselves the short distance to the royal palace (in the same splendid coach drawn by six white horses which had delivered them to the church). The newly-crowned monarch meanwhile, proceeded on his white horse with its stirrups of pure gold to the so-called Diszter or coronation mount in the centre of the great cathedral square. The earth underneath it was drawn from the soil of all the sixty-three counties of the land. King Károly IV (as he was now known to his subjects) was called upon to follow the ancient custom by clattering up the mound, state sword in hand and the thousand years of Magyar history pressed in a wobbly jewelled band around his head. Once on the top, he was to brandish the blade in all four directions, symbolising the oath he had just taken 'never to reduce but if possible increase' the territories of his kingdom.

Even for an experienced horseman it was a daunting task, and the icy ground was no help; but Karl accomplished it with only a slight slippage of the crooked crown. Otto, who was watching, alongside his mother, through the windows of the nearby palace, could not contain his joy. The child's shout of 'Papa! Papa!' echoed in the square, to start up a fresh wave of cheering.

To the outside world, this was nothing but a display of medieval mummery. To those watching, and indeed to all Hungarians, it was actuality, because the Middle Ages – and indeed the Dark Ages – were moulded together into their present, like the striates of a stone. For the child, and his parents, the coronation had created a special bond with the Hungarian nation – closer than with any other of their thirteen peoples, the Austrians included. It was a bond which, for all three of them, was to last a lifetime. The oath of 30 December 1916 remained the father's most solemn pledge as sovereign. In exile, as we shall see, it became his one flickering hope of restoration. As for Otto, it was to be seventy years before he stood on Budapest's cathedral square again; but he had forgotten nothing, including the loquacious Uncle Ferdinand.

To the dismay of Budapest society – which had been rummaging in its wardrobes, removing family jewels from its bank vaults and sprucing up its town palaces for a week of coronation revelry – the newly-crown pair returned to Vienna that same evening with their son. The problems awaiting them in their Austrian capital were already too grave to brook delay. Things were to move from grave to desperate in the brief two-year span of Karl's rule.

Otto and the little siblings who were born during their parent's reign after him remained shielded, until the very end, from the dramas and sufferings of the war, and the growing shadow it threw across the crown.[5] Food rationing bothered them little because, even in peacetime, plain (almost spartan) tastes had been the order of the day. Nor was there any sudden descent from sumptuousness, again because simplicity, bordering at times on a solid bourgeois lifestyle, was what their parents had always preferred. The resplendent state apartments in the Hofburg and Schönbrunn palaces were, of course, kept on throughout the war, and used whenever required. But, for Otto and the other children, the Villa Wartholz remained the family home and it was largely from its broad terraces that he saw the war.

It was here, for example, and not on any palace courtyard or army parade ground, that he watched as the Monarchy's front-line heroes assembled to be decorated by his father with the Maria Theresia order, the highest award for bravery. Wartholz was also sometimes the stage for the high politics of the Four Power alliance.[6] Another vivid childhood image was the visit of the exotically-clad Turkish War Minister, Enver Pasha, and his suite. Frequent visitors to the villa, and often captured in family photographs, were two of the children's' Bourbon-Parma uncles, Felix and René. Both had grown up in Austria and had joined the Emperor's army in 1914. Yet the two older brothers, Sixtus and Xavier, for whom France and their great castle at Chambord was home, both became lieutenants in the French army, and were thus now enemy subjects. It was a difficult trauma for the young Crown Prince to grasp. Yet his sharpest memories of Wartholz remained those implanted by nature, not by war: the walks in the surrounding forests and mountains, and the swarms of wild cyclamen and gentian which in those days surrounded the house.

Perhaps the most extraordinary feature of this wartime infancy was the place he looked back on as 'the other home'. It was a modest building in the supreme army command at Baden, just south west of Vienna. This was not because his father wanted to instil martial discipline into his children. Quite the reverse: the object was to preserve something of a peaceful family life amidst the bustle of a military headquarters. Soon after his accession, he had moved the seat of his High Command back from Teschen to this agreeable Austrian spa town in order to put some distance between the Monarchy and its German ally, which had grown more overpowering then ever once war had broken out.

Karl now chose a simple two-storey yellow-washed house in the centre of the town for official and family accommodation combined. The study of this so-called Kaiservilla served as his office, where the generals made their reports and strategy was mapped out. Next to it was the very simply-furnished living room, with a small table and four plain chairs and equally plain armchairs behind. Upstairs were the dining and living quarters, and the children had to do with two small dark rooms overlooking the inner court. It was all very non-imperial; but that was the point. Karl had to spend most of his days here and he wanted his young family to be there with him. Wartholz was too far distant for a daily journey to and fro, so their third base was set up at Laxenburg,[7] as beautiful but also as unpretentious as any Habsburg castle could be, and less than half an hour's drive away.

The young Emperor who, as early as 2 December 1916 took over the supreme command in person, had to make frequent inspection trips from Baden. Wherever practicable, his wife and children also went along, almost as if it were a family outing. Sometimes, the little Crown Prince, invariably clad in white, could be seen, following his father by returning the salute of guards of honour.

> My sister Adelheid usually came with me when we travelled to these different places. We were already at that time, I would almost say, a team, as we remained ever afterwards, and I particularly remember our visits to the air force base near Wiener Neustadt. My father decorated some of the officers who had done an outstanding job. Meanwhile we were shown the aeroplanes which impressed me very much.

There were journeys which took them far away from the war as well. Memorable above all was the visit they all paid in mid-July of 1918 to Pressburg for the celebration of the Harvest Festival.[8] They left from their baroque shooting-lodge of Eckartsau (soon to play a large role in their lives) and travelled by steamer along the Danube. Originally, only Otto was supposed to accompany his parents, but the four-year-old Adelheid made such a fuss at missing the boat trip that she was allowed to come among. The festival turned into a spontaneous surge of monarchist feeling from the mainly Magyar population. The same shouts of 'Éljén a Király!' which had rung through Budapest's coronation church at the beginning of the reign came from the crowd now, and the King-Emperor led the singing of the Hungarian national hymn. There was a domestic touch even here. Otto, as Crown Prince, should have kept his head covered during the anthem. But he forgot and his father, erect in field-marshal's uniform, had to hold for him the broad-brimmed white hat in his left hand. This was the first time the family had ever travelled along the Danube. It was also to be the last time they were to appear anywhere together in power, in peace and in public.

'Is this all a dream?' Zita asked her husband as they returned to a trouble-laden Vienna. Her husband assured her sadly that it was. Indeed, by now, there were more insistent sounds in his ears than the cheers of the Pressburg crowds: loud creaks were coming out of the imperial edifice. For the first time, it seemed that the whole structure might be crumbling underneath him.

Portents of disaster were everywhere in that midsummer of 1918. To begin with, military defeat was looming ever larger and that, as Karl had known from the start, would bring about the downfall of the Monarchy. On the key Western Front, the German Emperor's great spring offensive, launched with much braying about 'final victory', had been decisively repulsed and the 192 German divisions involved had begun what was to be instead their final retreat – back to the homeland. The Eastern Front had been in limbo ever since March, when Germany and Austria had signed separate peaces with the neo-Bolshevik rulers of Russia. But the threat from Lenin's regime, which Karl had always predicted,[9] was nonetheless growing.

The news that Tsar Nicholas and his entire family had been slaughtered by the Bolsheviks at Ekaterinburg on 17 July sent a shudder down the spines of all sovereigns. For the Habsburg Monarchy, however, the menace of this new atheist crusade was already closer to home: that 'bacillus' of which Karl had warned the German High Command in vain was now at work among his own troops. Prisoners of war returning home from Russia after the peace treaty brought back with them strong doses of revolutionary fervour collected in Bolshevik-run camps. And, wherever there was close contact on the Eastern Front, the Slav soldiers of the Monarchy had been defecting by the thousands to their big Slav anti-war brothers.

The political outlook for the Emperor Karl was equally black. During the summer, the Paris-based Czech National Council, by far the most active of the exiled pro-independence groups, had been recognised by the Western allies as the '*de facto* belligerent government of Czechoslovakia'.[10] When, on 3 September 1918, the United States finally signalled its acceptance of the new policy, the Dual Monarchy stood disowned, even as an entity, by its enemies. President Wilson continued to be Karl's last hope as a peace-broker who might still save his crown and he even resorted to a direct appeal for an armistice to the White House, over the head of his German ally. Yet, despite this gesture of independent action, and all the desperate personal efforts Karl had earlier made to distance himself from Berlin,[11] the Monarchy was ending the war more than ever under the heel of Germany and that, for the Western powers, spelt its damnation.

In any case, it was already clear that the Quadruple Alliance was not going to win. This once-formidable coalition was breaking off at its rusting hinges. The first to pull himself and his country away from the structure was none other than that unctuous compère at the Budapest coronation, Ferdinand of Bulgaria. True to his nickname, 'Foxy' had been weighing up his own chances of survival throughout the summer, as the tide of war turned steadily in favour of the Western powers. On 25 September he jumped. At 7.30 that evening, a telegram reached the Kaiservilla in Baden in which the Emperor's German brother-in-law announced that he had unilaterally ordered the complete surrender of his forces to the Allied armies advancing up the Balkans from their Greek base. The self-styled Tsar of Bulgaria was simply dropping the crown for his son to pick up and legging it back to his native Coburg.[12]

Ferdinand himself was no loss, but Bulgaria was. Despite its modest size and dubious loyalty, it formed the land bridge to Turkey, the fourth member of the alliance, which was now cut off. Even more important was the blow to morale. Soldiers crossing the lines had become commonplace along the Monarchy's battle-fronts. Even whole units had vanished. But for a country to desert was something ominously new. A rot seemed to have set in that nothing could stop, and so it proved.

The pleasant routine of commuting almost daily between Laxenburg and Baden became a thing of the past, while visits to their beloved Wartholz were unthinkable. Instead, from the beginning of October onwards, the family based themselves at Schönbrunn. Maria Theresia's summer palace, built for leisure and pageant, had become a gloomy imperial bunker from which the dynasty's final struggle for survival was directed.

The Emperor's last throw on the political front was a 'People's Manifesto', issued from Schönbrunn in the early evening of 16 October. In it he declared that Austria should be transformed into a federal state.[13] Each racial component was invited to set up its own national council to take charge of its affairs and implement the proposed transformation under the overall supervision of the crown. It was a concept he had often outlined to his confidants before ascending the throne, but one he had deemed impossible to carry through in wartime. Now, the shock waves that Bulgaria's defection had started up among all his Slav subjects left him no choice. Perhaps this would persuade President Wilson that he was earnest about democratic reform.

The Western powers ignored the move: for them it was a question of 'too little, too late'. But at home Austria's Slav peoples leapt on the manifesto; for them it was a matter of 'What have we got to lose?' One by one, they set about setting up councils which the crown had empowered them to establish. And, one by one, Czechs, Croats, Slovenes and Poles, they started transforming these into independent governments over which the crown would no longer have authority. Things started to move even in Vienna, though in typically addled fashion. Here a 'Provisional National Assembly of German-Austria' was formed by the three main parties. In this early stage, only the Social Democrats wanted a republic, though most seemed to favour a tribal link-up with the Germanic north. As we have seen, the concept of Austria *per se* was both too dim and too fuzzy for its inhabitants to grasp.

So far, the children had been kept as far away as possible from all the chaos and commotion their Uncle Ferdinand had set in train. But by the last week of October their parents had decided it was time to think about the safety of the family as well as the future of the crown. On 23 October they left Schönbrunn all together in a convoy of cars to head for Budapest. One pretext for the trip was to open a new university at Debrecen, where the largely Calvinist crowds gave them a thunderous welcome as though the royal couple had decades of reign ahead, instead of the few weeks which now remained. But the real purpose of the journey was revealed by what had been piled aboard the cars: not merely enough baggage for a lengthy absence, but also a sizeable part of their jewellery. Karl had left one capital of his Dual Monarchy as Emperor, but was heading for its twin as King Károly IV. Budapest was deemed to be safer than Vienna; Hungary would surely prove the last bastion of the dynasty. The coronation oath still sounded in the ears of the royal couple.

They took up residence in Gödöllö, the lovely little baroque castle just outside the capital which had been such a favourite refuge of the ever-wandering Empress Elisabeth. It was still a peaceful setting now, with a park for the children to play in. But the three days the King Emperor spent there turned into a frenzied nightmare, as he tried to find a Prime Minister prepared and qualified to head a royal Hungarian government in the face of a mounting republican turmoil. Possible candidates came and went in a constant stream of audiences. Nearly all were aristocrats (an Apponyi, a Battyány, an Andrássy and a Hadik among them). They included the man Karl most dreaded but finally had to name to the post: the forty-three year-old Count Michael Károlyi, a radical populist reformer who was to betray his King and his class before being betrayed himself in turn by his illusions.[14]

Karl could not stay long enough in Budapest to sort out the Hungarian imbroglio on the spot. The last, and in some ways the greatest, crisis the Dual Monarchy was to face had just erupted on the Italian front, where the Allied armies had mounted an annihilating blow against his forces. The royal couple had to get back to Vienna without an hour's delay; but what was to be done about the children? The risky decision was taken to leave all of them in Gödöllö.

For the main reason, one must go back once more to that coronation oath in the Matthias Church. The crown laid on them there was the bond not merely with their Hungarian subjects of today but with nine hundred years of their history. If the entire royal family fled Hungary while not directly threatened, it would appear as abandonment, and a signal that they never planned to return. The presence of the children, hostages presented out of free will, would form a pledge. Moreover, with this new emergency on Austria's southern front, there was even less guarantee that Vienna would be more secure than Budapest – at least as seen from the tranquil perspective of Gödöllö. Finally, they were being left in good hands. A trusted lady-in-waiting, the young Countess Thérèse Korff-Schmising-Kerssenbrock (mercifully always known simply as 'Korffi'),[15] was to stay behind and the whole party would be looked after by Prince René, one of the two Bourbon-Parma brothers serving as officers in the Austrian army.[16]

None of this debate was ever communicated to the children. Nor when the time came, on the evening of 26 October, for the parents to leave and board the royal train back to Vienna did they show any of the anguish they felt. It was treated as any normal leave-taking. Otto recalled afterwards that this was exactly how he and the other children had accepted it. They were, after all, so used to their parents' comings and goings throughout the war years. This seemed just another of those sudden departures, with an early reunion ahead.

That reunion came earlier – and in far different circumstances – than expected. By the end of the month the mob, which Károlyi and his fellow-radicals had prodded into action to promote their cause, took the left-wing cause over. Magyar volatility displaced Magyar loyalism. Hungary's immediate future was being decided not in Crown Council meetings or even in Parliament, but in the streets. It was time for the royal hostages at Gödöllö to get out fast. The crown no longer protected them.

It was as well that they had a young army officer in charge, for the escape, made on 31 October, was planned along military lines. Otto always remembered the adventurous trip:

> My Uncle René followed our motor convoy with one car loaded with cans of petrol. His plan was to set this ablaze to block the road to any unit of the so-called Red Guards which tried to catch us. The notion of a Bolshevik revolution was already very lively. But in fact we were not followed and by the afternoon we

had reached Pozsony where all was complete peace just as it had been when we made that river trip from Eckartsau in the summer.[17]

A few hours later they were back in the relative safety of Schönbrunn.

The family reunion was the only cause their parents had for rejoicing. Everything else was gloom, high drama and chaos as the dynasty entered the last ten days of its life. As in September, the battlefront interacted with the home front in disastrous fashion. Within a week of launching their offensive the Allied armies in Italy, who had smashed the Austrian defence line along the Piave river, had surged forward to take nearly a 100,000 prisoners. The defenders had been reduced by their parlous supply system to little more than an army of hungry scarecrows before battle was joined. They were further enfeebled by a stream, now growing into a flood, of deserters from their multi-racial ranks as Czech, Slovak, Polish, Slovene and, above all, Hungarian units,[18] deserted en masse and tramped back to their homelands, now administered by their own National Councils.

All this might have been swallowed by the Austrian people (for whom the Italians were the enemy) as the bitter fortunes of war. But worse was to come. By a combination of Italian guile and Austrian muddle-headedness, the armistice which Karl was forced to sue for turned into a costly battlefield farce. The retreating defenders were given to believe that the ceasefire was coming into effect on 3 November, but for the Italians it was to begin twenty-four hours later. The result (the so-called 'victory' of Vittorio Veneto) was that, within a day, the Italians had netted another 200,000 prisoners, many of these captured while dozing next to their stocked arms. The fault lay somewhere between the Austrian negotiating team in Italy and their Ministry of War in Vienna; but the blame was laid on their hapless Commander-in-Chief in Schönbrunn. The dynasty, already reeling on its knees, had received one last vicious blow below the belt.

The only question which remained was when and, above all, how it would surrender. That surrender must come was made plain, during the first week of November, by the way in which Schönbrunn itself was being gradually deserted, not just by most of the court officials and staff but by its military guards. The first to go was the battalion from the 69th Hungarian Infantry Regiment which provided all the sentries. They simply marched off, obeying the order from the new Minister of War in Budapest to return home.[19] The two hundred so-called 'palace gendarmes' also gradually melted away, as did the soldiers of the Life Guards, despite their special oath of loyalty. Familiar faces among the courtiers were also disappearing one by one. Otto noticed in particular that his father's aide-de-comp Prince Zdenko Lobkowitz, whose plump and cheerful presence had been a daily feature of palace life throughout the reign, was suddenly nowhere to be seen.

Then something extraordinary happened. Out of the blue, and without being summoned, the young cadets from the military academies of Wiener Neustadt and Traiskirchen appeared, immaculate in full kit, to guard their sovereign. For Otto and his siblings, these boys, many of whom were barely in their teens, were not seen as new guards so much as new playmates. 'We were delighted about the young people from the Academies who, after all, were relatively closer to our own age. We played games with them in the gardens around the palace and it was all happy-spirited.'

For the children, this surrealist atmosphere of playing with these doughty toy soldiers as though they were all still in kindergarten lasted a few days longer while – far away from Schönbrunn – the last act of the Great War was completed. On 9 November, the German Empire transformed itself into a republic and its erstwhile Supreme War Lord was bundled off by his generals into Dutch exile like a piece of unwanted baggage. That cast the die for the Monarchy in Vienna. The National Assembly, fortified by a telegram just received from President Wilson congratulating them on 'throwing off the yoke of the Austro-Hungarian Empire', was finally prodded into action to remove their own monarch.

No angry mob surged down the Schönbrunnerstrasse to take the un-guarded palace by force. The lungs of Austria's revolutionaries proved stronger than their hearts. Moreover, the aura of Franz Josef still hung over the palace. Socialist Party leaders who led the call for abdication admitted afterwards that even they would not have dared to present it had that imperial Titan still been holding audiences at the palace. As it was, the formula respectfully submitted to Karl on the morning of 11 November by two of his own Ministers did not demand that he should renounce his throne. Instead, a manifesto was produced. Its terms had been agreed during forty-eight hours of hectic comings and goings between the new State Council of the republic which was about to be born and the last Cabinet of the empire which was about to die (*both* working in a ghastly parallel existence); the National Assembly; the Archbishop of Vienna, Cardinal Piffl; and, of course, Karl's own personal emissaries. Its two key sentences were: 'I recognise in advance whatever decisions that German-Austria may make about its political from ... I renounce all participation in the affairs of state ...' [20]

The Empress first needed convincing that this formula did not amount to formal abdication. Once her protests had been met, her husband took out the metallic pencil he always carried with him for signing documents and, with the brief word 'Karl' ended six and a half centuries of Habsburg rule.

Otto and the other children knew nothing of all these negotiations and it never even entered their heads that their father would ever be anything but the Emperor. But, the night before, they had at last been told how grave the situation had become for the family. Otto recalled:

> The last evening we were told by our parents that we had to leave the palace. It was made completely clear to us – by that I mean to Adelheid and myself – that revolution was breaking out and that we would have to get away from Vienna. It was a tragic thing and seemed to be happening all against a background of darkness. On the final day we first went with our parents to the palace chapel where Dr Seidel, who was the court bishop, conducted a short ceremony of prayer that we might one day return here. Then we waited for the cars to drive us away.

It was only then that the children learned of their destination: Eckartsau, the shooting lodge on the Marchfeld from where, less than four months before, they had set out on that memorable Danube trip to an ecstatic welcome at Pressburg. The Dutch and Swiss Ministers, representing all the neutral missions in Vienna, had offered the royal family personal protection to escort them abroad. But Karl had declined to leave what was still, to him, his realm. One courtier had suggested Innsbruck, the Tyrolean refuge whence his ancestors had fled when revolutionary tremors had last shaken Austria 170 years before. Yet, though closer to Switzerland, that was still too far from Vienna, where the drama was being played out. Eckartsau, on the other hand, lay less than fifty miles away and, being sited at the so-called 'Three Countries Corner', was right on the borders of both Hungary and Slovakia. Above all, it was indisputably the Emperor's private property and not just another state dwelling, like the Vienna palaces, which the new republic would soon be confiscating.

So, in great secrecy, a convoy of motor cars was assembled for the journey. This proved no easy task and it was not until 6.30 in the evening, an hour and a half after the appointed time, that the vehicles appeared in the small inner court. For the family and, above all, for Otto and the elder children, there was another heart-rending moment of leave-taking. Lining the sides of the arcades, drawn up in two perfect ranks, were their hide-and-seek playmates, the young cadets of the military academies, stiffly at attention but some with tears rolling down their cheeks. They, at least, had lived up to the motto their founder, Empress Maria Theresia, had bestowed on them: 'Alzeit Getreu' ('Forever Loyal').

It was a gloomy evening and the deserted palace was shrouded in a November mist when they boarded the vehicles. Otto squeezed into the back of the first car together with his parents and all the other children except the infant Karl Ludwig who rode with 'Korffi' and the nurses in the car behind. The remnant of the Emperor's court that had stayed behind filled the other vehicles. They did not risk driving out of the main gate of the palace. Instead, the convoy slipped out along the tree-lined gravel drive which led to the eastern gate. They reached Eckartsau late that night, without any challenge along the circuitous route chosen. For Otto, the main memory was again one of the darkness. 'Vienna had become a dark city now.' But at least they had made a safe escape, unlike the doomed flight in 1791 of that Bourbon ancestor of the Empress, King Louis XVI and his equally ill-fated wife Maria-Antoinette, a Habsburg ancestor of Karl. Though the same two dynasties were again involved as man and wife, Eckartsau did not become a second Varennes.

In later years, Otto recalled, they more than once discussed what he terms 'the complete abandonment' of the royal family in its hour of need by those who might have been expected to show support. Of the aristocracy – all of whom owed titles and estates to the dynasty – only one is remembered as having actually turned up at Schönbrunn bringing a weapon and ready to fight. This was Count Karl Franz Walderdorff, who had served with the Emperor as a brother officer in the Seventh Dragoons. The Count had been convalescing from war wounds at his Bohemian castle in Alt Bunzlau when news reached him that the situation in Vienna was turning nasty. He somehow managed to make his way to the capital with a hunting rifle concealed under his loden cloak and this was the weapon he offered to use.

The commanders of the imperial forces were equally scarce on the ground when and where it mattered. One who was ready to march to the Emperor's aid was Field-Marshal Boroevič, who had led part of his defeated army Group in good order back from Italy to Carinthia. But his two offers of aid, in telegrams addressed personally to the Emperor, never got further than the Ministry of War. As for the commander of the Vienna garrison, General Dankl, who knew of this and other offers from the field, he simply sat on his hands. He did not show himself once at Schönbrunn during the final crisis, let alone send any troops.[21]

One who did show up was an ambitious young naval officer who had been a guest at the Schwarzau wedding, Niklós Horthy. Now an Admiral, he had come to discuss the surrender of his entire Adriatic fleet to the newly-formed republic of Croatia. A moment of high Magyar drama followed as Horthy, tears in his eyes, raised his right hand and swore never to rest until his sovereign had been restored to his thrones in Vienna and Budapest. Karl was to feel the irony of this unsolicited oath less than three years later.

Finally, and most hurtfully, was the abandonment of the Emperor by his own Habsburg family. Most of its numerous Archdukes did not even have the pretext of active military service for staying away. But not one of them seems to have shown his face at Schönbrunn in its last weeks as an imperial residence, which might as well have become a leper hospital. As for the Hungarian-based members, these were already starting their own power game. It was all too much for the Emperor's Hungarian Court Chamberlain, Count Josef Hunyády, an utterly devoted official who was at his post until the end.

Otto was told in later years that, shortly before they all left Schönbrunn, the Court Chamberlain approached his Emperor and took up the correct position for giving a formal report: at attention, hands held stiffly downwards, the palms pressing against the sides of his braided trouser uniform. But the message he delivered, though couched in the correct style, was far from official. 'I beg most obediently to report: Your Majesty has a family that stinks.' [22]

There was no reproof for this rebuke of the missing archdukes. A few hours later, Count Hunyády took up his seat next to the chauffeur in the front car of the escape convoy.

4

Exile at Home: Eckartsau

For the Emperor and his band of companions, the court had simply trans-ferred itself from the great palace of Schönbrunn to the family's baroque shooting lodge on the Danubian water meadows. The monarchists left behind in the capital looked at it the same way, even if they were afraid to show the black-yellow Habsburg colours on their sleeves: there was too much revolutionary red about for that. Though the reality was very different – in terms of power Karl was now little more than an impoverished country squire – events in what had been his Dual Monarchy could still not move forward without him.

On 13 November, less than forty-eight hours after his arrival and the day after the 'Republic of German-Austria' had been proclaimed in Vienna, a delegation of Hungarian magnates turned up at Eckartsau to discuss with their King what should be done about St Stephen's crown. Ironically, it was led by the Prince-Primate Archbishop Czernoch, the same prelate who had placed that crown on Karl's head only two years before. Others in the party included Prince Nicholas Esterházy and Count Dessewffy, two pillars of the Hungarian feudal order that had cheered its new ruler to the rafters on that coronation day. Now their mission – on instructions from Prime Minister Károlyi – was to persuade the King Emperor to abdicate outright.[1] The emissaries were anxious to obey orders, if only to save their own skins. Not, it must be said, without reason: the fearless Count Tisza, the only statesman in the entire Hungarian imbroglio, had been gunned down in his Budapest villa at dusk on 31 October by three soldiers of the 'Red Guard'.

Karl remained unmoved, either by their credentials or their panic. He had three long sessions alone with them, stretching from noon to early evening and, in the end, they had to settle for a repeat of the Vienna formula: withdrawal from all participation in the current affairs of state but no abdication. When he signed a brief three-sentence statement to this effect, Karl had simply laid St Stephen's crown on his lap. He was never to take his hands off it.

Many more tense days lay ahead, and not a few hazards. Yet, looking back on these four months of domestic exile, Otto remembered them as 'extraordinary but still very beautiful'. One reason was that – like Wartholz, Laxenburg and Gödöllö – here too they had a large park around them. They took long walks around the estate and, despite the Red Guard units occasionally on the prowl outside the gates, they felt fairly safe.[2] They would sometimes drive for hours along the swampy paths in a small horse-drawn Victoria coach. The woods and water meadows of Eckartsau, which stretched down to the Danube's banks, had a particular appeal: everything from wild partridge to the fish-eating cormorants flew up around them. The illusion of normality was further strengthened by the daily routine of lessons which continued for Otto and his sister.

What the park gates could not hold out was Spanish influenza, which was raging on a pandemic scale in Austria, as throughout Europe, in these winter months.[3] All the children went down with the disease, though Otto and the others were not as badly affected as the infant of the family, Karl Ludwig, who was barely eighteen months old. His condition gave such cause for concern that his mother at one point considered somehow getting him out to Switzerland for proper medical care. If the Empress herself was a victim, she did not show it. The Emperor held out as long as possible, helping with the administration of his tiny 'kingdom', as well as continuing with the somewhat unreal business of giving audiences to whoever turned up at this phantom court.

He had shown no disposition to behave like a phantom Emperor towards his visitors. Otto particularly remembered one sharp rebuke his father delivered to an Hungarian aristocrat who had called at Eckartsau. During lunch, at which the little Crown Prince was present, the guest launched into a furious tirade against the Jews, who were playing a leading role in Budapest's revolutionary movement. Though he well knew this, Karl jumped immediately to their defence. Apart from the fact that many Jews had stayed loyal, he retorted they were all subjects of the Empire and, as such, had the right to be respected. It was a dual experience for the child and one he never forgot. For the first time in his young life, he had encountered anti-Semitism on the one hand, and how a fair-minded person should deal with it on the other.

On 15 December 1918, audiences and much else came to an abrupt suspension as Karl succumbed to a particularly virulent attack of the flu and had to take to his bed. The Christmas that followed was, therefore, a rather sombre festival. There was no difficulty in finding a tree for the traditional exchange of gifts on the evening of the 24th, but producing the gifts themselves was a problem. It was largely solved by the happy discovery of a trunk that had been deposited at Eckartsau containing an assortment of minor presents which the royal family had been given on their official journeys. These were now put in a small heap at the foot of the tree and labelled for distribution between children and parents. The domestic staff were given little scraps of chocolate and other precious food items which had been saved specially and wrapped up. Otto remembers that his father got up for the occasion but was so weak that he had to remain seated in an armchair and retired again to bed immediately afterwards.

Food was not the only thing in short supply, despite the game which could be shot in the woods. The electricity was more off than on, as the generator ran out of fuel; candles for use when the power failed were scarce; matches to light them scarcer still. Soap was another rarity, so much so that the Empress put her children as far as possible in dark-coloured clothing, to reduce the need for washing. The only commodity available in plenty that Christmas was good wine. This was ironic in view of the abstemious tastes the parents had always had. The Emperor, however, had been advised to drink wine to build up his strength. When Count Hunyády made a foray to the imperial cellars in Vienna with the request, the old palace cellarman, who still presided over the stocks, had urged him to take away all he wanted, with the hope that it would do the Emperor some good. Toasts to the royal family's health were, it seemed, being drunk that Christmas right across Vienna. All behind closed shutters in private; the old order did not dare to make even symbolic gestures in public against the new.

The turn of the year brought little cheer. To begin with, the Emperor's successors in power began to put political pressure on him. Karl Renner, the leader of the Austrian Socialist party and most prominent figure in the newly-declared republic of 'German Austria', turned up unexpectedly at Eckartsau in the first week of January to try and persuade the royal family to leave Austria of their own accord. Renner, who had once served in the imperial bureaucracy, should have guessed what would happen. As Karl had not abdicated and Eckartsau was still his miniature court, he resolved to play by the rules of the full-scale model. The visitor, having arrived unannounced, was served the best food available at luncheon downstairs but with only one of the Emperor's aides, Zeno von Schonta, for company. Otto and all the children were kept with their parents on the first floor and the one-time servant of the dynasty departed not merely empty-handed but outplayed.

The case which the visitor had presented over luncheon was a blend of unctuousness and veiled threats. These damp Danube meadows, he pointed out, were very bad for the royal family's health, especially during an influenza-ridden winter. The aide replied blandly that they could find no fault with the local air. Then came the hint of menace. It would be well for the family to leave, Renner went on, otherwise there might be 'unpre-dictable actions by impetuous elements'.[4] This was a more substantial argument than all talk of the climate. The security situation was indeed worsening. No member of the family came under attack, yet shots had been fired at the gamekeepers as they patrolled the boundaries of the estate. Moreover, food deliveries from Vienna were becoming increasingly erratic. It was a bleak February that came round. Then came an event out of the blue which transformed everything. On the 16th of that month, two British officers arrived by motor-car at Eckartsau and announced that they were taking over responsibility for the royal family's welfare and protection.

Of all the postscripts to the Great War, this was one of the most extra-ordinary. The helping hand from the ex-enemy had not been extended as a local gesture of sympathy from the British military authorities in Vienna, nor from the government in Westminster. This was the hand of King George V, stretched out from Buckingham Palace, as sovereign to sovereign. The King nursed a distinctly uneasy conscience over his reluctance to support a rescue bid for his cousin, Tsar Nicholas, the year before. The butchery of the Russian Emperor and his family at Ekaterinburg by Bolshevik thugs had brought soul-searching as well as shock. There was no blood tie between the houses of Windsor and Habsburg and, moreover, they had fought for four bitter years in opposite camps. But the King had not forgotten that, as Archduke Karl, newly-engaged to his Bourbon Princess, the beleaguered squire of Eckartsau had attended his coronation in London (indeed, for the procession, he had been placed in the carriage immediately in front of those carrying the British royal family). But the events of the summer of 1918 rather than those of the summer of 1911 were uppermost in the King's mind now. When told that Eckartsau could easily become a second Ekaterinburg,[5] he hastily arranged for emergency military protection.

The British officer who soon assumed total responsibility for this might have been machine-tooled for the task.[6] Lieutenant-Colonel Edward Lisle Strutt, a grandson of the first Lord Belper, was a British aristocrat with extensive pre-war social connections in the old European order. (By an extraordinary coincidence, one of the first things he noticed in the large bedroom allotted to him at Eckartsau was a photograph taken in pre-war St Moritz showing himself standing next to the ill-fated Archduke Franz Ferdinand.)[7] Strutt was also a Catholic, which was most appropriate in view of the fact that his august charges had been crowned Apostolic Majesties. He was also an excellent linguist, fluent in both French and German. As the Emperor's English was very indifferent, they were able to communicate freely in the other two languages, which was always convenient and positively vital whenever absolute clarity was essential.

Above all, unlike the charming but distinctly non-martial medical officer whom he replaced, Strutt was a warrior. The left-hand breast of his uniform jacket bore a broad swathe of ribbons, beginning with a cluster from the Boer War, and ending with more than half a dozen British, French, Belgian and Romanian decorations for bravery from the war which had just ended. He had been enjoying life at the Hotel Danieli in Venice when the telegram had arrived from the Allied military headquarters in Constantinople ordering him to 'proceed at once to Eckartsau to give Emperor and Empress moral support of British Government'.[8] He had no idea what 'moral support' meant (the term was indeed deliberately vague). He had even less idea where Eckartsau was. He could only assume that the telegram was referring to the Austrian royal family. Nonetheless, only five days later, he was driving into the courtyard of the hunting lodge in a large six-seater Austro-Daimler car procured from the Schönbrunn palace stables with the imperial arms on the panels discreetly painted out.

For the children, the arrival of this reassuring figure from what they had known, dimly, as the enemy camp, was a special thrill. He seemed capable of working near miracles. Only forty-eight hours after his arrival a British lorry carrying food rations from Vienna for the entire household (which Strutt estimated at nearly a hundred persons) came through the gates. There was great excitement over the white bread – baked in Padua a fortnight before but still palatable; it was the first the children or anyone else at Eckartsau, had seen since 1916.[9] There were other unknown delights, such as British army bully beef. The older children were reported to have polished off one tin apiece at the first opportunity.

In addition to food and fuel, Strutt was able to infuse into this beleaguered community of exiles something of the steel masculinity which the sick and devastated Emperor could not provide. Indeed, the lorry's supplies had barely been unloaded when the Colonel fell to discussing with Schonta (himself a naval officer) how Eckartsau could be defended in case of real trouble. Apart from Dr Schober's ten armed policemen, they reckoned some twenty servants might be of use in a scratch force under joint Anglo-Austrian monarchist 'command'. Strutt's devotion to the royal family (and especially to the beautiful young Empress, who had fairly bowled him over) was instant and, in the event, was to prove long-lasting. The young Crown Prince shared the sense of total trust in the stranger who was to become a life-long friend. In old age, Otto looked fondly back:

> I still think with great respect and great gratitude towards him. Recently, an English person asked me whether I was not full of resentment against the British for the way they had treated my father later on in his exile. I replied: 'But after all, there was Colonel Strutt'.[10]

Strutt could provide moral support as well as essential supplies and a degree of military protection. He could not, however, save his charges from the onward crush of politics. By a coincidence, the first British officers to come to Eckartsau had arrived on the very day, 16 February, that the new republic was holding its elections. On 4 March, its first Parliament, reflecting the party balance in that poll, had duly assembled. Ten days later, a seemingly stable government had been formed, the first of a series of Left-Right coalitions which were to reappear, like self-seeding plants, at intervals down the century. As leader of the largest party, the Social Democrats, Karl Renner became Chancellor. That same day, 15 March 1919, the British Military Mission in Vienna received orders 'to get the Emperor out of Austria without delay'. His departure was to be 'expedited with all possible means'.

This was no coincidence but simply an immediate recognition of the new reality. Full diplomatic relations would soon have to be established with this new Austrian government; in the meantime, Renner would be heading his country's delegation to negotiate formal peace terms with the Allies. The visitor whom Karl had so roundly snubbed in January now felt powerful enough to dispose of him as he pleased. Back in London, Buckingham Palace had to yield to the Foreign Office. King George was dissuaded from exchanging even royal courtesies with the beleaguered Emperor, let alone following up his urgent pleas for military support.[11]

Yet, thanks to Strutt, Renner was not to have things all his own way. The Colonel had hurried to Vienna to learn that the Coalition Government (including its formerly monarchist Christian-Socialist members) had agreed on a three-pronged ultimatum to Karl: abdicate all rights and live in Austria with his family as private citizens; be exiled if refusing abdication; and, finally, face internment if rejecting both abdication and departure. Strutt realised that the best he could do now for his royal charge was to ensure that he left his realm in style and still, if possible, technically as Emperor.[12]

He lost not a moment in organising the first part of that programme. That same afternoon he arranged for a special train to be assembled on receipt of a code-word at Vienna's Westbahnhof. He next proceeded to the Swiss Legation where, simply in the capacity of a British escort officer, he asked for (and later received) formal permission for the royal family to enter Switzerland. Now that the mode of travel and the destination had been fixed, only two problems remained, but each was tough: to persuade Karl to go; and to persuade Renner to let him go as Emperor.

The first hurdle took three days to clear and, in the end it was the Empress (whom the Colonel had always regarded as the effective head of the family) who helped him over it. The Emperor had flatly rejected any idea of leaving by himself and had even claimed that there was no need for any of them to leave Eckartsau at all, as they faced no real danger. This illusion was knocked on the head by an ugly incident which took place on 19 March. One of the carts sent to Schönbrunn to fetch coffee and sugar had been set upon on its return journey, pillaged and smashed to pieces. The driver, who had been beaten up, arrived back on foot, carrying a letter addressed to 'Herr Karl Habsburg'. It contained a receipt for the goods seized and a threat, couched in obscene language, that the attackers were also coming to get 'Karli' himself. More disturbing than the language was the signature. The missive was signed by a senior lieutenant in the newly-mustered army of the republic. It had been regular soldiers on patrol, not marauders, who had destroyed the cart on his orders.

To another regular soldier, the message was clear: Strutt realised that popular feeling was turning against his royal charges, destroying their last screen of security. He went straight to the Empress to have it out with her. At first Zita hesitated. The Colonel finally won her over by arguing for the long term. Republican frenzy – boiling over in Budapest and now bubbling in Vienna – would surely fade. There was no point in risking their lives, for a dead Habsburg was no use to the dynasty whereas live ones could, in better times, serve their purpose. To this argument he added the pledge that her husband would leave, under his protection, as Emperor. When that sank in, it was all over in seconds. The Empress smiled, shook his hand and agreed, for all of them, to act under his orders.

It still took Strutt two more visits to Vienna and two face-to-face confrontations with Renner, to get the Chancellor to drop his insistence that the Emperor must abdicate before leaving the gates of Eckartsau behind him. He succeeded by a mixture of Prussian-style bombast and poker-style bluff. At the first indecisive meeting on 20 March, he at least managed to shake the Chancellor, who was seated at his desk, by barking at him to stand up when a senior British officer entered the room. When Strutt arrived two days later (having already activated the escape train) Renner was already standing up. But he was (understandably) incensed at his treatment and resolved to make this haughty officer enforce the key demand for abdication. Had he but known it, his antagonist was standing on very shaky ground. Another sobering telegram had arrived from London making it clear that the British government could undertake no guarantees concerning the royal party's journey. Strutt was quite on his own, despite the fact that he had so far convinced everyone – from the railway officials up to the Swiss Minister – that he was acting on War Office authority.

When the Chancellor, who was showing more spirit, immediately declared that the Emperor would be interned unless he toed the republican line, the Colonel reacted with the classic technique of the gambler who is bluffing on a weak hand. He raised the stakes to the maximum by placing on the table a telegram on official British Mission paper, signed by himself and addressed 'en clair' to the 'Director of Military Intelligence London'. This proposed that, in view of the Austrian government's obdurate demands concerning the Emperor's departure, the Allied blockade should be re-established and all food trains should be stopped from entering the country.

Had Renner known anything about military matters, or indeed how parliamentary democracy worked, he would have seen through the bluff, for no mere intelligence chief could have issued such a drastic order on behalf of his entire government. But the Chancellor was ignorant on the first count and a novice on the second. This was just as well, for Strutt, sensing trouble, had only drafted the telegram himself a few hours before. It worked. In poker terms, Renner 'folded' and threw in his cards. With a gesture of despair and a pious oath, he agreed the Emperor could leave the country without any conditions being set. Strutt strode out, carefully re-trieving as he left the telegram which could never have been despatched.

Otto had, of course, been unaware of all these manoeuvres. In any case, to the boy, the debate mattered but little. He would not have known what the word abdication meant and could never have imagined it being applied to his father who was and, for him, always would be, the Emperor. But, for the children, the daily routine of lessons and walks in the park and the illusion of normality which they gave was now abruptly terminated. That night, when Strutt arrived back from Vienna with the news, they were told that it was to be their last at Eckartsau. As with all their sudden departures over the last few months, the drama was deliberately underplayed. The family were to move to Switzerland for a while until things at home settled down.

This departure, however, on 23 March 1919, was to be very different from that furtive flight from Schönbrunn. Again there were farewell prayers, but on this occasion they were said at a proper mass taken by Bishop Seydl with the seven-year-old Crown Prince acting as server. The small chapel was crammed to suffocation, mainly because of an influx of the local population. At the end, all joined in the National Anthem, destined to be the last time it was sung before an Austrian Emperor, who sat with his family in the gallery. Most of the congregation were in tears.

There was no time for sobbing after that. The business of packing, which went on at full tilt throughout the day, produced an atmosphere of adventure rather than sadness. For the children, the excitement became greater when, at 2 p.m., lorries arrived from Vienna bearing six British military policemen, resplendent in their special uniform, to load the vehicles and act as armed escort. Thanks to Strutt, the British presence was even more in evidence when, shortly before 7 p.m. that evening, the royal family and their tiny 'court' arrived at the local station of Kopfstetten. There, looking huge on the light railway track, was the imperial train in full array – three saloon carriages, one kitchen and one dining car, two luggage vans with an extra open truck to carry two splendid motor vehicles. And, between the Austro-Daimler and the Mercedes, flew a large Union Jack to suggest that the might of Britain was standing guard over everything. Strutt had kept his promise: Karl was indeed leaving as Emperor.

There was even a miniature military ceremony before he boarded the train. A crowd of some two thousand people had gathered in the pouring rain and a darkness illuminated only by car headlights. Karl, who was wearing his field-marshal's uniform, shook hands with each man in a small group of wounded Austrian soldiers who had turned up to say goodbye to their one-time Commander-in-Chief. Then, with the British military policemen providing the guard of honour, he boarded his saloon car. There were no shouts as the imperial train pulled out. Instead, what Strutt described as 'a sort of low moan' came from the crowd.

Their journey into Switzerland lasted nearly twenty-two hours. There were no demonstrations, republican or monarchist, en route: neither jeers nor cheers, as though the people were simply numbed by the sight of the last royal train steaming away out of Austria. Indeed, the only incidents on the long journey westwards involved Allied troops. At Innsbruck a crowd of scruffy-looking Italian troops – cigarettes in their mouths and uniforms unbuttoned – crowded the train, some climbing up on the shoulders on their comrades to gape through the windows. On an order from Strutt, the Austrian police cleared them off, helped by 'Gussl', the Emperor's favourite dog who had been allowed to travel with him.

The most memorable event of the whole trip occurred soon afterwards when they stopped at Imst to put on a mountain engine to climb the steep Fern Pass ahead. A guard of twenty-five British soldiers stood lined up on the platform;[13] as the train moved out, they presented arms to the royal family, who were watching from the saloon car windows. The only official salute during their voyage from homeland into exile had come, like their protection on board, from their ex-enemies. The spectacle proved too much for the Emperor. For the one and only time during the harrowing journey, he broke into tears.

The little Crown Prince was too young to grasp the poignancy of all this. Indeed, in order to go on projecting this train trip to the children as just another of their family voyages, the Emperor had behaved rather like a tourist guide. What Otto always remembered from their journey into exile was the beauty of the mountains of Tyrol, with his father naming for him all the principal ranges towering one after the other above them. The child had never seen them before; nearly half a century was to pass before he would see them again.

5

Swiss Dramas

Two things deadened the pang of leaving their homeland behind them – for the very first time, in the case of Otto and the other children. To begin with, the courteous efficiency of the Swiss authorities who awaited them had acted like a local anaesthetic. The one-time imperial train had crossed the Rhine and pulled into the Swiss border station of Buchs punctual to the minute at 3.45 in the afternoon of Monday, 26 March 1919. Soldiers stood motionless along the platform, a passive guard of honour. The official delegation of welcome was headed by a Monsieur Borsinger de Baden of the Swiss Foreign Office, who conveyed a message of greeting to Karl from his Federal President. Blue-coloured Swiss identity papers, which had been prepared in advance, were handed over. These gave the new arrivals un-limited permits of residence, subject to the standard condition of good political behaviour: Karl and his party must abstain from any activity which might cause embarrassment to their host government. Even this mild caution was tactfully passed on via the aide, Count Ledóchowski. It was hard to feel emotional when encompassed by such clinical protocol.

It was, by contrast, a time to give emotions full rein when, in a convoy of cars, they reached their first refuge on Swiss soil, the nearby château of Wartegg on the shores of Lake Constance. This was no official residence designated by the authorities but a family home. Back in 1860, the Parmas had purchased the property as a safe sanctuary on neutral territory to flee from the upheavals of the Risorgimento. Half a century later, it was their relatives and children, including the Princes Sixtus and Xavier, who formed the welcoming party. At Wartegg, the Habsburgs had now joined the Bourbons and the Braganzas as dethroned dynasties abroad. They, of course, did not think of it like that; for them it was a joyous family reunion.

This domestic idyll could not last for long. To begin with, the Swiss authorities were suggesting, still with impeccable politeness, that they would feel happier if the dethroned ruler moved to a canton much further to the west for his regular abode. (From the balconies of Wartegg, the mountains of Vorarlberg seemed almost close enough to touch.) In any case, the château was simply too small to accommodate Karl and his suite of aides, tutors and servants. From the first day, these had had to be put up in neighbouring hotels and pensions. It took more than two months to find a suitable alternative and it was not until 20 May that they finally moved into the Villa Prangins, near Nyon on the shores of Lake Geneva.

This was a building of monumental ugliness, whose façade displayed a mixture of Venetian-style watchtowers, French-style conical domes and Tudor-style chimney-stacks. Inside, however, it was well-proportioned and spacious compared with the cramped cosiness of Wartegg. The children and their parents occupied the whole of the ground floor. The floor above was given over to the 'court' – Bishop Seydl, the house priest who had accompanied the family into exile, Count Ledóchowski, the Emperor's aide-de-camp, and the Empress's two ladies-in-waiting, the Countesses Bellegarde and Kerssenbrock. One wing of the building was for the domestic staff; the other housed the 'chancellery', headed by the ever-faithful von Schonta and Baron Werkmann, who served as secretary.

Otto remembered that summer in Prangins with affection. The villa had a magnificent view across the lake to Mont Blanc and was enclosed by a large park where the children could walk and play for hours and try their hand at gardening. He also recalls taking up fishing with great enthusiasm, though his later life was to leave him little time to pursue this, or any other outdoor sport. But the most grateful memory was for this spell of ordered family life with everyone together for weeks on end, almost for the first time either parents or children could remember.

It was here, on 5 September 1919, that the Empress bore her sixth child, the first of three who were to be born in exile. It was another brother, to add to the three Otto already had, and the infant was christened Rudolph, after the nobleman who had founded their dynasty six and a half centuries before. It was fitting that Count Rudolph IV of Habsburg should have been a Swabian Swiss. The imperial family were returning to their humbler roots; this symbolised their new lifestyle, one in which, to all outward appearances, Karl was leading the existence of any prosperous Swiss country gentleman.

The deposed Emperor took long walks unescorted along the shores of Lake Geneva, read the fat Swiss newspapers from end to end, and was even able, for the very first time, to help supervise the education of his eldest children. Inevitably, Otto was the main target of this programme, which took on a truly international flavour. A teacher from the Tyrol was summoned to do the basic school synopsis; Bishop Seydl supplied religious instruction; a Mademoiselle Batard gave French lessons; and a Father Zsambóki taught Hungarian, vital for a child whom the family still hoped would one day wear St Stephen's crown after his father. And that was the desperate problem which was being grappled with underneath this cloak of normality.

Utter mayhem raged in the kingdom Karl had been forced to abandon.

On 21 March of 1919, when the royal family were preparing to pack up and leave Eckartsau, the short-lived regime of Michael Károlyi had already been brushed aside by a Communist *coup d'état* (the renegade Count having lost his balance by leaning too far to the left). But Bela Kun's six months of 'red terror' were to be replaced by an equally savage reign of 'white terror' when, in November of that year, a monarchist army which had gathered under French protection in the south of the country moved up into the capital to take over power. At its head was Niklós Horthy, who had attended Karl's wedding as a humble aide-de-camp and had then risen during the war to command the Emperor's fleet. Now a monarchist soldier of fortune, it soon became clear that it was his own fortune he was after. He was helped towards his ambition by the arcane constitutional muddle which surrounded the crown itself; and this was a problem which Otto was to inherit in later years.

At issue was the very nature of Hungarian kingship. For the Legitimists, the exile sitting on the shores of Lake Geneva had been crowned as Károly IV of Hungary, and that was that. But for the so-called 'Free Electors' (who had supporters among the Calvinist aristocracy and the landed gentry), the nation was entitled to choose its own monarch as its own historic symbol. If it had to be a Habsburg, then Karl had at least two rivals sniffing after the throne. One was the magyarised Archduke Josef, whom he had made his on-the-spot executor, or 'homo regius', during the upheavals of October 1918. Another was Albrecht, son of Karl's one-time Commander-in-Chief, Archduke Frederick, who had led the court camarilla against him during his brief reign.[1] But, if the 'Free Electors' had their way, need it be an Archduke? Why could not any distinguished Hungarian discharge the royal duties?

These were the mists through which Horthy drove his military chariot. On 1 March 1920, a cowed Parliament, surrounded outside and patrolled inside by his armed troops, elected him Regent by 131 of the 141 votes cast 'to carry out, for the time being, the duties of a head of state'. Horthy immediately sent protestations of loyalty to Prangins but, as the months passed, he became more and more evasive as Karl pressed him over handing back the throne. The ex-admiral took up residence in the royal palace on Budapest's Var Hill and immediately felt at home among the gold leaf and the chandeliers. Karl swallowed hard when Horthy declared himself, as Regent, to be a Duke and started receiving foreign Ambassadors as 'His Serene Highness'. It became too much when the Regent ordered all army officers to take an oath of personal allegiance to him: that spelled danger, as well as trampling on the fundaments of sovereignty. A face-to-face confrontation in Budapest could no longer be delayed. But how to get there?

At this point, Colonel Strutt re-entered the family saga. On 22 February

1921 the children were delighted, if a little surprised, to see their saviour from Eckartsau appearing at Prangins to go for hour-long walks with their parents around the park. The would have been even more surprised had they known what the two men were discussing. Karl confided to the English Colonel, who had been on a skiing holiday in St Moritz, that he had received a deeply secret personal pledge from the French Prime Minister, M. Briand. This was to the effect that, provided it were successful in Hungary, France would come out publicly and support a restoration bid. The promise was only verbal and had been issued indirectly via the Emperor's indefatigable brother-in-law, Prince Sixtus. Everything hinged on success; if the bid failed, M. Briand would flatly deny even having known about it.

The French leader was thus on a double-headed coin in his campaign to preclude any revival of German influence in Central Europe.[2] For Karl, the toss was far from certain. So would Strutt go to Sixtus in Paris to confirm all this, and also give some advice on the best travel route into Hungary? It was an extraordinary request to put to a serving British officer but Strutt, already considering himself a willingly coopted fighter for the Habsburg cause, accepted without demur.

The Colonel reported back in Prangins a week later, confirming the Prince's story and carrying a passport which Sixtus had conjured up for his brother-in-law's journey.[3] So, on the Easter Friday of 25 March, Karl crossed the French border on foot and boarded the Vienna-bound sleeper train at Strasbourg, travelling as a Spanish diplomat called Sanchez with all the necessary transit and entry visas stamped in. He passed through his old capital unnoticed in the throng of Easter travellers (despite giving his taxi-driver a tip of fifty Swiss francs – a sum so enormous in inflationary Vienna that the astounded man reported it to the police). But when, the next day, he crossed by taxi into Hungary, accompanied only by a boyhood friend, Count Thomas Erdödy, the Spanish diplomat had become one William Codo, an official of the British Red Cross. Strutt's hand must have been at work here somehow, though he never revealed it and his Foreign Office, for all their later enquiries, never got at the truth. At all events, when they arrived at the palace of Count Mikes, the Bishop of Szombathely, late that night (the taxi had broken down so the final stretch was done by peasant horse and cart), William Codo duly became the King of Hungary, here to reclaim his throne.

The Bishop was as astounded as that Viennese taxi-driver; for him, the King had simply dropped out of the skies. The setting was worthy of an *opéra bouffe*, despite the weighty issue involved. A member of Horthy's 'Cabinet of the Regent', Dr Vass, just happened to be staying with the Bishop that evening and he instantly put himself under the orders of

Hungary's crowned King. By a further coincidence, a far more important political figure was also in the neighbourhood: none other than Horthy's Prime Minister, Count Pal Teleki, who was spending the weekend shooting snipe on the estate of Count Sigray at Ivancz, only twenty miles away. A messenger was despatched to get him out of bed and bring him hot-foot (but still unenlightened) to Szombathely, where he arrived at 4.30 in the morning. When confronted at the Bishop's palace by the news, he was troubled as well as thunderstruck. Though he had stayed in touch with Karl through secret couriers, nothing had prepared him for this sudden descent out of the Easter skies. He scratched his left ear with his right hand passed behind his head – a characteristic mannerism whenever anything was bothering him – and was heard to mutter 'Too soon, too soon'.[4]

Unlike Vass, the Prime Minister of the day did not place himself at the King's disposal, and the advice he gave was a mixture of good and bad. He correctly pointed out that, if he did not decide to return at once to Switzerland (in view of the lack of any fixed plan), Karl then must go on to Budapest, for the country could only be taken from its capital. Less sound was his insistence that no military presence would be needed. A passionate loyalist, Baron Anton Léhar (brother of the famous composer) was the Colonel commanding Hungarian army troops in this western region and he had placed his forces at the King's disposal. But Teleki feared civil war if they marched. Moreover, he convinced Karl that they would not be needed: Horthy would surely step aside once confronted by his monarch in his own royal palace. This turned out to be woefully wide of the mark.

When Karl arrived on Var Hill of Budapest at two o'clock in the afternoon of Easter Saturday (escorted only by Count Sigray and two officers of Léhar's command), no guard of honour presented arms to the sovereign who had been crowned there five years before, and nobody waved a single flag in greeting.[5] The two-hour confrontation which followed inside the palace proved equally bleak.[6] Karl, back in his old study, but with his Regent now using the desk, formally demanded the transfer of power. Horthy's response was so astounding that he was asked to say it again. Unabashed, repeat it he did: what honours, he demanded, would he be offered in return? Inexplicably, instead of rebuking such effrontery, Karl started to bargain. He first promised the turncoat confirmation of the ducal title which the Regent had already bestowed upon himself; then the post of Commander-in-Chief; and finally threw in the Order of the Golden Fleece (from which Horthy, as a Protestant, was in fact automatically disqualified). After each bribe Horthy dug in his heels afresh, claiming that a restoration at this time would only pitch Hungary into turmoil and even provoke invasion from the so-called 'succession states' along its borders.[7]

Karl abandoned politics for the plain issue of honour. As an admiral and as a court councillor, Horthy had sworn him a solemn oath of allegiance, and this must now be redeemed. Not so, the Regent replied: everything had been superseded by the oath he had himself sworn to Parliament. Even Karl, who abhorred violence of any sort, began to ask himself whether he ought not simply to arrest this one-time eager servant of the crown on the spot for treason. Then, as he felt in his uniform, the King realised that, in all the confusion of the departure early that morning, he had left his revolver behind. This was perhaps just as well. Without even a handful of loyal soldiers to summon to his aid (a lorry-load of twenty armed men would have been enough to secure the palace), the spectacle of the King targeting the Regent with a pistol would have led to nothing but further fiasco.

So, soon after four o'clock on the afternoon of 27 March 1921, the two men parted; there was nothing for it but for Karl to return to his loyalist haven in Szombathely. To salvage some pride, the King ordered his Regent to report to him there within three weeks in order to review the position.[8] To further massage his preposterous vanity, the Regent asked his King to bestow upon him the Grand Cross of the Monarchy's ancient Maria Theresia Order. Now desperate at all costs to get away, Karl gulped hard and agreed. He then left his palace for the last time by a side entrance to board his waiting car.

This first restoration bid was over the moment the King retreated from his capital, especially as Karl had been struck down by a severe bout of influenza and bronchitis by the time he reached Szombathely. Horthy now held the reins of government even more firmly in his hands, and proceeded to negotiate directly with the Entente powers over the King's removal and return to Switzerland.[9] The sick monarch had become a piece of stranded royal baggage to be despatched on its way. Despatched it was on 5 April: Karl was handed over at the Austrian border to an Entente escort of three officers sent to protect him from republican demonstrators on his journey back into exile. He never came face to face with Horthy again and never lived to hear his treacherous Regent express remorse. That was left for Karl's son and heir to experience more than thirty years later when a dying Horthy – now in exile himself – begged the Pretender to come to his bedside.

Back in the spring of 1921, that son and heir, an eight-year-old boy, was waiting in Prangins, quite unconcerned, for his father's return from his latest journey. As at Schönbrunn, Gödöllö and even at Eckartsau, the children had been told as little as possible about the stark reality of their situation and nothing at all about its dangers. So when, on the early frosty morning of 6 April, they heard that their mother had left by car for the familiar frontier station at Buchs, they assumed she had gone to collect their father from a routine trip. Not till much later did they learn that he had tried, and ignominiously failed, to wrest back his crown on that coronation hill Otto remembered so vividly as an infant.

It was a very different story for them when the second, and final, restoration attempt was launched six months later. For, that autumn, both parents slipped away together from their new abode at Hertenstein,[10] and neither was ever to return there. As part of the deception plan, the children had been told that their parents would be returning that same evening, so Otto and the others ran alongside the car as it left the drive as though seeing them off for a family day trip. There was no return that evening nor during any of the evenings that followed. As the days grew into weeks and the mood among the castle staff darkened, it gradually became clear to the older children that this had been no routine journey, nor was it to have a normal ending. Indeed, everything about this second – and fatally decisive – restoration bid was extraordinary.

To begin with, when Karl and Zita left Hertenstein by car at 9.30 in the morning of 20 October, they headed not, as assumed, for the Parma family castle at Wartegg, but (after a change of cars en route) for the Dübendorf airfield near Zurich. Here they boarded a specially chartered six-seater Junkers monoplane hired to take a 'Mr And Mrs Kovno' to an unnamed destination. In fact, when the monoplane took off soon after midday, it was flying the crowned King and Queen of Hungary directly home to their kingdom to wrest back the throne by armed force.

Neither Karl nor his wife had ever sat in an aeroplane before. Moreover, Zita was heavily pregnant with their seventh child. The royal couple had no luggage, no identification papers of any sort – real or assumed – and were travelling in a plane which itself carried no documents, let alone a proper flight plan. Yet, apart from one alarming moment when the plane's single engine started to stutter over Bavaria, they over flew Austria without incident and landed safely on Hungarian soil only four hours later. Indeed, they came down exactly at their planned destination, the estate of Count Cziráky at Denesfa. The flight was about the only thing which had gone to plan.[11]

The first sign that something had gone wrong was that no flares had been lit in the castle grounds, the prearranged signal to guide them in. Much more ominous than the lack of welcoming flares was the lack of welcoming troops. Drawing the obvious lesson from the Easter fiasco, Karl had, for months, been devising a loyalist military march on Budapest from western Hungary. Colonel Lehár was still in command of the regional garrison there and in his possession was the King's field-marshal's uniform, its collar with the badges of rank removed. On 5 April, Karl had handed it to the Colonel as they parted at the little border station of Gyanafalva, telling him that he would return to launch an all-out restoration bid on the day Lehár received the coded message: 'Stitch the collar on'. This sounded romantically convincing; however, the problem was to be: which day exactly? Most of the advance planning had had to be done verbally, by couriers travelling ceaselessly between Hertenstein and western Hungary. But the date itself was hurriedly fixed and could only be announced by tele-gram.[12] 'Collar will be stitched on on 20 October' was the last message despatched from Karl. It never reached the officer in Lehár's forces to whom it had been addressed. There were mutterings at the time that its despatch had been deliberately delayed by a traitor in the Carlist camp. A more likely explanation was provided later on by the Empress Zita. So much coded traffic was passing along the telephone wires between border smugglers that the Hungarian post offices had orders to destroy at will any suspicious messages. The King Emperor's telegram had probably landed in one of their waste-paper baskets.

If the reasons for the muddle were obscure, its effect was all too plain. The railway trucks which had been assembled at Sopron for the journey to Budapest had lain idle (and unguarded) and most had been shunted away by the local peasants anxious to get their sugar beet crop in. It took twenty-four hours before Lehár's men, scouring the countryside for the trucks, had tipped the sugar beet out and reassembled them for their intended cargo of soldiers. Finally, at eleven o'clock on the night of 21 October 1921, the railway armada of four trains steamed off, to the cheers of crowds. On board were Lehár and Ostenburg with some two thousand men and a couple of artillery batteries; a 'provisional Hungarian government' of loyalist worthies sworn in at Sopron and, of course, the royal couple themselves. Their transport consisted of a Red Cross carriage whose beds were made up with soldiers' blankets and a 'dining car' with a plain wooden table and railway stools.

This happened to be their tenth wedding anniversary. No greater contrast could be imagined than between the spartan setting of this perilous mission and the relaxed and confident splendour of the Schwarzau ceremony back in 1911. But they were both probably as excited and as hopeful now as then. They were home again and heading for one of their old twin capitals. Moreover, it seemed that Hungary was very willing to fall again under the embrace of the double-headed eagle, which seemed to be scooping up the nation from the track. The only things thrown at their train on its slow journey east were flowers. As the convoy made its way, Horthy's garrisons along the line – Komarom, Györ, Tata, Totis and Bicske – declared themselves, one after the other, for the King. Nothing, it seemed would stand in his way. Yet it all came to a shuddering end during the night of 23–24 October after one miserable skirmish in the suburbs of Budapest.

What had gone astray in Sopron was more than a few railway trucks. Karl had lost the element of surprise, and with it, the initiative. As the little army was chuffing its way towards the capital (with far too many stops to receive ceremonial addresses of welcome and celebrate open-air masses), Horthy, now fully alerted to the danger, had laid his plans for survival. He first mobilised the backing of the Entente missions in Budapest and found an especially warm supporter in the British Commissioner, Mr Hohler. These missions duly received formal instructions from the Ambassadors' Conference in Paris 'to take forthwith all necessary measures to secure once more the expulsion of the ex-King from his former dominions'. This was followed up by an even sharper message which called on the Hungarian government (in effect, Horthy) 'to proclaim without delay the dethronisation of the ex-King Karl'.[13] The Regent thus had all the political firepower he needed from the biggest guns in Europe. By the morning of 23 October he also had his vital double agent at his side.

This was General Paul Hegedüs, the overall commander of Horthy's army in western Hungary, who had tagged along with the King's expedition in case it might prove successful. Once it began to falter, he decided to change sides and, as Karl had unwisely appointed him commander of the railway (because he outranked the modest Lehár), he was uniquely placed to sabotage the venture. On the pretext of moving forward to parley with Horthy's men who were holding the station of Kelenföld ahead,[14] Hegedus walked straight through the battle zone to the royal palace, where he put himself at the Regent's disposition.

The final betrayal came on the ground. Hegedüs returned to Karl that afternoon with peace emissaries and proposals for an overnight truce which, he claimed, would give him time to bring up loyalist reinforcements from the west. In fact, he used that night to scupper the King's best chance of a local victory. When drawing up demarcation positions for the armistice, he placed Horthy's men (partly armed students who had been told that it was the hated Czechs who were besieging Budapest) up on the commanding heights, leaving Karl's troops along the track below. To round off the treachery, Hegedüs had arranged that the Regent's medley of forces would break the truce three hours before the agreed 8 a.m. deadline. They duly swept down in the dark through the ranks of the King's exhausted men, who were getting their first sleep in forty-eight hours. Shots rang out, one of them hitting the royal train. Karl did not panic; he simply caved in, horrified as he had been all his life at shedding the blood of his subjects. From his carriage window he called out to his officers: 'I forbid any more fighting. It's all quite senseless now'. He then dictated a surrender order to be passed down the line to what remained of his miniature army. The train then pulled out slowly – backwards, for Bicske, pulling Karl back out of history with it. It had all been over in five minutes.

Any post-mortem must be full of 'ifs'. Had the crowned King led a group of his soldiers onward through the mêlée – preferably on a horse rather than in the cab of a train engine – it is possible that the road to his old palace would have opened up for him. Certainly had he possessed the mettle of his wife, who, throughout life, was disposed to take any challenge head on, he would at least have attempted the sortie. But how long he could have stayed in his palace is a moot point. Quite apart from the trouble which the Horthy faction could have caused him at home, a restoration Hungary would have faced the fierce hostility of the succession states which formed a ring around it. And behind these three jackals stood the three lions of the Entente powers.[15] Horthy shrewdly stepped aside and let them deal with his prey.

There was no question now of another return under polite escort to Switzerland, even had the Swiss government been disposed to readmit their troublesome guests. Britain was left to sort out the exit problem, which could best be tackled by its navy. There was a British Danube flotilla at anchor in Budapest and it so happened that a British cruiser, the 5000 ton *Cardiff*, was about to put in at the Black Sea port of Galatz. That vessel was to carry them into what the Entente hoped would be final exile. After a week-long voyage down the Danube, mainly on the British monitor *Glow-Worm* (whose captain treated his royal passengers as 'honoured guests', though they were, in effect, his prisoners), the royal couple duly boarded the *Cardiff* at eight o'clock on the evening of 6 November.

The cruiser had far better facilities to offer than the small Danube monitor and its captain, Lionel Maitland-Kirwan, made the most of them. Zita was given the admiral's cabin that the vessel boasted and Karl was installed in the commander's own quarters. They set sail for Constantinople, which the royal couple had last seen three and a half years ago, on their final state visit of the war. No one on board (and indeed no one on land) knew anything as yet of their final destination, a problem which was still being chewed over in Paris and London.

The Entente leaders were thinking only of islands, as though Karl were some latter-day version of Napoleon, needing a St Helena to contain him.[16] Malta was the first possibility discussed. It was rejected on the grounds that the Prince of Wales was about to make a visit there, while the British government was anyway reluctant to have this troublesome ex-enemy couple on their hands if an alternative could be found. Lord Curzon, the British Foreign Secretary, thought that some Spanish island – one of the Balearics or Canaries perhaps – would fit the bill. It was the French who finally found the answer: Madeira, part of Portugal, over which the Braganzas, the dynasty of Zita's own mother, had once reigned. The idea was accepted in Lisbon – provided that the Portuguese government did not have to foot any bills.

Not until the *Cardiff* put in at Gibraltar was the decision officially confirmed to her captain. But Maitland-Kirwan had anticipated it unofficially a week before. On the morning of 19 November, hearing a rumour that Ascension Island – a rocky pinhead in the tropical South Atlantic – was being mentioned in the telegrams, he ordered his ship to steam off straight away, with Madeira as its destination. The royal couple were put ashore at Funchal ten days later. The ship's officers had first served them champagne in the wardroom, saying they hoped that the *Cardiff* would soon be back 'to take them home'. In fact, Karl had arrived at his last resting-place.

What, meanwhile, of the children back in Switzerland? The details of the bungled restoration bid and its aftermath reached Prangins only slowly and in piecemeal form. Otto only remembers being told in the last week of October that his father had again attempted to regain his throne and had again failed. Only then was the mystery solved of that so-called 'day trip' which seemed to have swallowed up his parents for weeks.[17]

Colonel Strutt had again sprung to the family's aid, this time as a communications link between the royal couple on board the *Cardiff* and their family. On 8 November, he managed to send a telegram from London to the British warship, then in the Bosphorus, assuring the parents that all was well with their children, who had been moved out of Prangins and returned to the security of the familiar Parma château at Wartegg. It was the first news that the couple had heard of them for eighteen days. That same morning, Zita had written a short unsealed letter in French to her children saying that all was well and they would soon be reunited. The British diplomatic mission in Constantinople, who were consulted, declared that the letter must not be sent. The Royal Navy ignored such churlishness and despatched it, unread, on their own responsibility. The onshore Admiral merely asked that, as a precaution, the Empress should have the envelope addressed, not in her own hand, to someone who would forward it to Switzerland.

More than two months were to pass before they were all together again. The royal couple spent a sombre Christmas at the Villa Victoria (an annexe of Funchal's already famous Reid's Hotel), alone apart from Dom Joao d'Almeida, a Portuguese nobleman who had volunteered his services as an aide-de-camp and now represented all the 'court' they possessed. Meanwhile, back in Wartegg, Countess Kerssenbrock, signing herself 'Nanny to the royal children' was petitioning the Swiss authorities in vain to allow her seven small charges to leave. It was, of all things, the inflamed appendix of Otto's

six-year-old brother, Robert, which broke the deadlock. Local doctors tes-
tified that an operation was vital and, not without difficulty, Zita obtained, on
compassionate grounds, permission to travel to Zurich to be at his bedside.

It was only with cautious reserve that the Western powers agreed to the
Swiss government's decision. Zita's reputation was now forcibly established
in their minds and the mighty Entente feared more trouble at the hands
of this young woman than anything her broken husband could instigate.
Mr T. B. Hohler, the British envoy in Hungary, who seems to have developed
an anti-Habsburg paranoia, fed these fears with Cassandra-like warnings.
The most dramatic was a telegram to the Ambassadors' Conference in Paris
in which he reminded them that the Queen was again heavy with child and
that 'design attributed to her is to come once again to Hungary to be
delivered there, bringing with her her eldest son, Otto'.[18]

The idea that Zita could somehow pluck her son from Wartegg and then
get her hands on St Stephen's crown from the maternity bed of a Budapest
hospital was one of the wildest fantasies churned out of the local rumour
mill. But the Western powers took it seriously enough to urge the Swiss
authorities to place her under the strictest surveillance during her visit.
They duly complied. On arrival in Zurich, on 12 January 1922, she was
quartered in a nuns' hospital called Paracelsus, which was placed under
round-the-clock police guard. She was allowed to come and go at will, but
each time any of the sisters left the building a detective at the gate would
politely lift her veil – to make sure it was not the royal visitor slipping
away in disguise for some secret assignment.

The operation itself passed off successfully and, on top of this relief, came
the news, at last, that her children would all be allowed to join their parents
in Madeira.[19] Zita went on ahead. Otto, with four other of the children,
set out from Wartegg a few days later (leaving the convalescent Robert to
follow them in a fortnight's time). Otto remembers the long, long train
journey through Europe. They stopped at Bordeaux, where the French
prefect went out of his way to be kind (they were, after all, half of French
blood), and again at Subserra near Lisbon, where the Portuguese nobility
were 'particularly friendly' (their mother after all was half a Braganza). He
recalls that it was a British warship which took the children, like their
parents before them, into their new exile. The *Avon* spent four days on the
journey from Lisbon to Funchal. When it docked, on 2 February 1922, Karl
ran up the gangway and led the family down, the two-year-old Rudolf in
his arms. Despite acute money problems, they were now all happily together
until, two months later almost to the day, tragedy struck.

6

'Your Majesty'

The poverty which afflicted the exiles in Madeira had a dingy background. On 1 November 1918, ten days before the flight from Schönbrunn, Karl had despatched his Grand Chamberlain, Count Berchtold, to Switzerland with all the family jewels which could be collected together. They made a weighty package worth, quite literally, a king's ransom even on the buyer's market of the day. The centrepiece was the so-called 'Florentine Diamond'; at more than 133 carats, it was reputed to be the largest pink gem of its type in the world. It was indisputably a family and not a state possession,[1] and the same was true of the other treasures entrusted to the Grand Chamberlain. These included the 'Empress's Crown' made up of Lothringen jewels, eight Golden Fleeces in various jewelled settings, and an assortment of brooches, diadems and necklaces (not including the spectacular four-foot long specimen in large, perfectly-matched pearls which Colonel Strutt had so admired in Eckartsau).

Berchtold had been a disaster as Foreign Minister of the Monarchy, which he had helped to steer straight onto the rocks of the Great War. He was, however, a trusty courtier, and returned to report that the jewels were now safely deposited in the vaults of a Zürich bank. The same could hardly be said of a certain Bruno Steiner,[2] the Austrian lawyer to whom Karl had entrusted the custody of the jewels, to be disposed of as and when required and only on his authorisation. To begin with, the arrangement seemed to be functioning properly. The 50,000 Swiss francs which Karl had required to hire that Junkers monoplane in April of 1921 were raised, for example, by the sale of a single diamond trinket given to an obscure Archduchess in Prague or Budapest a century before. But it was a different story when Zita, on her trip to Zürich for her son's operation, had taken the opportunity to search out Steiner, in order to relieve him of the jewels and carry what remained of them back to Madeira with her. There was no trace of the treasure and no sign of the treasurer,[3] though he had been informed in advance of her arrival.

That disaster left their captors, the Allied powers, as the only feasible source of help. These, reasonably enough, had begun by tackling the successors to the Monarchy to come up with an offer of compensation for the huge assets they had taken over from the crown. The contents of a single room in any of the Empire's major museums would have sufficed to keep a dozen exiled rulers in comfort for life. Before the royal family had even reached Madeira, the so-called 'Successor States' – Czechoslovakia, Poland, Yugoslavia and Roumania – had accordingly been approached by the Entente to pay an equal share of a joint subsidy to meet the needs of the ex-Emperor and his dependants. The sum proposed was £5000, or 500,000 gold francs each, making an annual grant of £20,000. The British Foreign Secretary, Lord Curzon, urged his envoys in all four capitals to press hard for acceptance.

Not surprisingly, Edouard Beneš, now Prime Minister of Czechoslovakia, led the chorus of rebuttal. The man who had done more than any other political figure to dismember the Habsburg Empire so savagely at the peace conference now ensured equally savage treatments for its deposed sovereign. There was, he declared, 'neither a juridical nor a political basis for such a request'. In the event, not a farthing came out of Prague, Warsaw, Belgrade or Budapest. The tight-fisted Treasury in London then rejected outright Curzon's suggestion for some temporary aid from the victorious Allied powers, including Japan.[4] Italy and France dithered and finally dodged the issue. The Japanese merely smiled.

Karl had had problems enough meeting the bills at the Villa Victoria when he only had his wife and a single aide-de-camp to provide for. But once all six children returned from Switzerland, with Countess Kerssenbrock accompanying the last of them, a hotel existence became impracticable as well as far beyond his means. Some help came from Portuguese sources – understandably, in view of the fact that the royal couple both had Braganza blood in their veins, but this came nowhere near their needs, even for life on a modest scale. Back in the Monarchy there were loyal followers ready to send money, but it never got through: the Entente, so the British Consul in Funchal glumly informed the Empress, had taken steps to block the transfers.

The fear of the great powers, stoked up as ever by Beneš, was that if Karl received help on a large scale he would be tempted to launch a third restoration bid, which might in turn encourage the Bavarians to mount a monarchist *coup d'état* in sympathy. This prompted a pang of alarm even in Lord Curzon, who was not personally hostile to the exiles. If Karl should try to break out from Madeira, he warned the Paris Conference, this would automatically oblige the Allied governments to transfer him to definite imprisonment in one of their more remote island possessions. The historical parallel was plain, but misleading. Karl was far from being, in temperament, in personal magnetism or potential resources, the Great Corsair who had come so close to swallowing Europe up for a second time before being despatched to oblivion in St Helena. The Habsburg exile – exhausted, sick and broken in spirit – only wanted somewhere where he and his family could lay their heads and build a quiet life together.

It was a local Portuguese banker who provided the solution by offering the free use of his villa, the Quinta do Monte, which was perched high up above the bay. Karl jumped at the offer and, before February was out, the family had moved up into the hills and were in residence. Most of the furniture they required, together with all the bedding, linen, crockery, glassware and kitchen utensils, had to be borrowed from the hotel (this was no problem since their benefactor was a joint-owner of that establishment and, indeed, of most of the other hotels on the island). The only thing he could not provide for his guests at the villa was a healthy climate. This was pleasant enough in summer when the heat on the coast could be sticky and oppressive. But in winter the Monte seemed permanently shrouded in a fine mist whose damp penetrated everywhere and everything. For the frail, it was a death-trap.

Once again, one is struck by the contrast between Otto's childhood memories of an experience which had been filtered through the soft protective lenses of his mother, and the hard reality of the time. This was graphically described by an Austrian lady's maid who had been allowed to come and join the household at Christmas. She wrote home, soon after the move up the mountain:

There is no electric light, water only on the first floor and down in the kitchen ... Our only fuel is green wood and this, of course, smokes all the time. We wash with only cold water and soap ... The laundry is never boiled here as at home. The sun is supposed to do that, it is a tropical sun – when it shines. Unfortunately, we have had little sunshine so far; often we look down enviously to Funchal, where the sun is always shining. The house is so damp that it all smells of mildew ...

If only we knew of someone who has influence with the Entente, to arrange for their Majesties to rent a proper house. Their Majesties should be given sufficient means to ensure them of a decent livelihood ...[5] Even the necessities of life are lacking at every turn here. The children's tutor, who has a doctor's degree, lives in a tumbledown hut in the garden with only one scrappily repaired room. In another rickety one-room cottage, which is divided by a partition, live the servants with their wives ...

What seems worst of all to us is that the Empress is expecting a baby in May and they cannot afford to have either a midwife or a doctor ... I am terribly upset about this ... We all do our best to cope with the dreadful situation. Sometimes we do get very low and depressed but when we see how patiently Their Majesties accept all these ills, we carry on again with new courage.[6]

This doleful eyewitness account of life at the Quinta do Monte contrasts sharply with Otto's images of the place, as recalled nearly eighty years later. He well remembered the almost perpetual mists up on the mountain but, nonetheless, the Monte was for him 'still a wonderful place with plenty of flowers which have always been important to me in my life'.[7] Similarly, the only direct connection down to Funchal – a wickerwork basket hoist – looked primitive and unreliable to the adult eye but was 'a very amusing toboggan ride' for the children. Nor did the tutor seem affected by his quarters in the battered cottage. He was a cheerful Hungarian priest, Pál Zsámboky,[8] whom Otto describes as 'the key person in the tiny household'.

Above all, he remembers the long walks which he and his seven-year-old sister Adelheid took with their father up and down the winding green lanes of the island. It was on these excursions that the exiled ruler passed on what amounted to his political legacy to his eldest son and heir. It was a message of tolerance even towards many of those who had injured the dynasty and, above all, of gratitude towards those who had, even passively, supported it.

> He stressed that what had happened to us was not the act of the nations in general but of the relatively few who were in power. He told us that we must continue to feel responsible towards those who had been so loyal, towards the soldiers who had sacrificed their lives and happiness in defence of the homeland, and that we must always do everything in our power to act for these people. This has remained very much with me and has helped me a great deal in my own life. Perhaps this has also been the motivation which brought many of us, Adelheid and also my brothers, into political activity in favour of the nations of the former empire. People have often thought that this was because we were aiming for a restoration of the monarchy. That, of course, was true to a certain degree and at a certain period. But in the long run that thought was no longer dominant but rather the feeling of responsibility towards those who had stayed so loyal.
>
> I knew that certain things needed to change while my father was on the throne but I only learned about the details of his reform plans later. Both parents always kept the big problems to themselves ... The main reason for this was that they did not want us to feel, later in life, resentment towards certain individuals so that we could one day meet them without thinking too much about the injustice towards our parents.

Otto strove to keep to that precept throughout his life. He sometimes found it hard to swallow and, once or twice, impossible.

It was one of these cherished family walks which cost Karl his life. On 9 March, he set off with Otto and Adelheid to go down to Funchal to buy some toys for little Karl Ludwig, who was about to have his fourth birthday. Someone ran out from the house with an overcoat which he decided not to carry: it hardly seemed necessary, for they could see the sunshine gleaming up from the town. But on the way back he was enveloped by the chill mists of the mountains and caught a cold. He refused at first to take it seriously. Five days later, fever and a severe bronchial cough forced him to take to his bed. The damp air of the Monte had started the illness; their poverty caused its fatal progression. For a whole week he refused his wife's pleas to send for medical attention. The household purse, he told her, was too empty for such needless expense. By the time a local doctor was summoned up from Funchal, pneumonia had set in. His heart had long been weak; now the lungs were giving way.

Zita tried to have their one-time royal physician, Dr Delug, sent from Vienna. Permission was either refused, or too late in coming. The Portuguese doctors (there were now two at the bedside) did all they could to halt the disease. But their remedies were basic (plasters of linseed and mustard accompanied by injections of caffeine and camphor), while the oxygen bags produced to ease the patient's breathing were too primitive to give more than seven minutes of relief. To add to the stricken household's problems, two of the children – Karl Ludwig and Felix – went down with a milder version of the pneumonia which was ravaging their father while a third child, Robert, developed a gastric infection; most of the staff had influenza. Only the lady of the house seemed immune to it and undaunted by it all. It was, in many ways, a repeat scene of that Christmas of 1918 at Eckartsau. But now there was no Colonel Strutt to bring them provisions and muster the royal train for a comfortable journey into safety. Moreover, this time, Zita was already almost eight months pregnant.

Otto seemed to have escaped, like his mother, the germs and ailments which swirled around in the villa. She, as usual, screened the children as far as possible from any sort of household woe. Thus, it was not until 27 March that he realised his father was dying and not just laid up with another of his all too frequent bouts of illness. That evening, as Karl received the last rites from Father Zsámboky, Otto was called, by himself, into the sick-room, which looked out on to the garden downstairs. There were no dramatics and no final testimony, beyond the message already conveyed during those long walks and which was now Otto's to discharge. As Karl told his wife afterwards, he had risked bringing the boy into the infected room so that he knew 'how one conducts oneself in such situations – as Catholic and as Emperor'. (Throughout their time together, the father was holding the crucifix in his hands.)

The end came five days later. That first of April was, for once, a sunny day and the children were playing in the garden when Otto was suddenly summoned again by his mother to come inside. By now his father was too weak to speak, too weak even to raise up his crucifix. His heir was at his bedside, when, at 12.23 p.m., the last of the Habsburg rulers died. Otto got quite a shock when, soon afterwards, he first heard himself addressed by the tiny household as 'Your Majesty'. For the moment he could not take in what had happened: 'I thought this was somehow wrong. His Majesty had always been my father. That was surely still my father.'

The change was soon brought home to him. On that final day of his father's life, his mother had been in a rose-coloured dress when she came into the sunlit garden to call him in. It was the last time he was ever to see her with any touch of colour in her clothes. She was to wear nothing but black for the rest of her long life, even at the hundreds of family birthdays, weddings and christenings which lay ahead.

It was just as well that neither the widow nor her first-born read what passed for the ex-sovereign's obituaries in the newspapers of Vienna. Even the most prestigious of them, the solidly bourgeois *Die Presse*, gave him little credit for what he had struggled to achieve, both as a peacemaker and a reformer, and suggested instead that it was his inexperience and indecision which had helped along the collapse of his empire. The essay summed it all up on a note of self-indulgent sorrow combined with reproach:

> How far off behind us do those days now seem when ex-Emperor Karl reigned and how much has changed since a powerful earth-tremor swept through Central Europe, toppling so many thrones and blotting out so much splendour. With his death, there vanishes a piece of history of which we were all a part. His death on a distant and remote island must bring a pang of nostalgia to all those who recall what we had lost, lost through relentless fate but also, in part, through him.[9]

This was mild stuff, compared with the vicious treatment meted out to the dead sovereign in the official organ of the Social Democrats. *Die Arbeiter Zeitung* devoted a whole page to trampling on his memory. For the editorialist, Karl was the last remnant of a dynasty which 'set the torch to the blaze which had destroyed the world'. (No mention of the Sarajevo assassins who had really lit the fuse, nor of the almost single-handed efforts of the 'Peace Emperor' to douse the flames in 1917, with his secret approach, via his brother-in-law, Prince Sixtus, to secure an armistice deal with France.) Moreover, Karl had forfeited any claim to respect, even in death, for refusing to accept his fate and behave as a private citizen in exile. Not that, according to the paper, he would have turned out any better as a family man than as an emperor. 'Karl was neither suited to bring up his children as capable people nor was he willing to support them through his own efforts.' The paper's final epitaph read: 'The Habsburgs, and he in person, have got what they deserved. Their fate is the revenge of Nemesis for their doings.'[10]

By 1921 the Social Democrats had been driven back into a battle of ideology because they had already lost the political one. At the elections of the previous October they had been driven from their brief tenure of power by the Christian Socialists. Henceforth it was the right wing, in various combinations and aberrations, which was to rule the First Republic until Hitler pounced to snuff it out. But even after his 'Thousand Year Reich' had been smashed and the Second Austrian Republic had emerged from the ashes, this virulent anti-Habsburg invective continued unabated for another generation – as Otto was to find out to his cost.

There had to be some ceremony, even in republican Vienna, to mark the passing of the ruler it had toppled and shunned. Fortunately for the family, the Chancellor of the day happened to be the right-wing Johannes Schober, the same man who, as the capital's police chief, had done so much to help and protect the beleaguered royal family during those months of internal exile. Five days after the news of the exile's death reached Vienna, Schober led his Vice-Chancellor and several of his Ministers into St Stephen's Cathedral to attend a requiem Mass. It was celebrated by the same Cardinal Piffl whose ambivalence, during the autumn upheaval in 1918, had contributed to the Emperor's political demise. Ministers, Field-Marshals and leading bureaucrats mingled in the congregation with members of the old aristocracy – now in press reports identified, according to the politically correct phraseology of the republic, without their titles.

When the service ended, a monarchist demonstration (mainly of young students, led by a certain Kuno Honnigg) formed up and paraded through the streets of the capital crying 'Down with the Republic!' and 'Long Live the Habsburgs!' and singing the empire's lovely old anthem. But when the demonstrators reached the Parliament building, the good reception they had so far received from the crowd turned sour. It was on the steps of this building, after all, where the death of the empire had been proclaimed. Predominant now were shouts of 'Long Live the Republic!' and 'Down with these Dynasty Lovers!'. It was a foretaste of much that was to happen in the capital in the years ahead.

Though Dr Schober had led his Ministers into the cathedral for a mass, he did not venture to send any formal message of condolence to the widow on Madeira; indeed, in Vienna, there was no official reaction whatever to the death. It was a very different story in the other twin capital of the old empire. Within hours of the news reaching Budapest both the Regent and the Prime Minister, Count Bethlen, had sent telegrams of sympathy to 'Her Majesty the Empress and Queen Zita' in Funchal. The widow

probably tossed Horthy's message into the waste-paper basket. Count
Bethlen's telegram she may well have kept. It anyway sounded more
genuine:

> The nation has been deeply shaken by the news of the passing of His Majesty
> King Karolyi IV. The whole Hungarian people mourns alongside Your Majesty.[11]
> I would like you to accept the expression of my deepest sympathy in the name
> of the royal Hungarian government.

Austria was now a republic and its Emperors had always only called themselves Archdukes. Hungary was still a monarchy and the dead man had
worn its crown. No wonder that it was towards Budapest that mother and
son looked with what consolation and hope remained.

The people of Madeira also paid their tribute to the Emperor who had
died among them. When the funeral was held five days later up on the
Monte, almost the entire population of Funchal seemed to have come up
the mountain for the ceremony, which was conducted by the local bishop
in the little pilgrimage church of Nossa Senhora do Monte. It was just as
well that this lay only a few hundred yards away from their villa, for the
funeral cortège was embarrassingly plain. No horse-drawn hearse could be
provided, so the plain coffin had to be loaded on a two-wheel hand cart
pulled by men of the household.

Only three things suggested that this was the ruler of a once sumptuous
empire who was being laid to rest. The first was the presence of Bourbon
and Habsburg relatives (his mother, Maria Josefa of Saxony, and his brother
Max had both been living in Bavaria and so were able to journey to Madeira
unhindered). The second was the insignia of the Golden Fleece hung round
the imperial Austrian army uniform in which he was buried. The third was
the mass of prestigious bouquets laid around the provisional mausoleum
which had been built inside the church. Foremost among them was one
from King Alfonso XIII of Spain. It was this kinsman who was soon to
send to Madeira something far more substantial than a bunch of flowers
to ease the family's plight.

There had been speculation that Karl's body would be brought back to
Vienna to lay alongside those of his ancestors in the imperial vaults of the
church of the Capuchins. Another rumour had it that the widow would
now be allowed to settle peacefully in Austria with her family. Both stories
were very wide of the mark, the second even further than the first. Quite
apart from the domestic problems which such a homecoming might cause
in the republic, the Entente powers, who had a morbid fear of the political
problems the widow might cause for them throughout Europe, were determined to keep her safely screened off on Madeira. Zita was equally

determined to leave, so that her new child, whose arrival was now imminent, would not be born in what amounted to enemy captivity. King Alfonso cut the Gordian knot which had, as ever, been tightened round the Allies' hands by the implacable Edouard Beneš. Having first sounded out London by diplomatic channels, the King made it clear to the Ambassadors' Conference in Paris that, whether they liked it or not, he would send a Spanish warship to Madeira to bring the exiles to Spain. At that, the British government gave in. They even dropped a provision they had originally insisted on, namely that the Empress, before leaving Madeira, should give a pledge that she would 'refrain from any intrigue in favour of a Habsburg restoration'. On 17 May, the Ambassadors' Conference in Paris was informed accordingly.[12] A week later, the *Infanta Isabel* dropped anchor in Funchal to take the family to Cadiz and thence by train to Madrid. King Alfonso was waiting at the station to greet his guests, who were then escorted with a military guard of honour to sumptuous quarters in the Prado Palace. Within a few days, it was here, on 31 May 1922, that Zita's last child was born. She was christened Elisabeth, after the lovely but doom-laden wife of the Emperor Franz Josef. It was Karl who had picked the name long in advance, claiming that he knew their new baby would be a girl.

Alfonso tried to persuade the Empress to stay on at the Prado, and even send the children to school in the capital. But however grateful she was for the rescue, Zita would have none of all this. Madrid was already in political ferment, hardly the educational background for Habsburg children, who anyway spoke no Spanish. What their mother needed was a home of their own, where she could supervise the academic programme herself, through house tutors whom she would select. Above all, she wanted to be closer to France, the home of her ancestors, and the country which had given her husband all the covert help it could in his vain struggle to reclaim his crown. It took a year to sort out the problem but the ideal solution was finally reached when, on 6 June 1923, she moved (not without difficulty) into the Palacio Uribarren, overlooking the Basque fishing village of Lequeitio.[13]

The six years that they were to spend there were the happiest and most tranquil period of their exile. It was at Lequeitio that Otto grew up into his teens and from this point onwards the story of his life enters the family archives (the relevant files all marked 'S.M.' or *Seine Mäjestat*). Even more informative are his own memories which, from now on, became steadily sharper and fuller. For him Lequeitio was, above all, 'hard work and lessons'.[14] He started at six every weekday morning with homework from the previous day. Then, after a break, came the first of the daily lessons: three and a half hours of them before lunch; a further three hours until teatime, after which he was allowed to go on working by himself until books were closed and pens laid down for the day at seven in the evening.

It was a ferocious schedule and a formidable battery of teachers had been assembled by his mother to carry it through. The greatest and steadiest contribution came from Hungary, where the abbot of the Benedictine order of Pannonhalma, Remig Bárdoss, sent a succession of his best teachers to instruct the youth he regarded as his King. But there were a stream of others: Father Weber ('very stern and very difficult') and the Austrian Professor Neideracher for German and the classics; a Miss Street for English and Miss Sépibus for French. All the children were soaked in this cascade of lessons, though the volume diminished the younger they were. One carefully posed family picture shows the entire royal brood reading around a table with the mother gazing approvingly from the centre. She developed the attractive habit at the time of having all eight of them photographed in a line, with Otto, the tallest, at the left, descending almost geometrically, down to the tiny Elisabeth at the far right. Otto's ration of tuition matched his height. Despite the cycling trips into the countryside, and boating outings in the bay, it was the tutorial regime which dominated. He wryly commented later on that it had made him a workaholic, adding that he had been happy to remain one for the rest of his life.

Though no nearer as the crow flew, Lequeitio brought them that much closer to their homeland. Travel had by now become much easier and, as this was the time of the great pilgrimages to the Spanish church of Limpias, most of the pilgrims from Austria and Hungary called to pay their respects at Lequeitio on the way. The Habsburg family itself was less in evidence. 'There were only a few Archdukes who came to visit us. This was understandable because both the branches of Archduke Friedrich and Archduke Josef were not exactly in favour,[15] while the Toscana branch had been excluded from the family on the orders of my father for submitting to the Austrian Republic.'[16] Among the handful who did show up were the Emperor's younger brother, Archduke Maximilian (with whom the widow did not always see eye to eye), and the venerable Archduke Eugène, who felt very at home in Spain since his sister was the Queen Mother.

It was the Queen Mother who, on what was to be the last of her regular visits, sounded the political alarm bell for Zita:

> She told my mother of her anxiety abut the future of Spain. During her time as Queen it was she, rather than her husband, who had kept up personal contact with all the left-wing leaders like Azana and Leroux who were later to proclaim the republic. She warned that if she were to die, she was very much afraid that the monarchy in Spain would come to an end within the next six months.[17]

King Alfonso XIII himself – who was also a frequent visitor to the family he had rescued – never seems to have expressed such dire pessimism. Nor did his British-born wife Queen Ena,[18] despite the fact that spots of blood from the nearby victims of a would-be assassin's bomb had stained her wedding dress as she left the ancient Madrid church of Los Geronimos after their marriage on 31 May 1906. Indeed, the King's visits only buoyed up the spirits of the exiles as well as underlining Otto's position as heir to the Habsburg claims. Whenever, for example, he stood to receive a delegation or review some local parade, Alfonso always placed the young Prince at his side. But a move from Lequeitio there had to be before the decade was out, and not just because of the political storm clouds gathering over Madrid behind them. They now had to think about university courses, above all for the sixteen-year-old Otto, who was about to sit and pass the qualifying 'Matura' examinations (in both German and Hungarian). A four-year academic course in Spain was even more unthinkable than the idea of a Spanish school had been when they first arrived from Madeira. It was, in any case, time to move on from this Basque village where, as Otto put it 'whatever happened was rather too far removed from the world'. A move closer to the centre of things was also part of his mother's long-term plan for the family: 'She felt that if, step by step, we moved to places with broader horizons, this would finally end the feeling, which still existed for some of us, that we were living in a semi-prison.'

But where? That was the problem facing the young matriarch with the heavy Habsburg mantle on her shoulders. For her, France would have been ideal; but the republic, having got rid of its own Bourbons, might not take kindly to the Regent of another banished dynasty settling there, especially in view of the unabashed monarchist activities of her two brothers in Paris. England, the Netherlands and the Scandinavian countries all still had monarchs, but their Protestant reigning houses had no family links with the Habsburgs. A strong link did exist with Luxembourg, for Felix, another of Zita's many brothers, had married Charlotte, the reigning Grand Duchess. They now stood eager to help in any way (Prince Felix had already acted as his nephew's guardian when Otto did a spell at Clairvaux to perfect his French), but the principality was simply too tiny to bear the weight of Zita's burgeoning ambitions. Mussolini's Italy was out of the question. Portugal, for all the official friendliness shown in Madeira, had deposed her own mother's dynasty and was, in any case, too far away from Europe's centre of gravity.

By process of elimination, that left Belgium. Here there was a family link of sorts (King Albert was married to a cousin of Zita's, Princess Elisabeth of Bavaria). Brussels itself was well situated for a discreet political base, not too important, not too insignificant. Above all, Louvain (or Leuven) which was close to the capital, was among the finest Catholic universities anywhere on the continent. Yet again, the Princes Sixtus and Xavier set to work appealing successfully both to King Albert and his Prime Minister, the Count de Brockeville. King Alfonso regretfully authorised the transfer from Spain and, in September 1929, the family packed up and said goodbye to the little fishing village which had taken them so much to its heart (an affection which was to bear unexpected fruit some ten years later). Among those who came from their homeland to attend the leave-taking were a troop of Hungary boy scouts, a Hungarian university professor and Baron Stritzl, who administered the Habsburg assets in Vienna (still minute but growing modestly). From all accounts, no archdukes appear to have turned up.

After four months of 'house-hunting' (during which time the family lived as guests in the spacious Brussels mansion of Count d'Ursel), Zita decided on Ham Castle, just outside the little Flemish village of Steenokkerzeel. It was not the sort of place to fall in love with at first sight. Ham was a gloomy-looking moated fortress surrounded on three sides by a lake that promised mosquitoes in the summer and damp all the year round. The facilities inside were almost as medieval as the stones: there was neither proper heating nor running water. On the other hand, it had space enough for a household which was expanding again.[19] Above all, it was ideally placed: close to the capital and on the road to Louvain University. After the owner, the Marquis Jean de Croix, had completely modernised the interior for her, Zita agreed to rent the sprawling edifice. In January 1930 the family moved in for what was to prove a spell of more than ten years. It was a decade of tranquillity for the family and growing hope for the dynasty – both shattered at the end, along with the peace of Europe.

Before the first year was out, Ham saw its first great event, at least in the domestic sphere. On 20 November 1930, Otto's eighteenth birthday, the young student, who had just begun his studies in law, became of age and, according to the family statutes, the head of the House of Habsburg. It was largely a technical change, for his mother, though no longer Regent, was to carry on running affairs until he had finished his four-year course. But, for all that, on the day, all the solemnity and splendour that the exiles could muster was paraded in the main salon of the castle. Zita, wearing only the diamond brooch of the Star Cross Order to light up her 'uniform' of black, declared her son, following the last depositions of his father, to have become 'in his own right, sovereign and head of their reigning house'. She then bowed to the young man and put her signature below the written procla-mation. It was followed by those of Archduke Robert, Otto's eldest brother and the next in line; his uncle Archduke Max; his grandmother, the ever-present Archduchess Maria Josefa; Count Degenfeld as head of the household; and a sprinkling of names from the old nobility. Stefan Rakovsky, one of the leaders of the first restoration bid, was among those who had come to sign for the Hungarian monarchists.

There was no figure of equal stature from Austria. Indeed, the contrast between the two halves of the vanished Dual Monarchy resurfaced in ghostly fashion again here, in two carefully posed photographs of this gathering of the exiles. The group picture representing the Austrian half is plainer and smaller in number, with some faces in the front row looking, symbolically perhaps, in different directions. The one taken to commemorate the Hungarian half has a very different impact. Whereas, before, Otto had posed in an anonymous black suit, here, again at the centre, he appears in splendid Hungarian gala dress, a broad band of silk running down from his right shoulder across the tunic. His mother appears much more involved and regal, holding what looks like a miniature staff of office in her right hand. Everyone – except Zita's mother – is looking straight at the camera. It is yet another reminder that the family title Otto had inherited directly from Vienna was Archduke of the Austrian Domains. The one he had taken over – and still possessed – from Budapest, was that of the Apostolic King of Hungary.

Yet, in the decade ahead, it was the Austrian claim that moved to the centre of the stage. It was put there, and kept there, by Adolf Hitler, who was about to burst on the European scene. The Führer feared a restoration bid in Vienna even more strongly than the exiles themselves expected it. He became obsessed with the threat, and so, the eighteen-year-old youth who had just become the head of the House of Hapsburg became also a key figure in the power game of the 1930s.

7

The Conundrum of the Crown

Before the move to Belgium, Zita had paid a private visit incognito to King Albert to discuss arrangements for the family's stay. He had made one important request: there should be no overt political activity while the exiles were on Belgian soil. Above all, Hams should not become another Hertenstein, the launch pad for an outright restoration bid. Zita was happy to give that specific undertaking but general abstention proved impossible. The household at Steenokkerzeel was bound to become a monarchist centre and, even if they had remained passive, Europe, in the shape of the Nazi menace, was reaching out towards them. Throughout the Lequeitio years, Nazism had remained a small brown stain on the European horizon. By now, it was threatening to absorb Germany and spread wider. Inevitably, Habsburg and Hitler would be locked in a battle for their common Germanic homeland.

The first thing to determine was how close Hitler was to winning the complex struggle for control in Berlin. In the winter of 1932–33, Otto was sent to the German capital to find out. The semi-pretext for the visit was to attend a course at the Agrarian Institute of Professor Sering, which was the leading German-language academy of its type in Europe. But even more significant than the Professor's academic fame was his political platform. Sering was a member of the Prussian Landtag, a Conservative, and a dedicated opponent of Hitler's. It was through him and Count Galen, a Landtag member for the Centre Party and another enemy of Nazism, that Otto's reconnaissance was prepared. As things turned out, Hitler became just as keen to inspect this twenty-year-old Pretender as the young man was to examine the Führer's prospects. Otto has given his account of this previously unpublished episode:

> I was first approached to meet Hitler by Prince August Wilhelm, the fourth or fifth in line of the Hohenzollern brothers. I had tried, if only as a matter of courtesy, to meet all of them. One afternoon, after I had had lunch with the Crown Prince, his younger brother invited me for a talk in his own house. He was not only a member of the Berlin Landtag but also an officer of the Nazi elite corps, the *Sturmabteilung*, and he received me in his SA uniform. In our talk, he sang the praises of the party and spoke only of its 'Führer', whom I always

pointedly referred to as 'Herr Hitler'. He then came out with the invitation. His
Führer had told him that he wanted to talk to me.

At that, I told the Prince that I was in Berlin to study ... and that consequently
I was avoiding political conversations. Of course, this was not true because I had
already met many personalities of the Democratic Conservative Party. But it was
the best reason I could give. Later on, Göring himself (who at that time was, of
course, President of the Berlin Landtag) made another approach through Baron
Pereira, in whose apartment I was lodging. The message was the same: the Führer
still wanted to meet me. I gave the same answer as before, and that was the end
of it.

Prince August Wilhelm was, in my eyes, a convinced Nazi but all the Hohenzollerns shared the illusion that Hitler would reinstate the monarchy once in
power. I was certain that Hitler was only using them as a means to attract
monarchist voters. I had seen how the Crown Prince had already supported Hitler
against President Hindenburg and that fundamentally he wanted to do exactly
the same thing with me as regards the Austrian voters. I had the great advantage
of having already read *Mein Kampf* from start to finish and knew what his aims
were. All this only reinforced my refusal to meet him ... On the other hand, it
would have been an interesting experience. In fact, this was the only interesting
conversation I ever avoided in my life.[1]

One unforgettable encounter Otto did have before leaving Berlin was
with the legendary Great War hero, Field-Marshal Hindenburg, then President of the fast-crumbling Weimar Republic, which he was about to deliver
up into Hitler's hands. The old man who had stood so resolutely on the
battlefield was wavering uncertainly on the political stage. For this meeting,
however, he displayed a sense of old world courtesy that would have had
the Führer foaming at the mouth. To meet the young heir to the Habsburg
dynasty, alongside which Hohenzollern Germany had fought as allies, the
Field-Marshal had put on an Austrian imperial army uniform which he
had preserved from the old days. The only decorations pinned to it were
the Austrian ones which Otto's father, and earlier, the Emperor Franz Josef,
had bestowed on him during the war. The conversation, Otto recalls, avoided
current politics altogether. Instead, Hindenburg talked mainly about his
days as a young officer and especially of the Franco-Prussian War of 1870,
in which he had fought, culminating in the triumphant victory march into
Paris. Otto was told afterwards that he was almost certainly the last non-Nazi
to be received by the President before he relinquished office.

That fateful event took place a few days later, on 30 January 1933, when,
after the Nazi party's victory at the polls,[2] the President was persuaded to
step down and hand over the reins of power to its leader, Hitler. Only a
few hours before that event, Otto had left Berlin. His departure did not
signify deliberate flight, but was, he claims, pure coincidence: his studies

under Professor Sering had been wound up at the end of that month, and he was due back soon at Louvain. He soon realised, however, that he was already in danger.

> I was again on German soil immediately after the election victories of the Nazis but only to pass through Bavaria, going from Lindau to Munich. I had first been at Mittenwald just inside Germany where I held meetings with leading Austrian monarchists and, during the two days I was there, I witnessed how the local Nazis took over power in the municipality.

He still did not connect any of this with himself but was given a shock the next day when he went on to Gaisl-Gasteig, the village right on the border where his grandmother, the ubiquitous Archduchess Maria Josefa, had a house.

> On the very evening of my arrival, a gentleman from Hitler's Gestapo came to call on us. He was a Croat who had become a German citizen and risen to high rank in the police. He came to warn me to leave at once because that same afternoon the Nazis had stormed the editorial offices of a German newspaper *Der Gerade Weg*. It was a weekly, and ferociously anti-Nazi. I had been on very friendly relations with its editor who had just been murdered. The Croat told us that the Nazis, having seized all the editor's correspondence, would have learnt of this relationship and might well come for me. I left by the next train for Belgium and did not see Nazi Germany against until after its defeat in 1945.

It was very fortunate for Otto that the Gestapo official had once been a Croatian citizen. In the days of empire, the Croats, alongside the Jews, had been fanatically loyal to the Emperor in Vienna. The reason in both cases had been self-protection: the Croats, for example, seeking amelioration of the second-class citizen status which the Hungarians had imposed on them.[3] In the different world of republics and dictatorships, the Croat blood in the German Nazi still could not stand the thought of this young Prince, son of the last Emperor to sit in Schönbrunn, being delivered up into the Führer's hands. But what was sinister was that, only weeks after declining, politely but firmly, to meet Hitler, Otto had become a target for his vengeance. Over the next ten years, the young Habsburg was to rise to the top on the Führer's wanted list of Austrian nationals.

The little court to which Otto hurried back at Hams now faced a totally new situation. The advantage of knowing *Mein Kampf* became a troubling asset now that its author had become the leader of a largely mesmerised German nation. In the second paragraph of the very first page, Hitler had given his pledge over the destiny of his native land: 'German Austria must return to the great German motherland ... One blood demands one Reich.'

The Hungarian half of the old Monarchy could, for the time being, breathe freely. No one could pretend that the Magyars were of German blood and, in any case, Regent Horthy, soon to become Hitler's ally, would always block Otto's path to Budapest. Vienna was both a natural target for Hitler and an easier one. So, from 1933 onwards, maintaining Austrian independence against that threat became an even greater priority for the exiles in Ham Castle than a restoration bid – unless the two could be linked. The search for support had to be redoubled, both inside and outside the boundaries of the old Monarchy.

Mussolini had long been the obvious choice among the European leaders. While Hitler was still clawing his way up the ladder of power in Germany, and even for a while after he had consolidated his hold there, the Duce remained the most powerful dictator on the continent. Moreover, he was determined, as a matter of vanity, as well as of policy, to reassert that dominance over any challenge from the brown-shirted upstart in Berlin. In midsummer of 1934, the challenge flared up over Austria itself. On 25 July, in a bungled attempt at a Nazi putsch in Vienna, the Chancellor of the day, Engelbert Dollfuss, was murdered by a band of rebel thugs in his office at the Ballhausplatz.[4] The diminutive peasant leader had developed his own brand of authoritarian extra-parliamentary rule of which the Führer might have approved had it not been for three grave disqualifications.

First, it was too mild: locking up opponents instead of killing them; shooting only when shot at; and failing to persecute the Jews. Secondly, 'Austro-Fascism' came wrapped in a blanket of Catholic fervour which was consciously anti-Nazi. Only three months before, its pious founder, who had once swung the incense-burner in his village church, produced a draft constitution which would have turned the republic into a would-be Kingdom of God on earth – the first and last such attempt the century was to witness. Finally, and even more distasteful than this mystical allegiance to the Almighty, came the allegiance (which Dollfuss had almost been obliged to invent) to an Austrian patriotism, the assertion that his people were a nation in their own right. That ran slap in the face in the second sentence of *Mein Kampf*. Dollfuss had to go before this pollution of the pure Germanic creed could spread its germs. So Dollfuss duly went, though how closely Hitler was personally involved in the abortive coup was unclear.

What became immediately clear, however, was that Mussolini, who had taken Dollfuss under his wing, was in no mood to have Italian influence in Austria swept away. It was around 3.45 p.m. that Dollfuss succumbed to his wounds in his shuttered Chancellery. Only fifteen minutes later, when the first firm news of the attempted 'putsch' reached Rome, the Duce ordered the Italian army to advance north in strength towards the Tyrolean and Carinthian borders. The next day, these forward troops were put at

1. Emperor Franz Josef with Archduke Otto. (*ÖNB*)

2. The wedding of Archduke Karl and Princess Zita of Bourbon-Parma, at Schwarzau, 21 October 1911. (*ÖNB*)

3. The end of a legend. The funeral of Emperor Franz Josef in Vienna, 30 November 1916. (*ÖNB*)

4. The new Crown Prince follows Franz Josef's coffin, flanked by his parents. (*ÖNB*)

5. The coronation in Budapest, 30 December 1916. (*ÖNB*)

6. Empress Zita with Crown Prince Otto.

7. Karl and Zita with Otto, Adelhaid and Robert. (*ÖNB*)

8. First World War. Otto and his sister Adelhaid, with their parents. The Emperor and Otto return the salutes of the troops. (*Private Collection*)

9. March 1919. The Emperor's journey into exile under English escort. (*ÖNB*)

10. October 1921. The hopeful beginning of the restoration attempt in Hungary. (*Private Collection*)

11. In prayer, just before the decisive defeat at the gates of Budapest. (*Private Collection*)

12. Karl and Zita in the park at Hertenstein. (*ÖNB*)

13. November 1921. On the way to exile in Madeira.

14. Wartholz, 1917. Zita (right) with Otto and Adelhaid. With the Duchess of Parma and Princes Felix and René of Parma. (*Private Collection*)

15. Otto and his mother at the funeral of the Emperor Karl, Madeira, April 1922. (*Private Collection*)

16. Otto as a young hunter. (*Private Collection*)

17. Otto in Hungarian dress uniform. (*Private Collection*)

battle stations. Mussolini's vaunted 'Watch on the Brenner' had begun. Though it eventually declined into a watch with binoculars only, at the time it carried a firm military warning to Berlin, which Mussolini now set about reinforcing further on the political front.

Four months before his death, Dollfuss had signed up to the so-called Rome Protocols. These linked Austria with Italy and Hungary in a new right-wing grouping to counter the Western-backed Little Entente of the inheritor states: Czechoslovakia, Yugoslavia and Roumania. A year later, Mussolini succeeded in adding provisions for military cooperation onto the original economic agreements. This had given Austria some framework of protection against Nazi Germany, as well as against the hostility of her smaller neighbours. After the Dollfuss murder, the Duce sought to strengthen that protection through an understanding with the Western powers. He was the moving spirit behind the pact of the so-called Stresa Front, signed between Italy, Britain and France in April of 1935, whereby the three powers pledged to 'consult together' in the event of any threat to Austria's independence. This was paper support only (and, in the event, was to prove paper-thin). But, together with the Rome Protocols, it showed the Duce at the height of his influence and ambitious as the power-broker of Central Europe.

This pivotal role had been anticipated well in advance by the royal exiles. As early as January 1931, Zita had been persuaded to take soundings in Rome to see what help her dynasty might expect from the Italian dictator. Yet again, it was her brother, Prince Sixtus, who had swung into action to do the persuading. In an eight-page memorandum penned to his sister, he stressed that Mussolini's grand strategy was the same as that of imperial Vienna, namely the containment of Serbia; moreover, the Duce might well neutralise or even influence Germany in the matter of a Habsburg restoration. Zita should accordingly pay a purely private visit to the Italian royal family, while despatching trusted emissaries to discuss European politics with the dictator.[5]

Zita took his advice. Both her emissaries who talked with the dictator that year (Count Nikolaus Revertera in January and Count Colloredo Mansfeld in June) were agreeably surprised by the warmth of their reception by the Duce, if rather taken aback by his very specific interest in the Habsburg dynasty. He heaped praises on Otto, describing him as good-looking, well-mannered and serious in disposition ('such a change from other princes who are wandering around the world'). He then came out with it: the young Habsburg Pretender would surely make an ideal match for Princess Maria, the youngest daughter of King Victor Emmanuel of Italy and his statuesque Montenegrin wife. Indeed, as Otto's mother would be calling on the Italian royal family at their summer residence in San Rossore, why could Otto not come along as well, so that the two young people would get to know one another?

Both of Zita's spokesmen made politely evasive answers, which was just as well, for the Duce's efforts as a matchmaker were both clumsy and misguided. Otto had not the slightest intention of marrying the sixteen year old, and his mother was also strictly against any such match. (Eventually, Princess Maria was to marry one of his uncles, Prince Louis of Bourbon Parma.)

Sixtus accordingly shelved his Habsburg propaganda efforts in Rome but only to substitute for them a much more ambitious project for London. King Alfonso XIII had been obliged to give up his throne in the spring of 1931, following the creation of the Spanish Republic, but he was turning out to be an extremely active and seemingly cheerful exile. In June 1933, he teamed up with the French Prince to promote the idea of launching Otto across the Channel. The King was about to pay a fortnight's private visit to England, his wife's native country, so why should Otto, travelling perhaps as the 'Duc de Bar' not follow in his wake? [6] Alfonso assured Sixtus that he could not only present the young man, suitably turned out, at Buckingham Palace, but could also arrange for him to meet informally leading figures in British political life. Zita needed no encouraging to suggest the visit in a personal letter to King George V, despatched from Hams on 22 June.

The sponsors of the project took success almost for granted and Alfonso, who had gone on ahead to make final preparations, reported back that both King George and Queen Mary were expressing delight at the idea. Everyone had reckoned without the cold and heavy hand of Whitehall, which had to be consulted in the matter. A decade before, the Foreign Office had opposed the restoration bids of Karl because of the disturbance they might well create in the wobbly power balance of the post-Versailles continent. They used the same arguments now to veto the visit of his son. Otto, they pointed out, was virtually a Pretender; his incognito could not possibly be preserved; his presence in London could therefore have undesirable political implications.

King George had little option but to cave in. On 29 June, he sent to Hams Castle an apologetic reply which bore unsmudged fingerprints of government drafting. If Archduke Otto were to visit England in 'the existing unsettled condition of Central Europe', the King obediently wrote, this was only likely to cause political embarrassment 'not only to my government but possibly also to you and your son'.[7] It was little consolation to Zita that the letter, penned in French according to prevailing custom, treated her as fulsomely as if she were still on the throne. The King signed himself off as 'Your Imperial Majesty's Good Cousin'.

Otto recalled later that he had been 'much less interested in the London idea than his mother, since I had the feeling that ... we could not count very much on help from England'.[8] Instead, he intensified his existing contacts (orchestrated by Sixtus) with French leaders. England may have been the dominant Western power (at a time when the United States was both uninterested in, and largely ignorant about, European affairs); but it was only in Paris that the Habsburg cause found sympathetic ears. The politicians Otto cultivated ranged from Louis Marin on the right to Anatole de Monzie and Edouard Herriot on the radical left. But it was the independent leader, Georges Mandel, who proved his most valuable supporter, and, later indeed was the man who was to help save the entire royal family when Hitler's Wehrmacht drove France to capitulation.

Yet French sympathy – now as at the time of the restoration bids – could only be translated into outright support once the exiles had regained a foothold in their homeland. Everything hinged on their success and that depended first of all in solving the riddle: how many monarchists were left in the old Monarchy, and what were they prepared to risk for their faith? Before descending on Paris with his scheme to take Otto with him to London, the peripatetic King Alfonso had been to Austria and, if his political verdict could be relied upon, the riddle was already solved. Vienna, he enthused, was in thoroughly loyalist mood; the old imperial capital felt that it now stood on the threshold of the restoration. As someone who had so conspicuously failed to read the republican mood in his own country, the ex-ruler of Spain was not, perhaps, the shrewdest observer of dynastic prospects in another republic.

Shrewd or not, the problem for the exiles was that all such estimates had to be judged by them at second-hand. As Otto commented, looking back at the problem many years later:

> We received all types of reports but there was no way we could verify them. You can only gauge the mood of a country when you can breathe in its air yourself, all around you, go into its inns, for example, and have contact with everyday people right on the spot. Judging from a distance is incredibly hard.[9]

Though it is unlikely that King Alfonso visited many inns, there were signs, at the time of his visit, of a remarkable upsurge of grass-roots support for the young Pretender, especially where the grass grew greenest, in the provinces of Tyrol, Styria and Carinthia. The first seed had been sown in the little Tyrolean village of Ampass on 6 December 1931, when the Mayor, Josef Kaltenhauser, and his councillors announced that Otto von Habsburg had been declared an honorary citizen of their community. The beautifully illuminated deed, worthy of the scribes of a medieval monastery,[10] set out their motivation. The first reason was to protest against the anti-Habsburg laws, still in force in the republic, which confiscated without compensation the property of the dynasty and banned its head from setting foot in his homeland. The second reason was subtly expressed: 'to give the house of Habsburg some small moral recompense for the injustice it had suffered'.[11]

The seeds of Ampass were soon sprouting everywhere in the Austrian countryside. By the time of King Alfonso's visit, several hundred villages had followed Mayor Kaltenhauser's example. An annual register of the so-called 'Emperor-Communities' was compiled, and the total eventually reached more than 1500. But what, exactly, did they signify? They were not formally affiliated to any right-wing parliamentary group and, like the monarchist movement as a whole, could not function as a separate party, since their cause was held to be above the political arena. This reflected the dilemma of the Habsburg camp in Austria, whose many separate elements were difficult to muster under any common organisation. There were the ex-soldiers and civil servants of the empire, who had to watch their step if they were still serving the republic or relying on it for their pensions; the devout Catholics, who revered the Habsburgs primarily as Apostolic Majesties; the great landed families who owed their estates to the dynasty but depended on republican goodwill to hang on to them; the Jews, as ever the unconditional supporters – unless they were in the Socialist ranks, in which case they could be the most rabid antagonists; and finally a swathe of sympathisers from all sections of the population moved mainly by nostalgia for a vanished national grandeur and a lost domestic stability. Not until the end of 1936 was Otto able to set up an umbrella organisation which, in theory, embraced all the monarchist elements. Called the 'Iron Ring', it had for its honorary president one of Archduke Franz Ferdinand's two sons, Duke Maximilian Hohenberg, with activists scattered throughout the province.

This is how the focus of their efforts reviewed the line-up many years later:

> Max Hohenberg was a key person. He was very active, held a great deal of meetings and often came to see us. He was also one of our most important links with the government, especially in the discussions over my possible return to Austria. He was unconditionally loyal, was an excellent orator and had the gift of being able to bring together people who were at odds with one another.
>
> Within the government, Baron Karwinsky, who was a Secretary of State, was one of our most valuable and trusted contacts. Also loyal and very active in Vienna was Colonel Wolff, who had actually founded a monarchist party, the

Kaisertreue Volkspartei, soon after the revolution. It never had great success, however, and Wolff himself, who was a strange person, did not help his cause by behaving on occasions imprudently.

Some of the main people in the movement were the activists in the provinces: General Englisch-Poparle and Major Serschen in Upper Austria; General Dankl in the Tyrol; Ingenieur Netzer in Vorarlberg; the Provincial Governor Reiter in Lower Austria; Dr Stepan of the Fatherland Front movement in Styria; and so on.

In the capital, Herr von Reichlin-Meldegg was an important figure and also – especially for mobilising Catholic supporters – Baron Zessner. But the vital figure, as regards not only liaison with us and the supply of information, but also the organisational side of the whole movement, was Baron Wiesner, a senior official in the Foreign Office. He was the Executive President of our 'Iron Ring' and who kept up the struggle until the end. Like Baron Zessner, Dr Stepan and many other of the monarchist leaders, Wiesner was to suffer for his beliefs in Nazi concentration camps.

As regards the strength of the 'Iron Ring', we estimated its actual membership at between thirty and forty thousand. It certainly had many more sympathisers than that outside the movement, though how many they were and how resolute they were was impossible to estimate. That would depend partly on the general political climate.[12]

That climate was to be set, throughout the final years of the republic's life, by the character and temperament of its last two Chancellors. The patriotic credentials of the first of them, Engelbert Dollfuss, were clear enough; they had been endorsed by his murder at the hands of Nazi thugs. Less evident at the time were his growing monarchist leanings. True, the 'First of May Constitution' which had proclaimed his new Catholic corporate state had also dropped some of the anti-Habsburg measures decreed by the Socialist regime in 1918. But it later emerged that, towards the end of his brief spell of power, Dollfuss had concluded that even patriotism – the primacy of nationhood over race – would not be enough to save his country from Hitler. The Habsburgs would also have to come to the aid of his 'Fatherland Front'. Only a few days before his assassination, he is said to have told Ernst Karl Winter, the Deputy Mayor of Vienna and himself a passionate monarchist, that Austria could only now be saved by a restoration and that he was going to do everything in his power to bring back the dynasty as swiftly as possible.[13] Calling on Austria's imperial past to the rescue of the republican present would have been a tough task to achieve, and not simply in the face of Berlin. The only man with both the courage and dynamism even to have attempted it was Dollfuss, and he was gone.

His successor, Kurt von Schuschnigg, had, for his part, always worn his monarchist feelings on his sleeve. The trouble for the dynasty was that that was where they were going to stay. Kurt von Schuschnigg incorporated in his being all the emotional muddle-headedness of the Austrian people and thus involuntarily sped their republic to an ignominious death. The only ones clear of this confusion were those who took up position at the extremes. At one far end stood Dollfuss, the first leader to launch an entire political movement based on the concept that Austria was not simply a southern branch line of Germany but a separate nation in its own right. At the opposite pole stood the republican descendants of Schönerer's 'Greater Germans' in the imperial age, sharing their conviction that Austria's salvation could only be found in extinction, through fusion with their northern neighbour.

Many on the left had stood in this camp if only because, in the confusing bedlam of the republic's founding years, Anschluss with Germany had also meant Anschluss with German socialism. Now, on the far right, came the Austrian Nazis and their supporters, for whom fusion was simply the fulfilment of that second sentence of *Mein Kampf* – the supremacy of race over nationhood. The mass in the middle were the ditherers, swinging now to one side and now to the other. Fatally for the Austrians, among those tugged both ways, and with the most violent swings of direction when the crunch came, was the Chancellor himself.

Schuschnigg's immediate pedigree was emphatically Austrian: he was a third generation Tyrolean whose grandfather and father had both risen to high rank in the imperial army, the latter being ennobled for his services to the dynasty. But, quite apart from the fact that three generations were not much of a lineage by Tyrolean standards, the family's true roots were Slav. They had started out as the Susniks of Slovenia and, like Catholic converts who can be more papal than the Pope, many Slavs of the empire, once Germanised, became more Teutonic than the pure stock itself. In the case of the young Kurt, this reverence for all things German was strengthened beyond breaking by the seven years of instruction he had had with the Jesuits of the Stella Matutina at Feldkirch. Though the school itself was on Austria's Arlberg Pass, the priests were mostly cultural émigrés from the German Reich and, on feast days, the single eagle of the Hohenzollerns was always hoisted alongside any Austrian banner.

The final paradox in the soul of this troubled man, which deepened his dilemma as a politician, was that Kurt von Schuschnigg was also a devout monarchist. This was partly due to the family's long tradition of military service in the empire, a tradition he himself had followed as an officer in the Great War – on the same Italian front and in the same elite regiment as Dollfuss. But his devotion also had mystically romantic elements: for centuries the Habsburgs had been rulers over what they had dubbed the 'Holy Roman Empire of the German Nation'. It was always a self-contradictory historical fantasy which Napoleon had anyway swept out of history with a single decree on 1 August 1806; yet even Franz Josef had felt its romantic pull down to the end of his enormous reign. The last Chancellor of the First Republic was thus in thrall at one and the same time both to the dynasty which was the very embodiment of the multi-racial concept and to a Teutonic creed which was now being turned into the all-out cult of the master race. In the 1930s, these two opposite poles were represented by the exiled young Pretender in Hams Castle and by Adolf Hitler in Berlin.

For the first half of his four-year chancellorship, Schuschnigg continued Austria's search for foreign support, and even managed to widen the arc. His first trip, made on 21 August 1934, only a few weeks after taking office, was to Florence to meet the Duce and thank him for the powerful support Italy had shown during the July crisis. He proved an uninspiring supplicant. To Mussolini, as to all the Western leaders the new Chancellor was to seek out, Schuschnigg cut a bleak figure compared with his predecessor. Apart from the fact that both men were upright and well-intentioned, the contrast between them was absolute, and all now to Austria's disadvantage. Even where Dollfuss had failed to win over minds abroad, he had always won over hearts. The diminutive figure had radiated warmth, humour and accessibility. For all the appeal exerted by his ready smile and the gaze of those large blue eyes, he conveyed a sense of conviction, of a man at ease with himself because he believed utterly in the course he had chosen. He was a born leader.

Schuschnigg, on the other hand, was the classic introvert, a professional figure without much personality, and not a gleam of that gift of Austrian birthright – charm. 14 He failed to convince because, as we have seen, he was at odds in his own convictions; yet this torment, like so much else, was suppressed. He was as impenetrable as he was vulnerable. No colleague ever managed to get behind those steel-rimmed glasses which he always wore.

Mussolini did not even try. The Duce repeated his promises of support and undertook to look into the grievances of the German-speaking population of the Alto Adigo (formerly Austria's South Tyrol). Yet neither at Florence, nor on follow-up meetings in Rome and Venice, was there any human empathy between the two men. Moreover, by the time of those later encounters, the strength of Italy's embrace was steadily loosening. As early as that summer of 1934, the Duce's mind was already focusing on his disastrous Abyssinian adventure (finally launched on 3 October 1935), and he wanted no distracting complications with Germany over Austria or anything else. The Stresa Pact, pledging the three Western powers merely to consult in the event of a threat to Austria's independence, was as far as he was now capable of going.

Before then, in visits to Paris and London during February of 1935, Schuschnigg had discovered for himself how badly balanced any Western front was bound to be. French foreign policy was in the hands of Pierre Laval, an unsavoury political opportunist who, a decade later, was to be executed for wartime collaboration with the Nazis. At the time of Schuschnigg's visit, however, his money was still on Mussolini in the European dictator stakes so, in this respect at least, Austrian and French alignments ran parallel. (This despite the fact that France was the sponsor and protector of the Little Entente, the three successor states to the Habsburg domains which formed a hostile Slavic ring around the Austrian Republic.)

In London, as in Paris, Schuschnigg was met with some politely pointed questions about the suppression of social democracy in his authoritarian state. The British also indicated, far more strongly than the French, that, though they desired Austria's independence, they were not prepared to roll up their sleeves to defend it. What they wanted was stability on the European continent, to enable them to administer their vast overseas empire in peace. Schuschnigg's responses in these exchanges included reassurances that, come what may, Austria would never take part in any anti-German alliance. This was dangerously categoric language that Dollfuss would never have used, especially after Germany had become synonymous with Adolf Hitler.

The restoration issue was not touched on directly in London, for the Foreign Office had made its views abundantly clear on that question when blocking Otto's projected private trip to England four years previously. But on every other foreign visit, official or unofficial, which he made, Schuschnigg faced searching questions on the future of the monarchy and the young Pretender's role in it. At that first Florence meeting, for example, Mussolini had asked him outright whether he intended to carry out a restoration and whether, in that case, Otto would be the man. While declaring himself a monarchist (for whom Otto was the only possible choice), Schuschnigg stressed that nothing could be attempted while 'external repercussions' remained as dangerous as they were. Yet, six months later in Paris, he had declined to give Laval a formal pledge that the Habsburgs would never reign again in Vienna. Austria, he said, had enough commonsense not to try any such experiments in the prevailing climate; nonetheless, he told the French that it reserved the sovereign right to choose its own form of government. This was the muted voice of the son and grandson of imperial army generals.

Needless to say, the Habsburg ghost loomed even larger when Schuschnigg travelled to the one-time capital of that empire. In Budapest, which he visited for the first time soon after becoming Chancellor, the Prime

Minister of the day was Julius Gömbös. True to form, Gömbös, a rabid anti-Habsburg, immediately demanded assurances that no restoration was being contemplated in Vienna. 15 Schuschnigg fell over backwards to oblige. Any active monarchist policy, he declared, was 'nothing but romantic nonsense'. (No mention here, as in Paris, of Austria's sovereign right to decide how she should be governed.) This seemed to satisfy both Gömbös and the Regent, though at a separate talk, Admiral Horthy assured his visitor that, if ever the empire were to be re-established in Vienna, he would 'walk on my two feet ... to offer my services again'. Unctuous hypocrisy does not come any thicker.

By his own admission, Schuschnigg had never felt comfortable on his visits to Western capitals and it was not hard to see why. Apart from the weak impact of his pallid personality, he was the very opposite of a cosmopolitan in either temperament or personality and spoke none of the languages of the host countries. (Mussolini talked to him in slow but grammatically correct German; in London and Paris, interpreters were needed.) If he felt more at home travelling around the old strongholds of the empire, this was not merely the pull of well-remembered landscapes and buildings (all unaltered) but the ease of communication. Gömbös, a graduate of the old Military Academy of Wiener Neustadt, talked German almost as fluently as his native Magyar tongue. When, in January 1936, Schuschnigg went on to visit Prague,16 familiar images loomed even larger.

Jan Masaryk, the founder and first President of Czechoslovakia, and the apostle of 'Austria delenda est', had resigned due to frail health the previous year. His successor was Edouard Beneš who, at the Paris Peace Conference, had come close to translating that maxim into reality. Now, however, Austria was needed as a counterweight to the massive pressure from Nazi Germany building up against Bohemia's borders. The three and a half million Sudeten Germans who lived on that border fringe were equal candidates, alongside the six and a half million Austrians, for absorption into Hitler's all-German homeland (and, indeed, were eventually to follow the Austrians down the Nazi maw). So the time seemed ripe to establish a political defensive link between Vienna and Prague.17

Schuschnigg could not have found a more congenial partner to discuss all this with than the man who had recently replaced Beneš as Prime Minister, Dr Emil Hodža. This former university professor from Slovakia was a child of the old empire, having once served as an adviser to no less a figure than the ill-fated Archduke Franz Ferdinand. Indeed, the Habsburg shroud seemed at times to be waving perceptibly in the background of the visit. There were even stories that, in order to block the German threat, Hodža might favour a restored monarchy in the form of a personal union, under Otto, of the crowns of Vienna, Budapest and Prague. The idea probably never existed outside the Central European diplomatic rumour mills. Yet it was prevalent enough for President Beneš to be attacked by some Czech newspapers for discarding what had been the trademark of his entire political life – denunciation of the Habsburg dynasty and all it stood for.

Certainly, when Schuschnigg pointed out to Beneš that legitimists should be cultivated if only as allies in the struggle against Nazism, the Czech leader was gracious enough to admit that Otto von Habsburg could not be put in the same category as Adolf Hitler. But both men skirted around the issue of a restoration. Schuschnigg assured Beneš that this could come into question 'for the time being' (a significant softening of the tone he had struck with Gömbös). Yet he also repeated his other mantra, namely that Austria would never indulge in any policy directed against Germany. All this was but the outward expression of his own personal dilemma. His inbred Teutonism made it impossible for him to deny that the Sudetens, like the Austrians, were of one and same German blood and, therefore, somehow belonged together. Yet his equally inbred monarchism made him feel that the crown was the surest defence against the swastika. Like the old double-headed eagle, he looked both ways at once.

Hodža made several cordial return visits to Austria. More could certainly have been achieved through these links than the paltry bilateral measures secured by Schuschnigg (trade talks and the expulsion of émigré Austrian socialists who had anyway already decamped from Brno to Paris). Prague was not merely a vital buffer against Nazi Germany.[18] It also embodied the only strong link Central Europe possessed to London, the capital Schuschnigg was most desperate to connect with. Yet he was even more desperate not to provoke Nazi Germany, so not even a protective mini-axis was set up between Vienna and Prague. Given that opening, his predecessor would at least have tried to exploit it, just as he would have exposed to the world Nazi subversion rather than played it down. But then, Dollfuss suffered from no Germanic complexes, while inside that pygmy body of his was the heart of a lion.

As it was, the only new diplomatic concept to be floated with Schuschnigg's backing was for a so-called Danubian Federation. This envisaged the linking up, initially on a trade basis, of the three countries of the Little Entente, with Austria and Hungary, their fellow neighbours along the banks of the great river. Geographically, this had always made sense. Historically, Danubian unity had a long pedigree. But to try and restore even the economic framework of the old empire in the world of the mid 1930s was to search after fool's gold. Hungary, already with one eye turned to Berlin, proved reluctant to move and, if Horthy dragged his feet, Hitler positively put the boot in. Germany promptly denounced the proposed pact while taking steps to circumvent it. As Schuschnigg had committed Austria never to engage in any anti-German policy, that was that. Again, there was no protest and no publicity.[19] Vienna simply backed away in silence, taking Prague with her. Austria's ignominious road to appeasement was opening up before her.

8

Meltdown in Vienna

Just before the end, a public outburst of pure Austrian patriotism was to come from Schuschnigg's lips. This upsurge was so uncharacteristic of the man as to be quite inexplicable; it was as though the spirit of the murdered Dollfuss had, for a few frantic days, taken possession of him. Too late; so much of what Austria's last Chancellor had done in the three and a half years before had served only to deaden nationalist fervour. Schuschnigg's handicap at home was the same which had hobbled him abroad. He had no clear vision of where he was leading his people and no strong personality to make even his muddled philosophy sound convincing.

Of the many figures who created trouble for him on the domestic front, two need singling out. Both were formidable, though in very different ways, because each had the dynamism and self-belief which he lacked. The first was the Vice-Chancellor he had inherited from Dollfuss, Prince Ernst Rüdiger Starhemberg. The Prince had risen to such high rank in the Fatherland Front government because he commanded the 30,000 strong Heimwehr, the most powerful of all the paramilitary political armies which had proved the bane of the First Republic's life.[1] It had been a Starhemberg, with the same forenames, who had commanded the beleaguered garrison of Vienna until its rescue by that great Catholic relief army which, in 1683, marched down from the Kahlenberg Hills to break the long Turkish siege of the capital. He had helped to save the cause of Christendom as well as the skins of near-starving defenders.

The descendant of this illustrious warrior also wanted to create a stir in Europe by rescuing his fellow countrymen. He was never quite certain, however, what it was they needed rescuing from and, even less, which horse he should mount in the attempt. To cap it all, the 'Playboy Prince', as he was dubbed, sometimes fell to wondering whether the whole thing was really worth the exertion. In those moods, he would abruptly quit the political scene for the pleasures of the chase and the flesh.

He began his somewhat clownish political career convinced that, whoever it was who threatened Austria, it was not Adolf Hitler. Quite the contrary: in the 1920s, the young Prince had fought in the Munich streets as a volunteer in the Nazi ranks, taking part in Hitler's abortive Bavarian putsch of 1923. As late as 1931, he was confronted with an offer from Germany's future Führer to lead a new movement which would absorb Austrian Nazi dissidents into his own Heimwehr. He declined, if only because by then Starhemberg had found another hero and role model in Benito Mussolini, still unchallenged as Europe's foremost dictator. Though the Duce always insisted that his brand of Fascism could never be exported, an authoritarian state, held in place by an adoring Heimwehr prince, was the most appealing scenario across his northern border. By 1934 it was the Heimwehr leader, far more than the doomed Dollfuss, who was recognised as Mussolini's man. This prestige was redoubled when, after the July putsch and Italy's 'March to the Brenner', his patron emerged as the protector of his country. As Vice-Chancellor, he anyway stood next in line for the office of the murdered man (and actually presided over the first emergency cabinet meeting) so that the Austrians took it almost for granted that Starhemberg would now be given the helm in Vienna. But that post lay in the gift of the Federal President and, for Wilhelm Miklas, a solid bourgeois patriot from the old Christian Socialist camp, the Playboy Prince was personally and politically abhorrent.

However unassuming this balding baby-eyed figure looked, Miklas was a man of resolute principles. He had demonstrated that back in 1918 when, along with only two other members of his conservative party, he had refused to disavow the crown they had all been vociferously supporting until the final collapse of the monarchy loomed up. He was to give the ultimate proof of that mettle when another final collapse, that of the republic, came round twenty years later. Now, in July 1934, he did his best to secure his country's immediate future by keeping it out of the hands of an idle political adventurer. Schuschnigg, the dour former Minister of Justice, seemed the safest choice, and Miklas saw the nomination through.

For a while Schuschnigg was obliged to share power with his deputy, who was formally appointed supreme leader of the Fatherland Front, including all its assorted paramilitary formations. This dichotomy, of Cabinet versus extra-governmental movements, was only ended nearly two years later by a neat manoeuvre of the Chancellor's. Schuschnigg had kept for himself the key portfolio of Minister of Defence (where Otto's champion, State Secretary General Wilhelm Zehner, was in day-to-day charge). On 1 April 1936 the two men introduced compulsory military conscription for all Austrians of arms-bearing age. A new national militia and this new national army would in future train and control all the country's paramilitary forces. At a stroke, Starhemberg's Heimwehr had ceased to exist as an independent power base.[2] A few weeks later, its leader obligingly dug his political grave by sending a telegram of congratulation to Mussolini, now the pariah of the Western world, over his 'victory' in Abyssinia.

By now, however, the Prince was being tempted by another possible avenue to power. It was one, suggested by the legitimists, which ran above all party politics. Given the deadlock over the restoration of the monarchy, might not Prince Starhemberg take over the royal mantle, for the time being, as 'Duke of Austria' or *de facto* Regent in Vienna? The project, however flattering, was never a starter. It would have needed the backing of a plebiscite to gain validity and the support of both Schuschnigg and Otto even to be launched. Neither would have entertained the idea, which, after a while, Starhemberg publicly rejected. Otto was certainly in intermittent touch with the Prince over the restoration question, which was discussed when Starhemberg called on the Pretender while on his way home from attending the funeral of King George V in January 1936.[3] But what Otto sought in the then Vice-Chancellor was support, not replacement.

As for Regents, he was to be given further proof of how 'temporary' and how nauseating their hold over power could prove when Horthy paid an official visit to Vienna later that year. One of Otto's trusted aides in the capital, his lawyer, Baron Stritzl, sent a horrified report to Hams Castle of the visitor's behaviour.[4] To begin with, he had 'had the cheek to appear everywhere in his old Imperial Admiral's uniform'. This had been enough to cause all the Austrian ex-naval officers from the days of the Monarchy to boycott his programme. At the gala opera performance given in his honour (the Baron was further able to report) the high aristocracy had joined with the naval officers in leaving their seats empty. Partly as a result of this snub, the visitor cut his visit short and departed in a huff by overnight train for Budapest.

Before leaving, however, he had pulled off one little trick which left the royal exiles fuming. Though it had not been in his programme, Horthy had arranged for himself, via Schuschnigg's office, to pay a special visit to the burial crypt of the Habsburgs underneath the Vienna's church of the Capuchins. The priest in charge of this cramped and fusty mausoleum of the dynasty, Father Gottfried, had been officially instructed over the telephone to receive the visitor and show him round. When Horthy appeared, shortly afterwards, he was again dressed as an Imperial Admiral and accompanied by a sizeable suite, many also in uniform. Their purpose was to form a line behind him so that His Serene Highness could pay his respects undisturbed. Horthy began by laying a wreath at the ornate tomb of Emperor Franz Josef, who had first given him his officer's commission. He then knelt on the bare tiles, refusing the priest's offer of a stool, to recite a long prayer of devotion. Finally, he moved on to the tablet recording the death of the

Emperor Karl.[5] He read the inscription, bowed his head, and left. This time, there was no wreath, and the renegade Admiral neither knelt nor prayed to the King he had supplanted.

The reaction from Otto was a written request to Father Gottfried to refer any future applications for visits to the family grave to Baron Stritzl for clearance with the exiled court. Had Horthy's intentions been known, the letter went on, the Capuchin priests would have been ordered to close their crypt for the whole day to any visitor.[6] As may be seen from the incident, Otto did not need another Regent in Vienna. The one already implanted in Budapest had proved more than enough.

This year, 1936, was notable for far more, as it concerned Austria, than leadership squabbles and dynastic rumours. It saw crucial shifts in the European balance of power, all of them tilted against Vienna. It was not merely that Mussolini, Austria's erstwhile military protector, was now running for cover himself before the worldwide uproar against his Abyssinian adventure.[7] The wrangle over how wide and how deep the punitive sanctions against him should go was tearing apart even that cardboard protection for Vienna which the Stresa Pact had offered. France was now in confrontation with England, which was refusing to implement the one sanction that would have hurt: the closure of the Suez Canal to all Italian vessels. Meanwhile, as the Stresa Front disintegrated, Hitler's grip on the European continent grew stronger. On 7 March 1936 his army, under his personal orders, marched in unopposed to reoccupy the demilitarised zone of the Rhineland, set up under the Versailles Treaty as a key containment buffer to keep the threat of renewed German militarism at bay. The Führer later admitted that, if the French army had resisted, he would have withdrawn his forces and called the gamble off. Its success almost invited him to raise the stakes for future ventures, especially as the cards in his hand were getting stronger by the month.

Mussolini now had to face the fact that he was no longer the strong man of Europe. The same gloomy reality had to be accepted by the royal exiles in Belgium. Even after the Abyssinian affair, Otto had maintained indirect contact with the Duce. His principal link was through the Austrian Minister to the League of Nations, Imre von Pflügl, a capable career diplomat who had married a wealthy American woman. This enabled him to live in sumptuous style in a castle overlooking Lake Geneva, which duly became the scene for many meetings Otto had with Austrian leaders attending the League's proceedings. It was here that Pflügl also gave the Archduke a first-hand account of the Venice encounter between the two dictators in 1937, the first at which the changed status between them became all too apparent. The Duce's resentment had spilled over into an outburst of vituperation. Mussolini showed Pflügl a photograph of himself and his visitor taken during the talks. Pointing to Hitler, he shouted 'Look at this face – it's a disgrace for humanity!' ('Guarda questa faccia – è una vergogna per l'humanità!'). The Duce, Pflügl reported, was a changed and broken man. Quite apart from the Abyssinian fiasco, health problems were also probably responsible for the decline (Mussolini was by now believed to be suffering from syphilis).[8]

The year 1936, when Hitler had imposed his will on the Western powers, was also the year when he made a decisive step forward towards the subjugation of Austria. It had been engineered for him by that other principal bane of Schuschnigg's chancellorship. Neither an Austrian nor, like Starhemberg, a political dilettante, Franz von Papen, Hitler's nominee as his new envoy to Vienna following the débâcle of the Nazi July putsch,[9] was a veteran of the power game who had served briefly as German Chancellor in 1932 before allowing Hitler in as his successor a year later. Quite apart from his heavyweight status, he was to prove an inspired personal choice for the task of rebuilding relations between the two German-speaking peoples. The attempt to bludgeon Austria into submission had failed. Papen's job was to lure her there peaceably, step by step, through a campaign of what would later be called psychological warfare.

For this, he had all the credentials. As a friend of the German industrial barons, he could talk round their impressionable Austrian counterparts. As a pronounced Catholic, he was acceptable to the church and many conservatives alike. Above all, he fitted in, like a sword into its sheath, with Austrian society. An accomplished rider and sportsman, he was soon at home in any of the country estates which invited him (as nearly all did). As a man of wide tastes he fitted in with the cultural life of the capital, where his embassy, whose hospitality was buttressed by lavish funds, became one of the city's social fulcrums. Untrustworthy fox though he may have been, he exuded both wit and charm. In all of these attributes (except the Catholicism) he was different from and more effective than Kurt von Schuschnigg.[10] The contrast could only help Hitler's oleaginous emissary to achieve his dual task: to make Europe forget about the Austrians and to make the Austrians remember they were Germans.

The first objective was wearisome and long-term: Austria's Nazi extremists had to be kept quiet and their links with Berlin carefully pruned. But he could get to work on the second aim immediately after presenting his credentials.[11] The approach, endorsed by Hitler, was to be copied later on by many a political predator stalking his prey: embrace the victim first, then strangle him. The instrument devised for the process was also to prove popular: the so-called 'Treaty of Friendship'.

For months on end, draft and counter-draft of the text passed between Papen's residence in the Metternichgasse and the Ballhausplatz, which housed both the Austrian Foreign Office and the Chancellery.[12] Hitler in Berlin was, of course, kept constantly informed; so, though in less detail, was Otto in Belgium, whom Schuschnigg had promised to inform and consult on such matters.[13] But it was Mussolini who finally pushed the wavering Schuschnigg into a decision. At a meeting in Rocca delle Caminate in June 1936, the Duce told his guest bluntly that if he wanted to count on further Italian help (the word 'protection' had dropped out of use) then Austria should make things easier all round by improving her own relations with Germany. A month later, on 11 July, at a festive ceremony in his Chancellery, Schuschnigg put his signature to the fateful pact.

That part of the declaration to be published the same day showed Schuschnigg's Austria in its (by now familiar) pose of looking in both directions at once. On the one hand, it welcomed Germany's pledge to recognise its 'full sovereignty'. On the other, it accepted without demur that Vienna's foreign policy would always in future 'conform to the basic principle of Austria's recognition that she is a German state'. A strange sovereignty indeed being told by a foreign power how it was in future to behave. But, of course, for Schuschnigg, Germany was not a foreign power but the blood brother across the border.

It was the section of the pact not published on the day of signature which showed the true extent of his capitulation. This was the so-called 'Gentlemen's Agreement', a separate protocol and intended to be kept highly secret. Like all such secrets in a Vienna dedicated to gossip, led by a government full of informers, it duly leaked into the open. One clause committed Schuschnigg to what was almost a full amnesty of his Nazi political prisoners. In the event, Papen was able to report to Hitler, 17,045 were released, including thirteen serving life prison terms for treason, while 213 left behind bars were to have their sentences reduced. The next clause showed that, in addition to turning thousands of Nazi trouble-makers out onto the streets, Schuschnigg had been forced to admit 'representatives of the so-called nationalist opposition in Austria' into his cabinet.

The two men selected for admission were not Nazis but so pan-German that, in effect, they served Hitler's cause without donning a brown shirt. One more or less selected himself: General Edmund von Glaise-Horstenau, the Director of Austria's Military Archives. He had been a wartime liaison officer at Hindenburg's High Command and was determined, as a leading member of Vienna's 'German Club', to tie his country as closely to Berlin in peacetime as she had once been in war. The other choice was a surprise: the young lawyer Guido Schmidt, who had become one of Schuschnigg's closest confidants in the Chancellery, was now catapulted into the post of State Secretary at the Foreign Office, charged with the day-to-day running of Austrian diplomacy. A political opportunist above all else, Schmidt strode down the pan-German path because it was the broadest and most inviting. Its doctrines had anyway been hammered into him in his youth: like Schuschnigg, he had been reared at the Stella Matutina school.[14]

The July pact not only marked a big stride towards Austria's surrender of her sovereignty. Equally ominous for the future was Schuschnigg's campaign to persuade the outside world of the opposite. Towards the end of June, the first circumstantial reports that Austria and Germany were in negotiations over a secret agreement were leaked to the world (via, of all channels, a Russian émigré newspaper printed in Paris). The French government (at the time in the hands of the strongly anti-Nazi socialist Prime Minister Leon Blum) sent an alarm signal to London, combined with a call for joint action to block the move. For once, Whitehall departed from its traditionally *laissez faire* attitude towards Central Europe. The Foreign Secretary, Anthony Eden, agreed to join his French colleague, Yvon Delbos, in a bid to head Schuschnigg off: they invited the Austrian Chancellor to meet with them in the corridors of the League of National General Assembly in Geneva.

Here at last was a possible lifeline thrown out by the West, if only diplomatic in nature and if only coming from two of the Stresa Pact partners. Schuschnigg let it drop and excused himself. One reason was that the third party to that pact, Mussolini, who was now firmly under Hitler's thumb,[15] advised him against going to the meeting. But the Chancellor was anyway disinclined. He had persuaded himself that Papen and the Führer were negotiating in good faith and that this understanding between the two German Chancellors was indeed an agreement between gentlemen. The delusion was made official when, on 10 July 1936, the day before the pact was signed, the broad outline of its terms was transmitted to the principal Western powers. The main text was presented as a great success for Austrian diplomacy and a safeguard of future peace in Europe. There was no mention of the secret protocol.

To be fair to Schuschnigg (who, as always, had a difficult hand to play), his negotiations had gone so far with Germany by the end of June that to have suddenly abandoned them would have been impracticable. But he should surely have attended that Geneva rendezvous, and passed on the main terms of the proposed pact then and there with the promise that, if Hitler showed any signs of betraying the agreement, he would alert London and Paris immediately, and call for help. 'Les absents ont toujours tort.' By turning down the meeting Schuschnigg had created the impression that he was already reconciling himself to the inevitable at Hitler's hands. When the Führer's totally misnamed 'Rape of Austria' finally took place, the Western democracies could be excused for thinking that Austria had voluntarily begun to disrobe herself for the taking nearly two years before.

If one looks back at the July Pact from the German side, what is striking is how it was regarded in Berlin above all as an insurance policy against the Habsburgs. Despite the enormous difficulties – constitutional, international and plain practical – which the dynasty faced in reclaiming its crown in either Vienna or Budapest, and despite the unresolved squabbles in the monarchist camp as to how, when and where this was to be attempted, the Nazis harboured a loathing and dread of the double-headed eagle. Papen, the chief architect of the 'Gentlemen's Agreement', gave his Führer three reasons why it would prove such a success. The first was that it would help to keep Austria off the international agenda (a process which, we have just seen, Schuschnigg was himself to help along). The second was very specific: it would put a stop to the 'constantly increasing efforts towards a Habsburg restoration'. The third depicted a broader dividend ranging from preventing the growth of any specifically Austrian culture to blocking the country's search for some sort of international guarantee. But, in this process, Papen could not help adding, 'the restoration question would be laid "ad acta" '.[16]

It is time to return to Hams Castle and see how the Pretender was himself faring in this tug-of-war between Germanic race and Austrian nationhood. The very idea of any 'understanding' between Schuschnigg and Hitler was disturbing, but Otto had been horrified when details of the secret protocol of the actual agreement were passed to him by the Chancellor. He had also been angry over the timing.

> Schuschnigg had promised me that if he did anything which would change the status of the Nazis in Austria or affect relations with Germany, he would always inform me beforehand, so that I could comment. It was two hours before midnight on 11 July 1936 when his courier Hofrat Weber arrived to pass on the information. Of course, the thing had already been signed. I always felt that this was hardly loyal, but it was just another sign of his weakness. I immediately, that same night, issued a sharp protest against the agreement, which Weber took back to Vienna. By then, of course, it was already too late.[17]

There was little doubt in Otto's mind that Austria had now set herself on the slippery slope to extinction. Could a restoration halt the slide? Inside Austria, only Schuschnigg could face up to that question and only Schuschnigg could answer it. It was time to find out once and for all. Papen's conviction that the restoration had been laid 'ad acta' by the July Pact could not have been more misplaced. The short-term effect of the pact had been to bring that issue, in the greatest secrecy, to the top of the pile.[18]

For the first unreported meetings between the two men, that secrecy was guaranteed by a Count de Bourbon-Busset. He was a distant kinsman of the Archduke's, but, more importantly, a senior officer in French intelligence. One of the 'safe houses' run by the service was at Mulhouse, in Alsace-Lorraine, which lay close both to the German Rhineland and the Swiss frontier at Basle. Otto remembers the building, the Hôtel du Parc, as the most secure of all the locations he was to enjoy in life for a secret encounter of any type. Even the gardeners in the grounds outside as well as the domestic staff inside were on Bourbon-Busset's staff. It was here in 1935 and 1936 that Schuschnigg was smuggled in for preliminary discussions about the future role of the Habsburg crown. The Chancellor had already shown his monarchist credentials by repealing, in July of 1935, the republican laws which banished the royal family from its homeland. All its members, except Otto and his mother, were now given the unrestricted right of return. The Pretender and the ex-Empress also enjoyed that right in principle, though, in practice, they agreed to get the Chancellor's permission beforehand. This lawyer's device of Schuschnigg's had so far been the barrier to keep them out. Could agreement now be secured for re-entry and, moreover, could the return be a dynastic one?

The meetings at Mulhouse had been positive in tone but inconclusive in substance, like other lower-level contacts on French soil. The decisive head-to-head encounter was held in a far more remote setting than Bourbon-Busset's hotel: the Swiss convent of Einsiedln, tucked away in the mountains above Zürich. It was here, on 7 January 1935, that Schuschnigg, accompanied by his alter ego, Guido Schmidt, arrived incognito to meet Otto, his mother and his trusted secretary, Count Henry Degenfeld. In all his post-war writings and apologia, Schuschnigg made no reference to the event. Nor did Schmidt, even in the depositions at his long and detailed post-war treason trial. In view of their behaviour a little more than a year later, both men would doubtless have been glad if the pledges made at the convent that day were buried and forgotten. So they would have been, had not Count Degenfeld taken down the proceedings in an 'Einsiedln Protocol' which has survived in the Habsburg archives.[19] It is headed, without more ado, 'Preparations for the Restoration', and begins by recording Schuschnigg's unequivocal promise 'to carry out the restoration as soon as possible in the coming year ... even if this should eventually lead to a serious European conflagration'.

Otto had always hammered home to the Chancellor that the threat of a

German Anschluss was bound up inextricably with the threat of a European war. He added that, if the Austrians were to hold their heads up after that war, they should resist occupation, however hopelessly the military odds were stacked up against them.[20] Schuschnigg first tried to square this circle by producing the somewhat harebrained idea that all might pass off peacefully provided that Hitler's acquiescence to a Habsburg restoration could be secured in advance. Otto rejected the notion outright. Quite apart from the fact that, if the moment should ever come, he wanted the Austrian people, not the German Führer, to place the crown on his head, the proposal flew in the face of everything that was known, or suspected, about Hitler's designs. His cardinal aim was to block any restoration, not bless it. Schuschnigg accepted the rebuff, promising to 'sort his ideas out' and communicate again on the subject later that month.

The last entry in Degenfeld's on-the-spot jottings turned out to be the most ironic. Just before taking his leave of the man he had addressed throughout as 'Your Majesty' ('Eure Mäjestat' in the even loftier German usage), Schuschnigg of his own accord gave his personal pledge that 'Any form of aggressive action on Germany's part against the independence of Austria will be resisted with force of arms'.

These were literally fighting words. Fortunately perhaps, in view of disappointments lying ahead, they created few illusions among his audience, who remained doubtful whether the words would be converted into action. The Empress summed it up long afterwards by saying that Schuschnigg had the goodwill, but not the willpower. Her son's judgement ran on similar lines:

> Schuschnigg was certainly an honourable man and he was certainly loyal to the dynasty. But he was hesitant, and had none of the dynamism of Dollfuss ... Of course he had a certain vision of the future but it was along the lines that the restoration would finally lead to the re-establishment of the Holy Roman Empire. In this sense, he was a romantic ... while I, in my talks with him, stressed the reality, and the priority of mobilising resistance against the threat which was approaching.[21]

The weeks after the Einsiedln meeting stretched into months and there was still no further word from the Chancellor showing that he had 'sorted his ideas out'. Not that he had let the matter rest. Indeed, when Hitler's Foreign Secretary, Baron von Neurath, came to Vienna for talks on 23 February 1937, Schuschnigg opened up with the restoration question. In view of the great affection in Austria for the old ruling house, might not a return to monarchy, he suggested, be the best way of quieting the domestic political scene? The German Minister's reply could not have been blunter.

To restore the Habsburgs, he declared, 'would be the best way for Austria to commit suicide'.[22] Incredibly, Schuschnigg still pressed on, repeating the idea – turned down flat by the royal family only six weeks before – of wanting to consult Germany beforehand over any action. The Führer's spokesman just shrugged. He must have wondered whether the Austrian Chancellor was either hard of hearing or not quite right in the head.

9

Fatal Encounter

As the months passed, the danger signals multiplied, all pointing to the year ahead. Neither in Vienna nor at Hams Castle were they to learn about Hitler's strategic planning conference, held in Berlin on 10 November 1937. At this the Führer had pencilled in for his generals 1938 as the best time to subjugate both Czechoslovakia and Austria by lightning strikes, and thus shorten the Wehrmacht's lines of communication for more ambitious operations. But the victims earmarked in what later became famous as the 'Hossbach Protocol' did not need to read his minutes to see the looming danger.[1] Otto's own informants were producing evidence enough.

Thus at the League of Nations General Assembly meeting in September 1937, Guido Schmidt and other members of his Austrian delegation were reliably quoted as saying, in private conversations, that 'this was the last time they would be coming to Geneva in this way. Next year, everything in Austria would be different'. Two months later Göring, who was to take a leading role in the Anschluss, had made even more ominous remarks at a meeting of the leaders of his Four Year Plan for the German economy. By the spring of 1938, he informed them, Germans would have no more currency to spare to go on buying Austrian iron ore, so vital for rearmament. Steps should therefore be taken to make sure that, by that time, currency exchange would no longer be needed.[2]

That same month, November 1937, Göring handed out even blunter notice about German intentions when presiding over the lavishly-staged International Sporting Exhibition in Berlin (Hitler's plump Air Marshal also occupied and revelled in the post as Chief Game Warden of the Reich). Several Austrians were among the international throng who attended and they all came in for shocks. Those who visited Göring's sumptuous shooting lodge at Karinhall were invited to inspect a medieval style fresco of Europe which had been specially painted earlier that year. It showed no border line between Germany and Austria. Göring smilingly explained to his astonished Austrian guests, 'Good hunters know no frontiers apart from game boundaries'. They all, including Guido Schmidt, seemed too taken aback, or too overawed, to comment.

Schuschnigg, as a non-sportsman, had not been expected to attend

Göring's great game festival. But, by now, the decision seems to have been taken in Berlin to get hold of him as soon as possible, not as a social visitor but as Austrian Chancellor, for a tête-à-tête with the Führer. Papen, who had been canvassing the idea for some time in Vienna, increased his pressure after Christmas, arguing that only by frank talks between 'the two German Chancellors' could their differences be resolved. It was an encounter which the shy and indecisive Schuschnigg dreaded, and he demurred as long as he could. In the end, it was not Papen's blandishments that persuaded him to enter the lion's den but the clear and mounting evidence that Austria's radical Nazis – the Führer's surrogates – were plotting to depose him.

The villains of the piece were the members of the so-called 'Committee of Seven', which Schuschnigg had himself called into life. In the spring of 1937, he had agreed to the setting up of this special panel of leading Austrian Nazis and pan-Germans (the line between them being often finely drawn) to build a political bridge between their camp and the 'Fatherland Front'. It gradually became clear – as Schuschnigg ought to have realised from the outset – that the Seven's main purpose in life was to dynamite all existing bridges, not to lay down new ones. The final proof came to light when the Austrian security authorities, who had stumbled on the committee's cipher codes, raided their headquarters in Vienna's Teinfaltstrasse, known as the 'Brown House' of the capital. In the safe they found and deciphered the so-called 'Plan of Action for 1938'. This was designed to destroy the republic in three swift interlocking stages: first, a wave of terrorist and sabotage acts too violent for the police to control; second, an appeal to Berlin for protection the moment Schuschnigg ordered his military forces into action; and third, provisions for the German Eighth Army in Bavaria to respond to the appeal by marching in to 'restore order'. Dr Leopold Tavs, the most virulent member of the Seven, was also, at that time, Hitler's Gauleiter-designate for Vienna. He had clearly grown impatient of waiting;[3] so, it seemed, had his masters.

Rumination had been going on for some time in Vienna over the face-to-face encounter with the Führer that even Schuschnigg himself realised would have to come. It was during this preparatory phase that a second dubious counsellor joined Guido Schmidt at the Chancellor's elbows. This was Arthur von Seyss-Inquart, like Schmidt, a fellow pupil of the Stella Matutina but with the additional link to the Chancellor of having served alongside him as a fellow officer of the imperial army on the Isonzo front. Like Schuschnigg, Seyss was also an ex-lawyer and, like him, a devout Catholic and a withdrawn intellectual whose polished spectacles were equally difficult to get behind. But his political compass quivered a degree or two still further towards the magnetic German north. Indeed, it almost covered the mark. He envisaged an Austria which could still call herself by that name (thus still qualifying him as a patriot), but which to all intents and purposes, would be an appendage of the Third Reich – allowed perhaps to be its cultural centre as a reward for surrendering political, military and economic independence. Incredibly enough, he was to see this vision become an apparent reality, with himself at its centre; but only for forty-eight hours. The significance of Seyss-Inquart, however, was not his own mayfly spell in office, but the work he had done towards undermining the regime which had gone before – the chancellorship of his old friend, Kurt Schuschnigg. He played a key role in drawing up the so-called 'Punktationen', a list of ten policy concessions which Austria should offer as her maximum with-drawal line at the forthcoming encounter. (It never seems to have occurred to anyone in Schuschnigg's camp that his aggrieved country should actually try to advance, to protect, let alone demand.) The general tone of the Ten Points was wishy-washy and defensive, while the ninth – a willingness 'to admit members of the so-called nationalist opposition into sharing political responsibility' – opened the Cabinet door to radical pan-Germans and crypto-Nazis alike. The one reservation – that the Chancellor was allowed to select who came in – could never have bolted that door.

Seyss-Inquart, it was later revealed,[4] was already in direct contact with Göring in Berlin and taking his instructions from Hitler's right-hand man. What also emerged later was that, in addition to promoting the Ten Points, Seyss, on the eve of the Hitler meeting, had passed the gist of them by special courier to Berchtesgaden.[5] If treachery was not the conscious motive of his actions, betrayal was their result. Hitler now knew that the victim he was aiming to squash would oblige by actually lying down under the steamroller.

The story of the first (and last) encounter between the two Chancellors on the Obersalzburg needs only to be recounted here on such points as reflect Schuschnigg's own performance.[6] Before it even began, he had taken a small step backwards. Waiting at the frontier post to greet him and Guido Schmidt was the immaculately-dressed Papen who, as major-domo of the proceedings, announced that three of Hitler's generals would also be in attendance. These included Keitel, the newly-appointed chief of the Wehrmacht's High Command,[7] and von Reichenau, who commanded the Fourth Army Group at Leipzig, the very man who would be in overall charge of any military operations against Austria. Did the Austrian Chancellor have any objections? Schuschnigg said nothing to this blatant blackmail. A more resolute man would have either demanded their withdrawal from what were supposed to be political talks, or insisted on calling up some generals of his own from Salzburg, if only to have uniforms on both sides of the room.

He was rocked back on his heels (and never once lunged forward) from the moment, soon after 11.00 a.m., that the two men sat down in Hitler's first- floor study, whose windows looked down towards Salzburg and his Austrian homeland. Austria, the Führer boomed, had done nothing to help the German Reich; her whole history had been one of treason to the race. This must now be brought to an end by the Reich, and nobody would interfere if it 'restored order on its frontiers'. All Schuschnigg could think of in reply to this opening salvo was to point out that, after all, the Austrians had made their cultural contribution to the German scene. (He even spoilt this weak sally by citing Beethoven, who, as the Führer acidly reminded him, was a Rheinlander.)

Hitler then got away with complaining that Austria's defence works along the German frontier had recently been strengthened. He well knew that the prime purpose of this was to secure the border against incursions from the so-called 'Austrian Legion' – paramilitaries trained by the Reich to strike at the homeland which had expelled them. Schuschnigg failed even to point this out. Instead, he promised that he would have any such defence works stopped if they irritated his host. Such meekness only seemed to increase the irritation and Hitler then embarked on one of those semi-calculated, semi-spontaneous outbursts of rage which were becoming the hallmark of his performances:

> I only have to give one command and all this comic stuff on the border will be blown to pieces overnight. You don't seriously think you could hold me up, even for half an hour, do you? Who knows – perhaps you will find me one morning in Vienna, like a spring storm. Then you will go through something ... Do you want to turn Austria into a second Spain?

It was superb histrionics, especially given the audience it was aimed at. Shedding German blood was the stuff of nightmares for Schuschnigg. He neither protested against this blatant threat of invasion nor did he suggest that Austria would lift one finger to oppose it. All he could say instead was that a German march-in could lead to a European war, a remark that Hitler flattened by his standard *tour d'horizon* of the continent: France always too weak; England always too detached; Italy by now too compliant.

This two-hour morning session settled the outcome of an encounter which had looked unbalanced in advance and now simply toppled over onto the Austrians. There were more histrionics in the afternoon, when Hitler shouted for Keitel to join him in his study, while shutting his guests up alone in an adjoining room. His purpose was simply to let them fret with anxiety while Keitel merely stared at the ceiling. It worked: both Schuschnigg and Schmidt later admitted they feared arrest at any moment.

Even Papen grew nervous. Earlier, the Führer had employed the classic technique for breaking a man down – offering him the carrot as well as the stick. By signing the agreement that had been prepared, he said, the Austrian Chancellor would get a unique opportunity to have his name 'recorded in the roll of great Germans'. The Führer made it clear that he was himself 'perhaps the greatest German of all time', but Schuschnigg's dizzy thoughts were of entering the Teutonic pantheon of Bismarck and Frederick the Great.

Throughout, Hitler had addressed his guest, somewhat rudely, as 'Herr Schuschnigg'. Only once, when that guest made an oblique reference to the murder of his predecessor, did the Führer use the proper style of 'Herr Bundeskanzler' in his response, while admitting: 'Dollfuss stands between us'. Here, if ever, was the moment to point out that matters such as the Nazi conspiracy plot of Dr Tavs were also, to put it mildly, still an obstacle to better relations. Schuschnigg let the moment pass. The machinations of Vienna's 'Committee of Seven' were not even mentioned.

It was against this background of bombast and intimidation that, after a relatively conventional luncheon, Hitler presented his demands. Perhaps with conscious irony, they also covered ten points. Not surprisingly, all went much further than those ten Austrian 'maximum concessions' which had been leaked to Berchtesgaden in advance. The real shock lay in point three. This demanded the appointment of Arthur Seyss-Inquart as Minister of Interior and Chief of Security in a new Austrian Cabinet; he was also to supervise the appointment of selected Austrian Nazis into the leadership of the 'Fatherland Front' and 'other Austrian institutions'. Schuschnigg's old comrade-in-arms was thus to become, in effect, his warden. So insistent was Hitler on this key measure that, according to later testimony,[8] he had told his entourage that he would order the German army into action if the Austrian Chancellor even demurred.

There was no demur. During the afternoon, the Austrians succeeded, in talks with Ribbentrop, in getting some of Hitler's other demands for personnel changes in Vienna dropped or amended.[9] Furthermore, the number of Austrian army officers to be 'exchanged' with their German colleagues was reduced from a hundred to fifty; émigré Nazi radicals were to be excluded from a general amnesty; finally, a three-day extension was granted for the formal approval of President Miklas. These were relative trifles: by agreeing to the appointment of Seyss-Inquart – apostle of the 'evolutionary way' but now little more than Hitler's puppet – the only pass which might have guarded Austria's independence had been sold.

By now it was early evening. Savouring his victory, the Führer was in a benign mood and invited his guests to stay on for supper. They, very conscious of defeat, could not wait to get away from his mountain lair and, after polite farewells, boarded the half-track vehicles that would take them down the steep and icy path to their vehicles on the road below. Papen accompanied them all the way back to the Salzburg border post, where a greeting party of Austrian officials had been waiting anxiously for hours. The 'major-domo' of Berchtesgaden did his best to sound cheerful about his master's terrifying performance that day. 'Well,' he said when taking leave of Schuschnigg, 'that's how the Führer can be ... but the next time you will get on much better. Believe me, he can be absolutely charming.' That next time for Schuschnigg was to be courtesy of Hitler's Gestapo.

Back in Vienna, Schuschnigg had to tackle two immediate problems. The first was what to say publicly about the Berchtesgaden meeting. The Führer had dictated and issued on the spot a brief communiqué of his own. This referred merely to an 'unofficial meeting reflecting the mutual desire to discuss all matters affecting relations between the German Reich and Austria'. It was alarmingly bland and the Viennese rumour mill, fed by official leaks, was soon hard at work filling in the blanks with horror stories which went even beyond the hidden facts.

To calm a mood of near panic, the Austrian Chancellor issued his own version on 14 February. This contained no mention of the Führer's demands (let alone his threats) and not a single detail about the long list of concessions. Instead, by agreement with Papen, it harked back to the pact of July 1936, under which Hitler had at least paid lip-service to Austrian sovereignty. The Berchtesgaden meeting, it went on, had taken steps to ensure 'the smooth execution of this agreement, thus ensuring a friendly relationship between the two countries, corresponding with their common national traditions'. As a description of an encounter which had mangled the July pact beyond recognition, trampled on Austrian sovereignty, ordered the Chancellor of a still independent state to change his Cabinet and threatened invasion if he refused, this was *suppressio veri* at its worst. As an exercise in news management it was anyway futile. The truth, though disguised in Schmidt's diplomatic guidance telegram, was soon buzzing around all the Foreign Offices of Europe. The Western powers could be forgiven for believing that the Austrian Chancellor was prepared to go to any lengths to keep the smile on the face of the tiger. Unfortunately, they were to be proven right.[10]

The second, and even more urgent problem, concerned the future of the present Austrian government, and of Schuschnigg himself. Three alternatives presented themselves to the Federal President: to call for a completely new government which would not be bound by the Berchtesgaden capitulation; to carry on with the existing Cabinet but with a new Chancellor, or, finally, to execute the agreement with the government as it stood. It was only after many debates over the pros and cons of each alternative that Dr Miklas decided to leave it to Schuschnigg to deliver up to Hitler what he had promised. There was, of course, another possibility: to denounce before the world an agreement that had not yet been finally ratified by the President and square Austria's shoulders for what might come. It was raised, but dropped without more ado.

The main reason why Schuschnigg was asked to carry on (apart from his personal integrity and his long involvement with the Nazi menace) was that the President was quite simply at a loss how to replace him. Even before Berchtesgaden, when Austria's doleful advance list of concessions was being prepared, questions had been raised in the Fatherland Front camp as to whether he was tough enough for the challenge. Now, after what had amounted to his capitulation with barely a squeak of protest, those voices became louder. Might not Richard Schmitz, the pro-monarchist Mayor of Vienna be a better leader in such a crisis, or even Dr Michael Skubl, the capital's doughty police chief who was to stay on even under the new security regime of Seyss-Inquart?

The difficulty was that neither man was keen on taking up this most unenviable of jobs at this most perilous juncture in the country's fortunes. Nor was any other willing candidate forthcoming from the old Christian Socialist camp. Then, out of the blue, a volunteer did emerge. Just over a week after his return from Berchtesgaden, a heavily-sealed letter, which had been brought to Vienna by secret courier, was put by hand on Schuschnigg's desk. When he opened it up, it was to find that the man he always addressed, and thought of, as 'Your Majesty', was offering to return from exile to take over his post and try to steer Austrian through the storm.

10

Takeover by Telephone

Otto had only learned via Baron Wiesner that Schuschnigg had agreed to go to Berchtesgaden the day before the Chancellor set out. It was thus too late to take a stand, though the Pretender was well aware of what the visit meant:

> It was quite clear to me that this was the beginning of the end. Schuschnigg tried hard in his messages to stress that there was no danger and that, on the contrary, this would lead to a peaceful outcome and to a lessening of the tensions inside Austria. I never believed this and neither did Wiesner or the others working with me.[1]

When, again through Wiesner, he learned what had actually taken place on the 12 February, the truth exceeded even his worst fears. It was obvious that Schuschnigg had simply buckled under pressure and that, if that pressure were renewed and intensified, Austria's Chancellor would collapse altogether, and take his country down with him.

All the grim details of the Berchtesgaden humiliation reached Hams Castle on 14 February. The next day, the twenty-five-year-old Pretender took the first major independent initiative of his young life. Without telling his mother what he intended to do, Otto shut himself in his room for the whole evening and night, working at draft after draft of a personal appeal to Schuschnigg to rescue the situation. Only when he was satisfied with the final version did he emerge and show it to his mother. The matriarch gave it her full blessing and only minor amendments were suggested. On 20 February both the letter, which was dated three days earlier, and the means for placing it on the Chancellor's desk, were finalised. Apart from the little court in exile, nobody – not even Wiesner – knew its contents.

The method worked out for the delivery was Byzantine.[2] The courier chosen to take the missive to Vienna was the young Count Heinrich Eltz. He was not, however, to make the final handover; this task was to be discharged by another loyalist trusty, Baron Franz von Mirbach. The letter was to be handed over to him between nine and ten in the morning at the Vienna Jockey Club in the Pallavicini palace, with a special seal to close the envelope. Even Mirbach could not act without agreeing the exact date of delivery with the indispensable Baron Wiesner and he was still *en route* from Belgium. (This was yet another example of that classic Austrian maxim: 'If there is a complicated way of doing something, why make it simple?')

In fact, the letter did not reach Schuschnigg's hands until the 25 or 26 February.[3] Acting on instructions, Mirbach made only one comment when putting it on the Chancellor's desk. This was to say that the courier, whom he did not name, would be staying on in Vienna for another forty-eight hours, in the hope of taking a prompt response back to Hams Castle with him. It was a vain hope. What Schuschnigg found himself reading was not exactly cut out for a snap decision.

After a sombre *tour d'horizon* of the dangers which Austria now faced, Otto addressed three pleas to his 'Dear Herr von Schuschnigg ... as a man of unshakeable loyalty to his Emperor and his People'. The first two sounded relatively harmless: to make no further concessions of any sort either to Germany or Austria's nationalist camp, and to inform him immediately of any signs of further demands from these quarters. The third request was startling and the paragraph deserves translating in full:

> However unexpected what now follows may appear, it has been just as carefully considered in this critical hour of acute danger. Should you feel unable to withstand further pressure ... I ask you then – whatever the situation may be – to hand over to me the office of Chancellor. I am not demanding a restoration of the monarchy, which would require a long drawn-out process of recognition by the Powers. I call on you only to give me the Chancellorship so that we could gain the same advantages achievable through a formal restoration of the Monarchy but without any change in the constitution or any new recognition.

The writer assured the recipient of his message that this proposal 'did not spring from the hunger for power of an ambitious young man'. On the contrary: 'I am acting as I do because I see it as my duty that, when Austria is in peril, I, as the heir to the House of Austria, should stand or fall with my country'. For good measure, Schuschnigg's oath of loyalty to the dynasty as an officer in the old imperial army was invoked by Otto – though this approach had done his own father little good when confronting Admiral Horthy in Budapest.

The Chancellor would have been moved by much of this, and especially by its ending: 'Otto, in a foreign land' ('in der Fremde').[4] But he was not sufficiently moved to get up and leave his chair. Admittedly, Austria was facing disaster as it was and its chances of wriggling away from the Nazi clutches looked bleak. But even these slim hopes might well have been dashed, not resolved, by this strange proposal. It amounted, after all, to a restoration without the crown, and both Baron von Neurath and Göring had assured him that, if the Habsburgs tried to return to Vienna, the German Army would march. Not for nothing was its rudimentary project for an invasion code-named 'Operation Otto'.

Then there was the constitutional problem itself, which Otto had more or less dismissed. Schuschnigg's office was simply not in his own gift to transfer. Appointing Chancellors was the sole prerogative of the Federal President and, as we have seen, Dr Miklas had a mind of his own. He was a conservative and also a one-time monarchist. Had Schuschnigg resigned and pressed for the Pretender as his successor, the President would have been torn between nostalgia and realism. The young Prince had not seen his native country since leaving it as a child nearly twenty years before. The Austrian Republic was a stranger to him and, until the arrival of Dollfuss and his 'Fatherland Front', a hostile stranger. So, for the President even to consider him as the new head of an emergency government, Otto would have needed the backing of the whole country – army, police, bureaucracy; the political apparatus in the capital and the provinces; and workers and peasants alike. In other words, it would hinge on popular acclamation rather than presidential appointment. But the Austrians were and are not the Magyars. National clamour is not their style. Thus, though Otto's letter showed immense personal courage, that very courage had blurred his vision.

It is, however, quite possible that this unexpected move of his had an equally unpredictable effort. It may well have helped Schuschnigg to gal-vanise himself into the first burst of nationalist fervour, combined with the first public display of anti-Nazi defiance, he had ever shown in his political career. During a whole fortnight, instead of shirking the limelight, he basked in it; instead of fudging decisions, he proclaimed them; instead of hedging his bets, he staked everything on one final gamble. He later admitted that even he could never quite explain what had suddenly come over him.[5]

The transformation had started on 24 February with a rousing speech to the ersatz Parliament of his corporate state. It was four days after Hitler had spoken in disappointingly menacing tones about Austria to his own Reichstag. Schuschnigg now responded with oratory which even the Führer might have envied.

There was a note of drama from the start. 'The one and only point on the order of the day is: Austria', he began. Then followed the rhetorical device so often used by Adolf Hitler – the historical retrospect to justify action in the present. Schuschnigg called the roll of honour of those who had fought to defend Austria's independence. He started with the Empress Maria Theresia and ended with his murdered predecessor, Engelbert Dollfuss, whose voice seemed to be coming from his lips. He came on to the confrontation with Hitler, and there was a Germanic echo when he called it 'this struggle of brother against brother'. But the fraternal touch was abandoned in what followed. At Berchtesgaden he had gone right up to that boundary line clearly marked 'Thus far and no further'. There would be no further retreat. To the Nazi sympathisers among his countrymen he declared: 'It is not Nationalism or Socialism which is the watchword in Austria, but Patriotism'. He ended almost in a shriek: 'Unto death! Red-White-Red! Austria!'

His performance brought the house down. The cheering spread to the streets outside where, for want of any other appropriate chorus (everything in Vienna having to be framed in music), the old imperial anthem broke out. At Hams Castle in Belgium, where the last candle flickered of that empire, there were more controlled feelings of delight mixed with bewilderment. Was this the same man who, they had always thought, had his heart in the right place but no stomach for a fight? For the exiles, the answer seemed to come in the letter of 2 March, in which Schuschnigg belatedly replied to Otto's offer to take over the helm. The response amounted to the most deferential rejection.

The Habsburg problem, he argued, could only await a long-term solution,[6] and this was not the time to act. He would be happy to inform His Majesty of any changes in the overall situation, but the present policy of the present regime in Vienna represented 'the only realistic and negotiation way forward'. These things, so difficult to judge from far away, could only be decided by those on the spot, and if Austria's path to the future were to be blotted out by wrong decisions, to reconstruct it again would be impossible in a lifetime. As regards the chancellorship, the lawyer Schuschnigg, not surprisingly, fell back on the legal argument: only the Federal President could discuss and appoint to the post. As regards a restoration, any such move not just for now, but in the foreseeable future, 'must assuredly, with 100 per cent certainty, mean the death of Austria'. After a pledge that the fight to preserve Austria was the sole motive behind all his decisions, Schuschnigg signed himself off 'In devoted reverence to Your Majesty'.[7]

The royal recipient of that response could not see in its contents much sign of devotion. He had opposed Berchtesgaden in vain and had been dismayed by Schuschnigg's tactics afterwards – smothering everything up instead of publicly protesting to the world about Hitler's blackmail. And now this rejection. 'It stood,' he noted, 'in direct contradiction to everything that Schuschnigg had clearly set out in his speech of 24 February. It amounted to a flat admission that he would offer no further resistance to German threats.'[8]

Those words were written on 6 March 1938, soon after Otto had got back from Paris, where he had been helping to mobilise French support for Schuschnigg's 'Unto Death' speech. The Pretender found he was pushing at an already opening door. In the French National Assembly's debate over the Austrian crisis, there was loud acclaim for the Foreign Minister, Yvon Delbos, when he backed Vienna's embattled Chancellor to the hilt.[9] All this made Otto doubly bitter to find Schuschnigg's letter of rejection awaiting him on his return. Yet, as he and the rest of the world were soon to find out, the Chancellor was already preparing an even bolder gesture of defiance against Hitler. It was to be his last, and Austria's last: one final giant firework which was to fizzle out before leaving the ground.

At Berchtesgaden, Hitler, at one point, had cuttingly referred to Schusch-nigg's Slav origins which, he pointed out, meant that he had more right to call himself an Austrian than his guest. And the Führer had continued: 'Why don't you once try a plebiscite in Austria in which you and I would run against each other? Then you would find out!' It was a plebiscite which Schuschnigg now decided to launch, though without the Führer against him on the hustings. It should, of course, have been staged much earlier – after the murder of Dollfuss in 1934, for example, or, at the latest, after the treacherous July pact of 1936. Be that as it may, there seemed to be several good reasons for trying it, as a last throw, in March 1938.

One positive factor was that, at long last, the 'Austro-Fascist' corporate state was touching hands with the Socialist trade union movements it had driven underground.[10] This was more of a clasp of desperation to save both sides from drowning, for the Austrian workers now saw, just as clearly as the Catholic right-wingers of the Fatherland Front, the reality of the Nazi danger which faced them all alike. The shadow of the noose still dangled between these two camps. It had been the same Kurt Schuschnigg, then Minister of Justice, who had enforced all nine death sentences passed on Socialist 'rebels' after the brief but bloody civil war of February 1934. Austria's left-wingers could neither forget nor forgive the humiliation of those days but, four years later, the Chancellor could reckon with at least partial support from their ranks. He was still their devil. It was just that a more terrible Lucifer had appeared in the north.

More important, however, were the negative factors pushing Schuschnigg to an appeal to the nation. The Austrian Nazis had already taken to the streets in the provinces while he was making his 'Unto Death' speech in the capital. In Graz, their 'flying squads' succeeded in storming the town hall, stopping the relay of his words by disconnecting the loud-speakers and even hoisting the swastika from the roof of the building before the army restored order. Other, less serious demonstrations spluttered on in the days that followed. Meanwhile, within the Cabinet, Interior Minister

Seyss-Inquart was turning a deeper shade of Nazi brown on top of his pale
Austrian Red-White-Red by the day. (Ominously, Vienna's shops were
reported to be selling out of brown-coloured cloth suitable for flags and
banners. The good citizenry was already hedging its bets.)

According to Schuschnigg's own account of these crucial days,[11] it was
the arrival in Vienna on 4 March of Dr Wilhelm Keppler, Hitler's Special
Commissioner for Nazi Affairs, that proved decisive. The special commissioner bore a blunt message: the Berchtesgaden agreement was no longer
enough and Austria must now go further down the road to compliance. In
a forty-minute session with the Chancellor, held in his private apartments,
Keppler spelt out the details. They overturned every single concession that
Schuschnigg had managed to get away with on 12 February. Specifically, the
number of Austrian officers to be exchanged with their German colleagues
was put back to a hundred from the compromise figure of fifty; German
party newspapers hitherto barred from Austria were now to be freely
circulated; and the two currencies were to be closely linked.

The most critical demand was the political one: henceforth, the National
Socialist movement was to be formally recognised in Austria; even their
extremists would no longer be 'illegals'. It seemed clear that Hitler's emissary
was deliberately throwing down the gauntlet. For the first and last time,
Schuschnigg, just as deliberately, picked it up. The Chancellor went straight
away to the Federal President to ask for his formal approval to hold a
nationwide plebiscite. It was enthusiastically given.

The Duce, who was approached through the Austrian Minister in Rome,
Ulrich von Hassel, expressed equally marked disapproval, but Schuschnigg,
still under his trance-like spell of defiance, was undeterred. Indeed, he put
on another bravura public performance when he announced his terms at
a mass gathering in Innsbruck three days later. The text had been hammered
out not in Cabinet (which was felt to be insecure) but in the Vienna
headquarters of the Fatherland Front where – it was optimistically assumed
– all secrets would be safe.

The voters were to be asked whether they wanted an Austria which was
to be 'free, German, independent, social, Christian and united'. (There was
no mention of 'democratic'.) The sequence of the words chosen says everything about the mind of Schuschnigg and perhaps also the mood of his
countrymen at the time. Second only to 'free' came 'German', which stood a
long way before 'Christian', with 'unity' bringing up the rear. Pan-Germans,
worshippers of either the Catholic God or the Socialist welfare state, patriots,
political bridge-builders – there was something for almost everyone here.
It was just as well, since nobody knew exactly what it was they did want
in those Ides of March.

What was hoped to be the magic formula for salvation was announced on the 9th to the world at large in the congenial setting of the civic hall in Innsbruck, capital of Schuchnigg's native Tyrol. It was another firebrand speech, and seemingly unrehearsed, as though those inner voices were still speaking out for him:

'We want a free German Austria ... We want bread and peace in our land, and equal rights for all who stand for nation and fatherland.'[12] Next Sunday, 13 March, he told his audience, he was calling a plebiscite because he simply had to know whether he had the people behind him at this critical juncture. It was, he made clear, a personal decision. 'I have taken responsibility for this decision entirely upon myself and I will stand or fall – with everything I strive for and believe in – by the support which the Austrian people declare ... I cannot imagine that any individual man or woman, aware of what is at stake, will cast a vote against.'

The speech had been punctuated at intervals with loud applause. When, in an inspired touch, he ended it in dialect with the rallying call of 'Mander s'ischt Zeit!' (Men, the time has come!), the hall and the crowd outside exploded. That had been the cry with which Tyrol's great freedom fighter, Andreas Hofer, had rallied his pitchfork army to do battle with Napoleon. The slim bespectacled man on the rostrum, though wearing the grey loden jacket and green waistcoat of the province, cut a much less inspiring figure than the black-bearded giant of legend. But the message, carried by loud-speaker and over the airwaves, had the same resonance: another invader from the north to be met by the same defiance. It sounded like the joyful cradle-song of a nation reborn. Nobody watching or listening could have believed that this was to be, in fact, a funeral anthem.

Had they but known it, the omens lay right there with the platform microphones. The radio broadcasts of the speech were being blotted out in neighbouring Bavaria and even distorted in some parts of Austria by heavy and systematic jamming from Germany. Hitler had heard all about Schuschnigg's secret in Berlin at least thirty-six hours before the would-be surprise was unveiled in Innsbruck. On the evening of 8 March the Austrian Chancellor revealed his plan to Seyss-Inquart, who had given his word of honour to keep it secret. Hitler's placeman must have been sorely tested to keep that pledge. In the event there was no need: the betrayal had already taken place and it came from the very heart of Schuschnigg's political bastion, the Fatherland Front. The woman secretary of the director of the Front, Guido Zernatto, had leaked an outline of the plebiscite project, which she had just taken down in dictation, to Viennese Nazis. They had rushed it by courier to Salzburg, where their ideological brethren on the frontier service passed it straight to Berlin via a special telex link with the German

Gestapo, together with the text of the propaganda posters. From that moment on, it was to be the Austrian Chancellor and not the Führer who was in for surprises.

None of this was, of course, suspected at Hams Castle, where Schuschnigg's rousing speech at Innsbruck was greeted, still in somewhat dazed delight, as a further sign of Austria's regeneration. Everything reported from Vienna on the following day, 10 March, seemed to confirm this. It was a brilliantly sunny day and the pavements of the capital were lined with cheering crowds as open lorries, flying Fatherland Front banners, chugged through the streets hurling pro-plebiscite leaflets into the air. The text was uncompromising: 'With Schuschnigg, for a free Austria!' Otto promptly flung himself into a fundraising campaign to help finance the referendum and received substantial support from, among others, the Jewish community in London.

The Chancellor himself felt serenely confident as pledge after pledge of support came in from anti-Nazi groups of all colours: the Heimwehr, the Jewish community, the monarchists, the Catholics and even, most significantly, from spokesmen of the underground Socialist activists. Even some paid Nazi demonstrators were torn in their greed. A group of youths who had been paid five schillings a head to shout for Hitler approached the Fatherland Front in a Vienna suburb offering to perform the same service for Schuschnigg at the special bargain rate of only four schillings.

The Chancellor even found time that day to write a long letter to Seyss-Inquart, who had done his duty by the Führer by questioning whether the plebiscite might not be in contravention of the Berchtesgaden Pact. On the contrary, Schuschnigg replied. It was the Nazis who were wrecking that agreement by their terror campaign. 'I am neither capable nor desirous of playing a puppet's role,' the letter continued, 'and I am in the fortunate position of being able to call up the whole world as a witness of who is right and who stands for peace.'

That evening, the two former fellow students and comrades-at-arms had a long private talk at which Seyss, after securing some technical changes over the poll, eventually promised to appeal to his own supporters to vote 'Yes' in the Sunday plebiscite. It all seemed cut and dried. The chastened Minister of Interior then went over to the Hotel Regina to report his actions to a secret emergency meeting of Austrian Nazi leaders who had gathered from every province in the country to discuss the plebiscite crisis. It was now that Seyss-Inquart first sensed, with a shock, that another and far bigger game was in play in which he might well be the puppet. The Nazi leaders seemed totally uninterested in his news about the agreement he had just reached with Schuschnigg. Moreover, when they retired to another room to talk among themselves, Hitler's chosen Minister of Interior found the door closed in his face. These were the men who were already considering themselves as the Führer's Austrian Gauleiters and, by now, they had good cause. At 4.30 that same afternoon, General von Bock, the German army commander in the Dresden district had received direct orders from his Führer to march into Austria at around midday on 12 March 'to restore orderly conditions'.

The order was the culmination of more than twenty-four hours deliberation at Hitler's Berlin Chancellery. This was never a tranquil place at the easiest of times but, now, under the impact of the Austrian crisis, things had moved at a frenetic pace. The Führer's first reaction to Schuschnigg's plebiscite plan showed shock as well as fury. When he sent his guest packing from Berchtesgaden almost exactly a month before, he had visualised him as a sort of political bluebottle, who would henceforth go buzzing round his Chancellery, quite harmlessly and without any sense of direction. Now, the bluebottle had suddenly turned into a hornet with a very venomous sting. It had to be swatted.

The Führer initially toyed with the idea of doing the swatting in a quasi-constitutional manner by allowed the referendum to go ahead, but with the option of voting for the Anschluss instead (the 'greatest of all the Germans' pitted against an opponent who was not really German at all). But when that opponent delivered his ringing speech of defiance at Innsbruck, Hitler put all such ideas out of his head and turned to the military option. This badly needed sorting out. When 'Operation Otto' was dug up from the files, it turned out to be nothing more than a theoretical staff study of measures to suppress a Habsburg restoration which had been gathering dust ever since it was first drafted the previous summer. Hitler dismissed it with a snort and substituted a proper mobilisation and march plan to be issued in its place. This, the so-called 'Instruction No. 1',[13] was a straightforward invasion campaign over which the Führer would be in personal control. The German Eighth Army was to attack 'with the immediate objective of occupying Upper Austria, Salzburg, Lower Austria and the Tyrol, as well as the rapid seizure of Vienna and the securing of the Austro-Czech frontier'. General von Bock was also given a political directive which reflected the uniquely strange nature of the operation. Though any resistance was to be 'mercilessly crushed', it should not be provoked, as 'we do not wish to start a war against our Austrian brothers'. The General was to have no worries on this score.

Seyss-Inquart, as we have seen, had remained in Vienna throughout these proceedings, though his fellow 'nationalist patriot', Glaise-Horstenau, who had been holidaying in Germany, was summoned to the Führer's presence.

The wretched General found himself called upon to deliver no fewer than three missives to his Chancellor. Two were produced by Hitler: first, a draft letter of resignation from Seyss-Inquart, as an act of protest against the plebiscite; and, second, the proposed text of a broadcast by Schuschnigg abandoning the referendum. Then Göring sidled up to produce the third and most sinister missive. This was a draft telegram to be signed by Seyss-Inquart and sent to Berlin formally requesting the despatch of German troops to 'restore order' in his country. The General remained enough of an Austrian, and a member of Schuschnigg's Cabinet, to refuse playing the postman in this dire game. Given the setting, and the two men at his elbows, this was a spirited gesture. Unhappily, it was an ineffectual one. The next day, whether he liked it or not, General von Glaise-Horstenau became one of Hitler's messengers of doom in Vienna.

11 March 1938 was to be the last day in the life of a free Austria. The story of that day's happenings in Vienna is a mixture of tragedy and farce. It is, above all, a chronicle of muddle and confusion, descending at times into sheer bedlam. These events however, have been well documented over the years and need only to be summarised again here before coming to the tale which has not so far been told. This is of the struggle of the royal exiles in general, and of Otto in particular, to raise the banner of resistance in their old homeland.

Schuschnigg's long day in Vienna started very early and very ominously. Before dawn, at 5.30 a.m., he was roused from his sleep by an emergency call from his Chief of Police, Dr Michael Skubl. The Germans had closed their customs post at Salzburg during the night and massive troops movements were being reported on their side of the frontier. Pausing only to offer a brief prayer *en route* at St Stephen's Cathedral, Schuschnigg was in his Chancellery soon after six o'clock to find his key officials already anxiously assembled. They handed over more grim news, a telegram which had arrived from their Consul General in Munich, Dr Jordan. It read simply 'Leo is ready to travel'. The lion was Hitler, for this translated in the secret code book as 'Preparations for an imminent invasion seem to have begun'.

By now there was a great bustle of activity at Vienna's Aspern airport. Before Schuschnigg had even reached his office, Papen had left by special plane for Berlin, preferring not to witness the final phase of the disaster he had engineered for Austria. Seyss-Inquart, for whom the Chancellor had been searching, was also at the airport where the dawn arrival traffic from Germany had been momentous. The first machine in carried only one passenger, a special courier carrying Hitler's surrender message for Schuschnigg. This was followed soon afterwards by the plane Seyss had gone to meet. It carried his comrade in perplexity, Glaise-Horstenau, who landed in the company of Göring's Austrian brother-in-law, Dr Franz Hüber. The Field-Marshal, it seemed, was taking a family interest in the drama.

As Hitler's personal message could only be regarded as an official document, Seyss had it collected from the German Legation and read it through with Glaise-Horstenau on their way to the Chancellery. No wonder they had solemn faces: the leader of a foreign power had issued an ultimatum to their Chancellor and it had fallen to them – two of his own Ministers – not only to deliver it but to help enforce it. Both declared they would resign (starting other unspecified measures in train) unless Schuschnigg agreed to Hitler's demand: postpone the plebiscite for at least a fortnight to allow for a 'legal poll' to be organised in its place.

It was now 9.30 a.m. and, for the next two hours, the three men tossed the issue to and fro between them. Hitler's ultimatum was timed to expire at noon, but Seyss-Inquart obligingly extended it, on the Führer's behalf, for another two hours. This was the first personal initiative that Hitler's chosen Interior Minister had taken throughout the crisis; it also marked the first intimation that he was considering himself to be Austria's next leader.

When noon came round, however, Schuschnigg was still in belligerent mood. Not only was he determined to defend his plebiscite, he was also taking energetic measures to defend his country. In a stream of emergency orders, he called up the 1915 class of Austrian military reservists; put the Vienna police and National Front militia on alert; had arms distributed to the security guards both of the federal railways and the key power plants of the capital; and even organised extra fuel supplies for the army's motorised units. This was fighting talk indeed; unhappily, it was to remain only talk.

When, two hours later, he summoned all his closest advisers to discuss the situation, it was Schuschnigg the lawyer who took over from Schuschnigg the warrior. Just as in the Berchtesgaden crisis, he put forward three possible courses of action (almost as though Schuschnigg, the devout Catholic, were subconsciously relying on the Holy Trinity itself as a model). The options ranged from total rejection of all Hitler's demands, coupled with an appeal to world opinion; a compromise in which only technical changes would be made to the plebiscite; and, finally, acceptance of the ultimatum. When those two terrible ideological twins, Glaise-Horstenau and Seyss-Inquart, flatly rejected any compromise, the Chancellor found himself boxed in, having to fight or to yield. He put the problem to President Miklas, who had hurried over from his office on the opposite side of the Ballhausplatz Square. When Schuschnigg rejoined his colleagues, it was to tell them, somewhat to their surprise, that he had decided to yield to Hitler's demands. It was now 2.30 in the afternoon. Only two and a half hours before, he had been rolling all the guns out for action: why the about-turn?

The only negative development over that lunchtime had been the failure of his repeated efforts to telephone Mussolini in Rome over the crisis. The Duce had simply declared himself unavailable. Yet this reaction was just as expected: Mussolini had flagged his intentions over any new Austrian crisis very clearly in advance. Nor, as Schuschnigg well knew, could anything beyond formal protest be expected from the two other members of the collapsed Stresa Front. France had chosen 10 March, the very day of the mounting crisis, to be without a government, so that its Foreign Minister, Yvon Delbos, a staunch friend of Austria's was now 'in statu demissionis'. London could have been a pressure point, for Hitler's new Foreign Minister, Ribbentrop, happened to be on a visit there and was actually lunching with the British Prime Minister, Neville Chamberlain, on 11 March when Foreign Office telegrams on the plebiscite drama were brought in. But Chamberlain, like Mussolini, wanted to keep his lines with Hitler open and not tangled up by complications in Vienna. The most that he delivered to his guest was a reproachful slap on the wrist.[14]

The truth of the matter was that, by suddenly caving in over the ultimatum, Schuschnigg had already decided his own fate, along with that of his country. The manner by which the *coup de grâce* came was, nonetheless, bizarre. To begin with, it was Göring, rather than Hitler, who now leapt into action to deliver the blow. The Marshal had always been fond of telling his visitors in Berlin that the Austrian question would have to be settled 'so oder so' ('one way or the other'); however, even he could never have imagined that he would become the first person in history to take over a sovereign state entirely on the telephone. Yet that was what happened in Vienna between 3 p.m. and 8 p.m. on the afternoon and early evening of 11 March.

To the ignominious end of his days,[15] the Marshal remained proud of what he had accomplished in those five hours, inspired, he felt, by some messianic impulse of racial destiny. 'I had an instinctive feeling', he told his Nuremberg judges, 'that here at last was the opportunity – so long and so passionately awaited – to bring about a final, clear-cut solution.'[16] For him, the moment had come after he heard from Seyss-Inquart of Schuschnigg's surrender over the plebiscite. The Chancellor and his mixed bag of colleagues had naively believed that this climb-down perhaps marked the end of the crisis. As they all learned twenty minutes later, it was only the beginning. At five minutes past three, Göring returned the call and, obviously with Hitler's blessing, dictated the following message:

In view of his breach of the Berchtesgaden agreement Schuschnigg no longer enjoys our confidence. The national Ministers in Austria [Seyss-Inquart and

Glaise-Horstenau] are to hand in their resignations to the Chancellor and to demand that he resign as well.

Seyss-Inquart was then informed that he was the 'obvious choice' to be appointed by President Miklas as the new Chancellor of Austria. He was given one hour to put everything through.

In fact, it was not to be before midnight on this seemingly interminable day that Seyss-Inquart was confirmed as Hitler's Chancellor. For nine hours, despite all the threats that Göring hurled at him, Miklas had rejected the nomination as a foreign imposition, while imploring a series of patriotic Austrian leaders to step into Schuschnigg's shoes. There were no takers, and finally, having run out of volunteers and with Nazi thugs gathering, unmolested, in the courtyard below, the doughty old President gave way.

However admirable this one-man stand for Austria had been, Miklas was defending a pass that had already been sold. By teatime, Schuschnigg had reversed his noonday military heroics by instructing his army commander General Sigismund Schilawsky to withdraw his troops from all border areas and order them to offer no resistance to any German forces marching in. [17] That had lowered the red-white flag to half-mast. At ten minutes to eight in the evening, Schuschnigg unhooked it and folded it. A microphone was rigged up in the so-called Corner Room of the Chancellery. It was only a few feet from the spot where Dollfuss had fallen to Nazi bullets four years before and now it was his successor who stepped forward to declare bloodless surrender to the nation. After briefly recounting the day's events, he announced without more ado that Austria was 'yielding to force'. He had issued the no resistance order because 'we are resolved that, on no account, and not even at this grave hour, shall German blood by spilled'. He ended with the choking cry 'May God protect Austria!' But he also took leave of his people by pronouncing along with his heartfelt wishes, 'a German word'. (His phrase, 'ein deutsches Wort', has the undertone of a pledge or vow.)

It seems that what had finally propelled him to the microphone was a report that German troops had already crossed the border. This turned out to be false alarm: the forces of Hitler's 'Instruction No. 1' did not march in until the following morning and then not to enforce surrender but to exploit it. Yet even this final irony touched the root of the matter. Schuschnigg did not yield because of his diplomatic isolation, which had long been anticipated, and was not finally confirmed in the telegrams reaching Vienna until *after* his resignation. Nor did he give in because he was a coward. His personal courage – and, perhaps, his total misreading of the future – was shown by his refusal to flee with colleagues across the Czech border while it was still open. His surrender was, quite simply, the ultimate sacrifice before his Germanic altar. He had knelt before it as a student, fought to defend it as a soldier, and continued to venerate it to the end as a politician.

As experienced by the royal exiles in Belgium, the fall of Austria was complicated first and foremost by the problems of communication. Göring could bark his commands down the telephone from Berlin to Vienna by priority calls which were connected almost as soon as he lifted the receiver. Normally, the lines from Belgium to Austria also went through the German capital. They could not, however, be used as they would almost certainly have been tapped, so that any identifiable caller or listener in the republic would automatically join the Habsburg Pretender himself on the Gestapo's wanted list. The only solution was to find a secure line going through Switzerland, which Otto arranged in frequent contact visits, from the New Year onwards.

Even before Berchtesgaden, Otto was preoccupied with two problems. The first was how to galvanise the Austrians into saving themselves. The second was how and when the banished dynasty might ride in to their rescue, without wrecking both itself and them in the process. Something had to be attempted, for Schuschnigg's promised *annus mirabilis* of 1937, the year when he had pledged to carry out the restoration, had passed with Austria even more in Hitler's grip than ever.

'We always ruled out the idea of a military *coup d'état*,' Otto recalled,

> which, even assuming it could have worked, would have been too provocative and set the wrong tone. But after Berchtesgaden, we explored the idea of a political shake-up. We had reason to believe that President Miklas would not be opposed to the formation of an emergency Coalition government of National Resistance which would take an altogether tougher line with the Nazis. So Baron Wiesner sounded out on our behalf Richard Schmitz, the Mayor of Vienna, and Josef Reiter, the powerful Provincial Governor of Lower Austria, to see if they would take the lead. But both demurred, saying the idea was 'no longer feasible'. It was that which decided me to write my letter to Schuschnigg offering to form such an emergency government myself, by taking over from him as Chancellor. That was turned down. [18]

During the final crisis of 10–12 March, Otto was in constant touch, over a safe Zürich line, with two key people. The first was General Zehner in the Ministry of Defence, whom he urged to organise some sort of resistance to a German march-in, even if only brief and symbolic. This was seen both as a matter of honour and as an historic marker to secure Austria's future. Zehner was all for it but Schuschnigg's order to the troops to pull back and simply sit on their arms squashed the idea flat.

On the political side, Otto concentrated on Dr Schmitz, pleading with him to step forward and instil some defiance into the tottering government. The Mayor's last words down the telephone in reply showed he had given up the struggle. 'Schuschnigg got us into this mess,' he told Otto, 'and now it's up to him to get us out of it.'

So, in the last forty-eight hours of Austria's freedom, the ultimate challenge had to be faced again. Should Otto simply board a private plane in Belgium,[19] descend on Vienna's Aspern airfield like a living ghost of the imperial past and gamble that his very name and bravura would persuade the nation to rally round him? The idea had been debated on and off ever since the beginning of the year but, by 10 March, with Hitler threatening and Schuschnigg wobbling, it was now or never. This produced what Otto always remembered as 'the one and only really flaming row I ever had with my mother'.

True to her indomitable nature, she insisted he should take the gamble, arguing that 'courage often carried the day regardless of the odds'. Moreover – and here she touched a chord in him – she maintained that 'it was our task as Habsburgs to stand by Austria regardless of what might happen'. And she again came out with her favourite maxim of the hunter: 'By not shooting at all, you also miss.'[20]

Otto's answer was that the target was, by now, quite simply out of range. In February, when he had offered to go to Vienna and take over the Chancellorship, a legal path was still open and a legal government was in place and still perhaps sufficiently stable to sustain even the startling change he had proposed. But by 10–11 March everything was crumbling. Even the monarchists had begun to waver, and with the security apparatus firmly in the hands of Seyss-Inquart, and the army now ordered to stack its arms, where was the physical or political basis for a Habsburg take-over?[21] As things stood in Vienna, he would merely be landing in Hitler's clutches.

Then, when she continued to press him, Otto was driven to remind her of October 1921. Then it had been she who had urged her husband on to attempt the subjugation of Horthy's Hungary with a miniature royalist army. That adventure, he reminded her, had ended in tragedy for all of them, and had helped to bring on his father's premature death. Did she now wish to murder her son? At that, for the first and only time in his life, he saw his mother break down. The subject was dropped and they watched helplessly as the curtain duly descended on the Austrian Republic.

There is a coda to all this. More than sixty years later, after reminiscing with a friend over the Anschluss saga, Otto added:

By the way, I was in Berlin a day or two ago, the first time I had seen it since the war. They showed me that dreadful yard in the Plötzensee Prison with the wire nooses hanging from butchers' hooks on which the leaders of the July 1944 plot against Hitler had been slowly strangled to death. As I looked, it suddenly struck me that I could easily have ended up on one of those hooks myself had I flown to Vienna in March of 1938 just before the Gestapo took over.[22]

11

Homecoming

Vienna now underwent a transformation which, in both speed and scope, was unparalleled in anything seen in the history of a Western capital. On the afternoon of 11 March, the streets and houses remained bedecked with the black crutched cross symbol of the Fatherland Front, whose plebiscite propaganda leaflets still lay scattered on the pavements. By the evening of the 12th, all these – and, for that matter, the plain red-white-red flags of the republic itself – were nowhere to be seen. In their place was the omnipresent Nazi swastika: set in red arm-bands on all official jackets and on many civilian ones; displayed in placards in shop fronts; stuck in car windows and even tacked onto bicycles; framed in banners streaming down from thousands of rooftops and balconies. It was as though there had been a complete change of stage sets put in place between two acts of an opera.

The sounds had changed as well as the scenery. Those of the previous day's performers still on view were now singing from different scores, while the chorus, more deafening than ever, had also changed its tune. 'Heil Hitler!' was already in use as a personal greeting as well as a mass rallying cry. 'Heil Schuschnigg!' was nowhere to be heard, no more (at least in pubic) than 'Long Live Austria!' or the old Habsburg anthem. A new act had indeed begun, one which was to last for more than seven years.

The classic image of Vienna's metamorphosis is that of the Führer, on 15 March, addressing a jubilant throng of some 250,000 of his new subjects from the great balcony overlooking the Heldenplatz, part of the newest wing of the former imperial palace. The ubiquitous swastika banners now trailed down from all windows of the Hofburg and a forest of arms raised in the Nazi salute greeted him from below. It is an eternal historical embarrassment, for any Austrian with a pulse of national pride or even identity. However many busloads of supporters were shipped in for the occasion,[1] they were far outnumbered by the native Viennese – enthusiasts out of fear and calculation as well as out of conviction. Yet this famous scene is not the truest portrait of Austria's downfall. For that, we have to go back three days to the German army's ceremonial march-in (to describe it as an invasion would be ludicrous) of 12 March. German patrols had slipped across the deserted Austrian border before dawn and, by breakfast

time that day, Hitler's Eighth Army had occupied all the key areas of
Salzburg, Passau and Kiefersfelden which, only twenty-four hours ago,
Schuschnigg had seemed determined to hold.[2] Not a shot was fired. The
only things thrown at the marching soldiers were flowers, in little bouquets
or single blooms.

This strangest of days became positively bizarre when, shortly before
four o'clock in the afternoon, the Führer followed his soldiers into Austria.
How, exactly, was he to enter? There had not been the tiniest of skirmishes,
let alone any proper military engagement, so he could not appear as a
victorious Commander-in-Chief to accept surrender. As the Nazi movement
in Austria was still technically illegal, he could hardly be joining in a party
rally. Moreover, as Austria still survived, on paper, as a state, certain rules
of procedure applied. This could not be treated as a state visit, because he
had not been asked in by the Federal President of the republic, Dr Miklas.
It could not even be regarded as an official visit, for no invitation had been
organised from his own puppet Chancellor, Seyss-Inquart. In his speech,
broadcast from Berlin before he left the capital that morning, by air, he
had declared: 'I, myself, as Führer and Chancellor of the German people
shall be happy, as a German and a free citizen, to enter once more the
country of my birth'.

It was as though Hitler had invited himself in, virtually as a tourist.
Indeed, in Berlin, the initial purpose of his visit was being officially presented
as 'visiting his mother's grave'.[3] The Führer was, quite literally, coming
home, and his intentions towards his native country seemed almost paternal.
The original constitutional blueprint for Austria under the new order (drawn
up in Berlin by State Secretary Stuckhart of the Interior Ministry) envisaged
a form of 'Personal Union' between the two countries. Hitler would be the
supreme ruler and the Nazi system would be the unchallenged instrument
of his rule. Yet there would be fusion rather than total absorption, so that
Austria would preserve some vague and undefined shadow of its national
identity. This was, in fact, close to that vision of *Zusammenschluss* of which
Seyss-Inquart and his fellow hopefuls had dreamt. But even had it survived
in practice, the dream was snuffed out within hours.

That evening, after a long drive in his open Mercedes Benz car through
the countryside of Upper Austria – cheering crowds lining the streets of
every town and village along his route – the Führer's motorcade entered
Linz, the provincial capital. Seyss-Inquart had flown there that afternoon
to greet him, in the sombre company of Wilhelm Keppler, Hitler's Nazi
Commissioner for Austria, and Heinrich Himmler, his executioner-in-chief
for the whole of the Reich. In view of what was about to unfold on the
stage, the prologue was a pure charade. Seyss welcomed their visitor in the

name of 'all Austrians' and was careful to describe him no more precisely than as 'the leader of the German nation'. When Hitler rose to deliver his reply from the balcony of the town hall, he, in turn, began with a threefold greeting to 'Germans, German racial comrades, and Herr Bundeskanzler'. The ghostly inter-state protocol still survived. What banished it, within minutes, from Hitler's mind, was the reception he now received from the crowd below.

The population of Linz numbered some 120,000 at the time and, of these, almost 100,000 had packed into the square. They greeted his emotional words with that mass hysteria which Hitler was so adept at producing, but with a seeming spontaneity of acclaim which matched or surpassed anything he had achieved in his Nuremberg rallies. His designs seemed to be changing inside him as the short improvised speech developed, for he ended by telling his listeners that one day, not too far distant, they 'would be summoned'. Then, he went on, they would have to 'pledge their vows', and, as a result, he would be able to 'point with pride at my homeland'. A plainer hint that their days as Austrians were drawing to a close could not have been given. Yet it only drew fresh storms of applause which left the Nazi cheer-leaders with little to do.

These cheers were to produce a fateful exercise in telepathy between the Führer in Linz and his deputy in Berlin. The Marshal had been glued to the radio to listen to his master's words at the town hall but, as the minutes passed and the uproar mounted, he became more and more gripped by the audience than the orator. For the man who had often sworn to solve the Austrian problem 'so oder so', such frenzy could only point to another of his trysts with destiny. The conquest he had embarked on the previous afternoon over the telephone to Vienna was seemingly being consummated for him in the main square of a provincial capital. The broadcast had barely ended before he had despatched a special courier plane to Linz to ask Hitler whether, in view of all this, they ought not to drop the plan for personal union and go the whole hog. His plane crossed in the air with another courier machine sent off by the Führer to ask his deputy what he now thought about a complete annexation.[4] The citizenry of Linz had driven the final nail in the coffin of the first Austrian Republic.[5] The next day, 13 March, Hitler first paid his planned visit to the family grave at his own birthplace, Braunau-am-Inn, and then turned to the burial of his homeland.

As usual with so many of the Führer's impulsive decisions, execution was at lightning speed. State Secretary Stuckhart was summoned overnight to Linz to draw up a new constitutional decree, this time for outright annexation. This 'Reunification Law' had already been drafted by midday on the 13th and by the same afternoon had been flown by Stuckhart to Vienna for promulgation. Dr Miklas, stubborn as ever, refused to sign it. His defiance was, however, blended with pragmatism, in face of the inevitable. He made over all his powers to Seyss-Inquart, thus placing responsibility for total capitulation where it really belonged – on the shoulders of Hitler's puppet Chancellor. At four o'clock, Seyss called his colleagues together, as submissive and shell-shocked a body of men ever to call themselves a Cabinet. He read out to them the new constitution prescribed for their country. Article Number One said everything: 'Austria is a land of the German Reich'. There was no discussion, let alone debate. Seyss simply declared the law to have been accepted and his 'Ministers' followed him in appending their signatures to the document. It had taken barely five minutes for the Austrian Republic to be wiped off the map of Europe – exactly as had been portrayed in that fresco on the walls of Göring's Karinhall shooting lodge.

The fiction that a non-existent Austria somehow still had a government was allowed to survive, for administrative reasons, for two more days. Then that government duly followed the country into oblivion, as its mayfly Chancellor was renamed Governor of the Reich's eastern province (an impotent role, eclipsed by the power of the Nazi Special Commissioners).[6] That was on 15 March 1938, the day of Hitler's popular enthronement at the Heldenplatz.

On the fairly safe assumption that not more than fifteen per cent of the Austrian population were Nazis (fanatics or supporters) before the German march-in, how was this minority suddenly able to present itself as an overwhelming majority once the Führer had appeared on the scene? It mystified, as well as depressed, the royal exiles at the time and has challenged analysis ever since. It is not enough to say that many among those delirious crowds of welcome were time-servers, opportunists or simply bystanders determined not to miss out on any great event.[7] Nor is it relevant, in this context, to stress the absence of those who had hidden away in fear (the 175,000 Jews of Vienna, for example) and the thousands on Himmler's wanted lists, many of whom had been bundled away by the Gestapo before the Führer had risen to speak. Amongst the quarter of a million Viennese who were present on the Heldenplatz (after all, one-seventh of the capital's entire population) a mass transformation of mood really *had* taken place. The reasons lie embedded in the history of the nation which has been traced out in earlier chapters.

Metal fatigue can break the wings of an aircraft which has flown for too many thousands of hours. By March 1938, the Austrian Republic had endured nearly twenty years of almost non-stop stress and vibration. Emotional fatigue had set in within the fabric of the nation as a result. To begin with, its citizens had had to absorb the shock of losing, within the space of a few weeks, the empire and the dynasty which had given them such identity as they possessed for centuries past. Then, in the panic of its insignificant isolation, their little republic had tried to join hands with the much larger German Socialist state to the north, also the successor to a fallen empire. When that bid was blocked, and the Austrians were forced to travel on their own, their national consciousness became riven even further by the ideological battle between 'Reds' and 'Blacks', fought out in February 1934 on the streets. Then along came Engelbert Dollfuss to tell them they really were Austrians, not Southern Germans, and should be proud of the fact. That message had hardly registered before it was muffled by his murder by the agents of a new and much more intimidating Germany, which, over the next four years was to draw Austria tighter and tighter into its maw.

The final two-way psychological wrench came, of course, in that extra-ordinary forty-eight hours which preceded the republic's demise. On 9 March, its people were suddenly being summoned to defy Hitlerism and resist the Germanic magnetic pull by supporting the Schuschnigg plebiscite. By the evening of the 11th, the sponsor of that referendum was himself telling them over the radio that it had been abandoned and hinting that a German takeover was now unstoppable. It was hardly surprising that, when the Führer and his war machine duly appeared in their midst, so many arms went up in dutiful salute and so many throats were hoarse with cheering. At long last, somebody had finally made up their minds for them. Prone anyway to rapid changes of mind, this smack of authority was something that the Austrians had always needed to shape their destiny. Napoleon had wound up their Holy Roman Empire for them; Bismarck had settled their ditherings over the German Confederation by simply booting them out of it. Now, their own native-born son had returned to tell them how to behave. Most of them were to help him, actively or passively, to carry out his orders over the next seven years.

There were, however, those who refused to kow-tow, and even more whose refusal had been taken for granted by the Gestapo. Just after the war, the resurrected Austrian Republic put the first wave of political arrests after the Anschluss at 76,000.[8] This turned out to be heavily exaggerated. A partial reason may well have been that accurate figures were still difficult to obtain at the time. But overlying this were political and propaganda factors. In view of the account of their behaviour traced above, the Austrians had been extremely fortunate to emerge after the war labelled as 'the first victims of Nazi aggression'. Not surprisingly, they made every effort to play down the substantial role they had been obliged to fill in Hitler's war machine, and to play up their sufferings at his hands.[9] According to the Gestapo – which certainly had no interest at that time in minimising its

activities – a total of 21,000 arrests were carried out during the whole of
1938, with only 1500 Austrians still under what was coyly described as
'protective custody' by the end of that year. Many of that original 21,000
would certainly have been struck off the Gestapo's Ostmark lists because
they had meanwhile been transferred to concentration camps elsewhere in
Hitler's Reich. Otto's supporters figure high among these victims, as he
learned to his growing dismay. Officials like Dr Hornbostel in the Foreign
Office and Dr Vollgruber at the Paris Embassy; peasant leaders like Leopold
Figl in Lower Austria; Fatherland Front leaders like Dr Stepan in Graz; and,
inevitably, the real head of the monarchist movement, Baron Friedrich
Wiesner, followed thousands of other listed anti-Nazis behind the barbed
wire fences.[10]

Eventually, Schuschnigg joined them there as well. His fate reflected the
gradual dissolving of the Seyss-Inquart dream during the spring and summer
of 1938.[11] To begin with, it seemed that, as one of the 'two German Chancellors', he would be spared the worst. In the early hours of 12 March he
was driven, in his old official car, to his old official residence in the pleasant
'Garden House' of the Belvedere Palace. Though SS guards were soon posted
at the door, he remained there, in reasonable comfort and tranquillity, until
23 May, when he was abruptly transferred to a room on the fifth floor of
Vienna's Hotel Metropole. This would normally have been an agreeable
billet. The hotel now happened, however, to be the Gestapo headquarters
in the capital and his stay there, which lasted nearly eighteen months, was
anything but agreeable, though he suffered no physical violence – then or
indeed later.

After the Hotel Metropole, Schuschnigg was swallowed up, like the
country he had once governed, into the Reich, which was now at war. From
October to December of 1939, he was in solitary confinement at the Gestapo's
prison in Munich (where he found the attitude of the Bavarian Nazis far
more sympathetic than that displayed by their Viennese colleagues). Then
came more than four years in three German concentration camps: Sachen-
hausen, then Flossenburg, followed by a brief spell in Dachau. He was to
be spared the horrors of these camps, however, and even accorded one
great privilege. This matched the courage by which it had been secured.
On 9 December 1941, the day he arrived in Sachsenhausen, his second wife
Vera sent a personal appeal to Himmler to be allowed to join her husband
and share his fate unreservedly. Even the overlord of the Nazi terror machine
was impressed by the request, which he granted.

At the very end of the war, the life of Austria's former Chancellor was
to be saved by an aristocrat serving in Hitler's now shattered army. His
final move, under SS guard, was to a hotel in the Pustertal where a group

of political prisoners of seventeen different nationalities had been assembled. At the end of April 1945 word got around in the neighbourhood that orders had come from Berlin to execute the most prominent among the hostages. In the nick of time a special Wehrmacht unit under Captain Wichard von Alvensleben surrounded the hotel, disarmed the SS guards, and freed the prisoners.

The manner of his liberation – an aristocratic officer of the old army disarming Hitler's SS – must have made Schuschnigg ponder yet again that key question he had wrestled with throughout the long years of imprisonment and to which he was constantly to return in books, speeches and letters after the war: should he have ordered military resistance to the so-called invasion of March 1938? His justification for not doing so was always the same: given Austria's virtual abandonment by all the Stresa Front leaders (including its erstwhile protector, the Duce), it would have been a battle against hopeless odds and therefore a pointless shedding of blood. But it was, of course, the German blood in the veins of both armies which he was refusing to shed. Even those two days of full battle which the Austrian general staff had promised him would have been enough to guarantee his country a form of co-belligerent status alongside the Western democracies in the great war which ensued. 12 That would have meant that in the spring of 1945 the four-power occupation of his country could not have been imposed as it was, and could never have been spun out by the Russians for ten years on the grounds that Austria had always been a willing partner in Hitler's plans. A few Austrian bullets in March 1938 might also have stirred the Western powers, including America, to sit up and take more notice of Nazi aggression. Finally, the actual timetable of that aggression might well have been altered. Had the Austrians given him, and the outside world, real cause for concern in the spring of 1938, Hitler would scarcely have struck again at Czechoslovakia only six months later.

All this is speculative. The fact remains that Hitler certainly had no cause for concern over his Anschluss, when the total lack of resistance surprised even the 'invaders'. The man who, but for Schuschnigg, would have given the order to fire, General-Inspector Schilhawsky, was to show his true mettle a few weeks later by refusing to take the oath of allegiance to Hitler. He was immediately pensioned off for his defiance. State Secretary General Zehner, who would gladly have passed down the instruction to him, was not even approached over the oath. Instead, on the evening of 10 April 1938, he was shot down in his Vienna apartment in front of his wife by two Austrian Nazi thugs who then attempted to present the killing as suicide.

Though there was a hard core of defiantly Austrian officers who resisted both the blandishments and the blackmail of the new regime, they remained in a small minority.[13] A six-page report sent to Otto soon after the Anschluss by an ardent monarchist, Dr Phillip, made sober reading.[14] After listing (in the main correctly) the names of the Pretender's supporters already under arrest, the writer turned to the behaviour of the Austrian Bundesheer. The stand taken by General Schilhawsky was exceptional. 'Most of the officers have behaved dishonourably by swearing allegiance to Hitler as soon as they were asked.' He cited the case of one middle-aged officer wearing the medals of the vanished empire who told the German military appointment board that he was now ready to render true service to the National Socialist cause though he had previously been a monarchist. Glancing at his medals, the board's chairman quietly replied: 'What else could you have been but a monarchist?'

Nor did the lower ranks escape censure in the report. It cited incidents where ordinary soldiers of the Bundesheer had saluted German officers on the streets of Vienna with the cry of 'Heil Hitler!' and the Nazi greeting of the upraised arm. In all cases, the officers had upbraided the men, ordering them to salute again, but in regulation army style. This seemed to reflect genuine distaste, and not simply the German passion for discipline.

So that all this popular frenzy could be translated for posterity into Nazi-style statistics, Hitler lost no time in ordering a plebiscite to be held. The wording was a great deal more precise, as well as more intimidating, than those woolly catch-all phrases in Schuschnigg's abortive referendum. The six and a half million inhabitants of the Ostmark were now called on to answer the uncompromising question: 'Do you acknowledge Adolf Hitler as our Führer and the reunion of Austria with the German Reich which was effected on 13 March 1938?' The poll was fixed for Sunday 10 April and it became clear, well before that date, that the pass had been sold to Nazism by more potent forces than the military.

The top echelons of the Fatherland Front and the monarchist movement were already locked away, together with all the revolutionary left-wingers, former trade union leaders and other suspected trouble-makers on the Gestapo's lists. There remained only the waverers to be corralled in for the poll and they were mainly to be found in two camps: the Catholic Church, which looked after the soul of the nation; and the moderate Socialists, keepers of its battered republican heritage.

The church had lost no time in 'rendering to Caesar' what this new European conqueror had just gratefully grabbed. While Hitler was still advancing on Vienna, its primate, Cardinal Theodor Innitzer, had sent him a message of greeting and ordered all the churches along his route to sound their bells. The petals strewn across the streets below were thus matched by the peals of welcome from above. Once Hitler had reached the capital,

Papen, who had dug Austria's grave for her, saw to it that the burial would be properly solemnised. Before the Heldenplatz celebrations were over, he had persuaded the Führer to meet the Cardinal immediately afterwards. The result of that meeting (held in the nearby Hotel Imperial) exceeded even Papen's expectations – and led to some raised eyebrows in the Vatican. The Cardinal declared his delight at 'the realisation of the old dream of German unity' and took it upon himself to pledge that Austria's Catholics would become 'the truest sons of the great empire into whose arms they had been brought'.

It is not without significance that Innitzer had some Sudeten German blood in him. Nonetheless, it was a remarkably agile somersault for the primate who, only a week before, had been urging the faithful to back Schuschnigg's plebiscite in his stand for 'a free and independent Austria'. Startling, but somehow understandable in the context of the centuries old tradition of leaving the body politic to its masters provided the church could look after its soul. Innitzer had simply struck a lightning concordat of his own. On 27 March, this was duly pronounced from all the pulpits of the land. The proclamation read out declared that Austria's bishops, as an 'obvious national duty', had declared themselves to be 'Germans for the German Empire' and that in the coming plebiscite the faithful would also behave accordingly. Had Engelbert Dollfuss remained a peasant farmer instead of becoming a politician, even his sturdy Austrian heart might have been swayed, listening to that in his village church at Kirnberg.

Only the moderate Socialists were now left to declare publicly for Hitler. The key figure here was the first Chancellor of the republic, Karl Renner, who was like a lay cardinal to his followers. He was put under sustained pressure, but it was not until 3 April, a week before the polls, that he finally fell into line. When it came, his endorsement proved to be less flamboyant than that of the bishops. In a newspaper interview,[15] he even began by expressing reservations over the methods by which the union with Germany had been brought about. But then came everything which the Nazi propaganda machine could have hoped for. The humiliations of the peace treaties had been put right and, in the process, 'the twenty years stray wanderings of the Austrian people are now over as it returns, united, to the starting point set out in its solemn declaration of November 1918'.

It had of course been Renner who, in those days, had declared his infant republic to be part of the unified state of 'German-Austria', only to have the concept banned by the victorious Allies in negotiations at which it was Renner himself who had endured the humiliation of a diktat. It is somewhat surprising, therefore, that this professional political pragmatist had waited so long to give Hitler his blessing. Yet now it had been bestowed and the tenement dwellers and factory workers had been given the same firm guidance from on high as the congregations in the churches. Innitzer and Renner, who so rarely agreed about anything, were now of one voice over the most far-reaching question ever to be put to the Austrian people.

Not surprisingly, when the urns were emptied on 10 April, over 99 per cent of the votes were counted as in favour.[16] Just under 12,000 of the four and a half million eligible electorate had voted against, while another 5776 hardy souls had spoiled their ballot papers. The figures may well have been somewhat massaged by the Nazi propaganda machine. Yet there is no reason to doubt that, for the variety of reasons outlined above, an overwhelming majority had endorsed the Anschluss in March of 1938, just as in February a comfortable majority would have voted with Schuschnigg against it.

The tiny Tyrolean village of Tarrent, cut off from the world in the mountains between Nassereith and Imst, became the sublime example of this mass swing of sentiment. On 13 March, the villagers, who do not appear to have had either a wireless set or a daily newspaper between them, were urged by their Mayor, Herr Kuprian, to vote on the question in Schuschnigg's referendum, despite the fact that it had been scrapped two days before. The result was 100 per cent in favour. On 10 April, when the villagers had been brought up to date by events, they voted again, in Hitler's poll. The result was 100 per cent in favour.

12

New Horizons

The exiled dynasty, as well as the people in their old homeland, now had to face up to some sober realities. On the day of the German march-in, Otto had acted as though he were still the legitimate champion of the Austrian nation. In a statement in French issued from Hams Castle on the evening of 12 March, he declared himself 'the spokesman of the ardent patriotic feelings of millions of Austrians'. He then called on the world 'to support the Austrian people in their unquenchable will for liberty and independence'.[1] As the heir to a dynasty that, in his words, 'had presided over the greatness and prosperity of Austria for 650 years', he could hardly have phrased things very differently. But, as that outside world knew, as soon as the eyewitness reports of their Vienna missions came in, the Austrian Republic, inside or outside the Chancellery, had demonstrated precious little will for independence once the final challenge was thrown down. What a difference it would have made to Austria's standing at the time had that declaration been able to refer to 'heroic resistance against overwhelming odds'.

But there had been no resistance; Austria had been swallowed up without a gulp and, with Czechoslovakia soon to follow, Hitler was firmly astride Central Europe. This meant that, even before the war which added to his conquests, the Führer had ruled out any possibility of that Habsburg restoration which had seemed so real during the eighteen months before the Anschluss. For the foreseeable future, Otto would have to abandon all thoughts of the crown. Instead, so far as Austria was concerned, he had to concentrate from his exile on preserving the notion of, and the belief in, her identity. That task was to be pursued, with any means and any helpers at hand, on both sides of the Atlantic for the next seven years.

It began in Paris, immediately after the Anschluss, with securing that most basic of all identity needs – identity documents themselves. The Daladier government was soon under the strongest pressure from Berlin to have all Austrians living in France – whether as established businessmen or as political refugees – documented as German citizens. Otto, who had by now established his headquarters at the Hôtel Cayré in the Boulevard Raspail, led the campaign of protest. He had a wide variety of helpers within the French political establishment: his uncle, Prince Sixtus; several members of Daladier's cabinet, including the Employment Minister, Anatole de Monzie, and the indispensable Interior Minister, Georges Mandel; party leaders such as Louis Marin, head of the Democratic Republican movement, as well as key figures like Secretary-General Rochat in the Foreign Office. As important as any was Martin Fuchs, who had been Press Attaché at the pre-Anschluss Austrian Legation, a post which he managed to hold on to after the legation had been absorbed into the German Embassy. As a result of the combined pressure, discreetly applied through all these channels, the French authorities allowed a special category of 'former Austrians' ('ex-Autrichiens') to be set up. This saved those concerned from being declared and treated as citizens of Hitler's Third Reich, which had already annulled their Austrian papers.

Unhappily – but not untypically – it proved impossible then, or later, for those 'former Austrians' to present a united front in France, or any other of the Western countries where they had gathered. Everywhere, the exile groups splintered against each other and among each other, fighting the old ideological battles between Socialist 'Reds' and Catholic 'Blacks', where the only colour that needed confronting was Nazi brown. Even the outbreak of war failed to knock all these squabbling heads together; this despite the fact that now, more than ever, the need arose for some sort of Austrian government in exile to be put together, to match the other émigré regimes made welcome in the West. However obvious and pressing the need, the solution stayed out of reach.

One basic problem was finding a leader of sufficient stature. Otto, who had never sat on a throne, was not a king in exile like Haakon VII of Norway, who had already worn his crown for thirty-five years before taking refuge in England in 1940. Moreover, though Otto was by far the best known of all the Austrian exiles and refugees, a Habsburg Pretender was simply not feasible as the head of a republican shadow government. Instead, he sponsored the candidacy of Hans Rott, the only former Minister amongst the Austrian colony in Paris. But Rott, a Minister without Portfolio in Schuschnigg's last government, had been a relatively insignificant figure even on the Vienna stage and was quite unknown to the outside world. He did, however, have one qualification as a possible bridge-builder between the rival ideologies in that he had belonged to the liberal wing of the old Christian Socialist party.

This made him acceptable to the moderates among the exiled Social Democrats, led by Karl Hartl in Paris and Heinrich Allina in London (where Otto's brother Robert was installed and very active). He would also have been approved by France's Socialist Prime Minister, Edouard Daladier, who, in a private meeting with Otto at Chantilly in July 1939, had encouraged the Pretender to revive and promote the concept of a free and independent Austria. But it never came to the test. The so-called Revolutionary Socialists, the ideological brethren of Otto Bauer, who had fled the Dollfuss and Schuschnigg regimes with him,[2] rejected outright the proposed nomination of Hans Rott as leader of the 'Free Austrians Movement' and de facto head of an exiled regime. Their pretext was that, as a junior member of Schuschnigg's authoritarian regime (albeit one whose task was to seek a common path with the Socialists), he was still defiled by its pitch and, therefore, politically untouchable. For a party which had been driven underground by 'Austro-Fascism', this resentment had to be respected, however out of date it had become. The trouble was that the real objection, which was undeclared, went deeper. At heart, these radical left-wingers rejected the idea of any independent Austrian government, either in peacetime Vienna or as a caretaker administration based in wartime Paris, London or anywhere else. Even in exile, most of them still pursued their pathetic dream of fusion with a Socialist Germany – pathetic because at no time was the German Republic willing to accept them.

Otto's attempts to raise an 'Austrian Legion' of volunteers to fight alongside the Allied armies suffered a similar fate. He had learnt all about the Czech Legion, raised from exiles by his father's most formidable opponent, Jan Masaryk, in the middle of the First World War. Its remarkable fighting record in the Russian campaign (during the summer of 1918 it controlled virtually the whole length of the Trans-Siberian Railway) guaranteed it a place, as a 'co-belligerent', at the Allied peace treaty talks – a privilege brilliantly exploited by Masaryk and Beneš at the expense of the Habsburg Monarchy. Now, already early on in the Second World War, another generation of Czech and Polish volunteers were flocking to the same Allied colours. How could the Austrians follow suit?

Ideological rivalries apart, there were severe handicaps. Masaryk's Legion had a firm military foundation, an entire army corps of Czech and Slovak nationals that had been fighting under Russian command since 1916. In contrast to this, the Austrian colonies in exile during the Second World War did not possess even a ready-made platoon of soldiers between them, let alone a single ex-officer of suitable rank and experience to assume command. As a result, an elaborate recruiting scheme drawn up by Otto's advisers in the spring of 1939 proposed that, once an Austrian volunteer force had been raised (to serve as part of the French army), its officers would be nominated by 'His Majesty, as Supreme War Lord of the Austrian Nation'. It was an expedient born out of an emergency, yet anything better calculated to drive all left-wingers away from the Paris recruiting offices could not have been imagined. It was hardly his own fault that the 'Supreme War Lord' was still in his twenties, and had never in his life fired anything more martial than a hunting rifle. Be that as it may, the 'Austrian Legion' never got even to the parade ground, at least on the European side of the Atlantic.

Thanks to liberal funding put at his disposal (largely by the head of the Paris branch of the Rothschild family, Baron Robert), Otto was able to make progress on the propaganda front. A newspaper, the *Österreichische Post*, was launched to counter the outdated revolutionary message spread by the Bauer camp, and radio broadcasting was prepared, both through existing French channels and over a separate Austrian station. One of the objectives of such propaganda was to encourage anti-Nazi resistance in the homeland. Here Otto came right up against a brick wall with very few loose bricks in it.

At the start, it had looked as though that wall could be shaken. On 7 October 1938, only six months after Hitler's plebiscite, a crowd of ten thousand Catholics gathered in Vienna's Cathedral Square, ostensibly to mark the Feast of the Rosary. This day had patriotic associations going back three and a half centuries,[3] but on this occasion the patriotism displayed had a marked contemporary flavour. The demonstrators, mostly boys or students from the Catholic Youth Movement, clashed with rowdies from the Nazi Hitlerjugend, exchanging rival slogans as well as blows. Austrian police eventually restored order, handing the Catholic cheerleaders over to the Gestapo. The younger schoolchildren were sent back to school for disciplinary action; dozens of the older ones were despatched to the more brutal discipline of the Dachau and Mauthausen concentration camps.

This large public demonstration against Nazism was to be the first and the last ever witnessed in Austria. But it pointed to one area where some sparks of resistance might be found. Otto did his best to kindle them. He later described how, after the Munich crisis, he developed strong contacts with Catholic resistance cells through a coordinating centre in Holland led by a Jesuit priest, Father Muckermann, and also, directly, with a young Bavarian priest, Rudolf Graber, who later became Bishop of Regensburg.[4] Attempts to set up similar direct contacts in Austria, as he ruefully admitted, were often frustrated because the modest resistance cells there were apt to betray themselves by talking too much.

It should be entered in their defence that, unlike the French, Poles, Danes, Norwegians, Dutch and all the other resistance movements of Nazi-occupied Europe, the Austrians shared a common tongue, as well as a common culture and history, with their new masters. This made them reluctant to contemplate resistance in the first place and vulnerable to

Gestapo penetration when they did attempt it.[5] Moreover, until the last phase of the war, they remained isolated and cut off from any outside help. Austria had no western-facing Atlantic coastline to provide an indestructible if hazardous link with the Allies. Yet, if Catholic resistance contacts failed to provide any immediate results on the ground, they did provide Otto with the next best thing – intelligence as to what was really going on inside the 'Thousand Year Reich'. It was this which unexpectedly led to a sudden transformation in the Archduke's fortunes. The catalyst for the change was the American Ambassador in wartime Paris, William Christian Bullitt.

Bullitt was one of the most extraordinary figures in the American foreign service, and was to have one of the most extraordinary careers. It had started at the Paris Peace Conference where he was serving among the vast flock of President Wilson's special advisers, dubbed by him the 'Argonauts'. Bullitt's job was the relatively humdrum one of preparing daily intelligence briefings on conference goings-on. But he caught the eye of Colonel Edward House, Wilson's alter ego, and in February 1919, aged only twenty-eight, he was despatched to Bolshevik Moscow on the intelligence mission of a lifetime: to examine if the Bolshevik regime there would survive and whether Washington could do business with it. He was treated as a VIP from the moment he stepped ashore at Petrograd. He held a long conference with Lenin himself, and returned triumphantly to Paris with a seven-point Soviet outline for negotiations. The fact that no talks were held did not diminish Bullitt's instantly acquired status as his country's leading expert on Russian affairs. In 1933, when the United States became the last of the western powers formally to recognise the Soviet Union, Bullitt was sent to Moscow as its first Ambassador. After his time there (during which his initial sympathy for the Communist cause had considerably waned), he was transferred to Paris.

This was the unusual but highly intelligent diplomat with whom Otto soon made contact and rapidly established a close relationship. Bullitt, unlike some of his colleagues back in Washington, was unreservedly anti-Nazi. He knew that President Roosevelt had shared his sentiments even before the outbreak of war. What he needed now was ammunition to feed this view to an uncertain White House. Bullitt, the intelligence gatherer who, as a young official, had tried to find out what Lenin was up to in 1919, now, as Ambassador twenty years later, wanted the same question asked about Hitler. This was where Otto's underground contacts proved valuable to both men. The Archduke passed on all he could learn about developments in the Third Reich without knowing that his reports were landing up on Roosevelt's desk. The most important item came soon after the Anschluss from Father Graber's Bavarian network: details of a secret briefing in which

the Führer had outlined to his party faithful his plans for the further
expansion of German power. When the President read that, he sent an
invitation to the Archduke, via Bullitt, to come over to America and meet
him. The invitation was to change the course of Otto's life – as well as, in
the short term, help to rescue himself and his family from Nazi clutches.

As a presidential guest, he had VIP treatment from the start. He arrived
in Baltimore on 4 March 1940 on one of Pan American's legendary 'Clipper'
flying-boats, the journey being, in itself, a sensation in travel even for the
much-travelled young man. A week later, on 10 March, he was at the White
House for his first talk with Roosevelt. A warm personal contact seems to
have sprung up at once between the ailing late middle-aged man, who led
the New World, and the energetic young Pretender from the dim recesses
of the Old. 6 As the head of the greatest of republics, Roosevelt could hardly
be expected to sponsor the cause of a fallen dynasty. It had been his
predecessor, Woodrow Wilson, who had authorised the dismemberment of
that dynasty. Moreover, Edouard Beneš, the Czech leader who had supervised
the process in 1919, was present again in America now – the most influential
of all the European exiles, with a pledge to restore the Czechoslovakia of
Versailles already in his pocket.

Yet these two men meeting for the first time had certain things in
common. Franklin Delano Roosevelt was himself of patrician stock and had
an inborn respect for tradition. He also had fond personal memories of the
vanished Habsburg Monarchy. Before the First World War, he had embarked
on a tour by bicycle across the European continent and his route had taken
him across Hungary and Transylvania at a time when the double-headed
eagle flew over both these lands. In the spring of 1940, with the United
States still a neutral, Roosevelt's main concern as President was how the
Second World War was developing and he questioned Otto closely about
the true strength of Hitlerism. The mere idea that France might collapse
in only two months' time was so inconceivable that the military situation
was not even discussed.

What they did talk about at length – at this and a second session at the
end of Otto's stay – was what would happen along the Danube's bank after
the war against Hitler was won. On restoration – which was never even
mentioned by name throughout – the Archduke took the line that future
state forms were not for himself or his family to decide: 'I make it quite
clear at the outset to Roosevelt that questions concerning the constitution
or the economic regime of any country could only be decided by the people
of that state, once its own sovereignty had been firmly established.' 7

What he did, however, solicit from the President was his help in reaffirm-
ing that sovereignty, both in Hungary, once it had shaken off Horthy, and

18. The family in exile in Spain. (*Private Collection*)

19. Otto and his brothers and sisters, in order of height. Right to left: Otto, Adelhaid,
Robert, Felix, Karl Ludwig, Rudolf, Charlotte and Elisabeth. (*Private Collection*)

20. Snowball fight in Lequeitio. (*Private Collection*)

21. Steenokkerzeel, Belgium, the family home during the dramas of the 1930s. (*ÖNB*)

22. Chancellor Kurt von Schuschnigg arriving at Innsbruck, on 9 March 1938 for his short-lived show of defiance against Hitler.

23. Admiral Niklós Horthy riding into Budapest in 1919 at the head of his anti-Communist White Army. The following year he secured his election as Regent.

24. The Pretender in exile in Belgium. (*Private Collection*)

25. Visiting an American film studio during the Second World War. (*Private Collection*)

26. With American soldiers during the shooting of a propaganda film. (*Private Collection*)

27. The
newly-weds,
Otto and Regina,
in the early
1950s. (*Private
Collection*)

28. Otto and his
brother Rudolf
in America.
(*Private
Collection*)

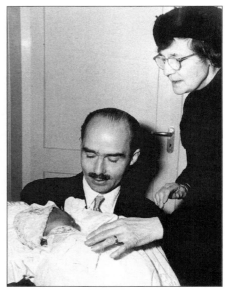

29. Otto and Count Degenfeld, his long-term adviser and secretary, 1957. (*Private Collection*)

30. Otto shows his mother, the Empress Zita, his first son, Karl. (*Private Collection*)

31. Family ski trip in the Bavarian Alps, 1969. (*Private Collection*)

32. Otto, Regina and the family, 1969. (*Private Collection*)

33. Otto and General Franco, Madrid, 1966.

34. Archduke Otto von Habsburg, during his twenty-year stint in the European Parliament. (*Private Collection*)

in Austria, once it had been prised loose from the Third Reich. The reaction was favourable though, as America was not yet in the war, its leader could hardly commit himself in advance about post-war settlements. The basis, however, had been laid – especially, in Roosevelt's case, for freeing Hungary from Hitler's military and political grip.

The White House meetings were both strictly private. By contrast, what Otto did in the weeks between was conducted in a blaze of favourable publicity, as useful to him as it was unusual. The nearest thing to an official appearance was an address to the United States Senate, which was received with a standing ovation. The wives of rich industrialists vied with invitations to 'His Majesty'. The editors of newspapers, news agencies and radio networks were just as keen to secure interviews, while describing him, less gushingly and more properly, as 'Archduke Otto of Habsburg'. The message he put across was essentially the same one he had communicated to the President: the need, after the war, to establish a federation of the Danube nations. Without raising the question of his own restoration, he was able to project to the American people a vision of Central Europe freed from Hitler's grip and united to preserve it from any future predators. The fact that most of the listeners and readers involved would have had difficulty in identifying the countries he was talking about was really irrelevant. The Americans have always been fond of 'The Big Idea'. This was a very big one to lodge, however nebulously, in their imagination.

Apart from the publicity, what Otto had gained were personal contacts. Some, like that with the Secretary of State, Cordell Hull, were to pay few dividends. Others, like his meetings with Senator Robert Taft and the Vice-President John Garner, were to stand him in much better stead for the future. But the burgeoning friendship with the President was the keystone of American support, especially after Roosevelt, on taking leave of his guest, offered the Archduke his protection for the exiled dynasty should they ever need it. Neither man had any inkling as they parted how swiftly and unexpectedly that need would arise.

Otto arrived back at Hams Castle just in time to join in the family celebrations for his mother's forty-eighth birthday. During that same night of 9 May, Hitler sent his own invidious greeting. As the prelude to his Blitzkrieg which was soon to crush France in its path, German paratroopers floated down on Belgian soil, one unit landing within a mile or two of Steenokkerzeel. The royal family, exiles for the past twenty years, were now refugees on the run. That Gestapo arrest warrant for the young head of the dynasty, hitherto treated with contempt, was suddenly a mortal threat. By noon, the entire household, which had been alerted by the Defence Ministry in Brussels, was packed up and gone. A few hours later, whether by accident or design, Göring's dive-bombers attacked the deserted castle, scoring a direct hit on the roof.

Otto later recalled that the Empress, together with himself and all his brothers and sisters, were equipped for the flight with Belgian diplomatic passports. These guaranteed free passage until rendered worthless on 28 May by the abrupt surrender of King Leopold III to the invaders. The rest of the household were travelling on special travel permits secured from the French government, thanks largely to the help of the family's guardian angel, Georges Mandel. It was a certain General Jouarre who helped arrange the transport.[8]

In the main convoy, seventeen passengers with their light luggage crammed into three cars: the Empress and her children (together with three more belonging to her sister) and key members of the staff such as Count Degenfeld and Countess Kerssenbrock. Otto and Charles broke off from the group for a few hours to see if anything could be done to help the Austrian colony in Brussels achieve the same special status he had secured for their opposite numbers in Paris two years before. Then there was time on his side. Now he had none. In a belatedly pathetic gesture, the 'League of Austrians' who numbered over a thousand registered members (nearly all registered expatriates) applied to the Belgian Foreign Minister, on the very day German tanks crossed the border, to be recognised as the official representatives of the Austrian colony in Belgium. In little more than a fortnight, there was no Foreign Ministry and indeed no free government left in Brussels to grant favours to anyone.

The two brothers rejoined the family in the early evening at a prearranged rendezvous. The convoy then headed south into France and by midnight reached Dunkirk, where they put up for the night in a hotel. The next morning, they split up again. Otto headed for Paris, which he reached on 14 May, and where he remained until the eve of the German march-in nearly a month later. The slow slide of France into surrender had already begun and there was precious little that an exiled Pretender, without a single soldier to throw into the struggle, could do to slow it down.

Otto used what he had in personal contacts to encourage resolute spirits as a substitute for his total lack of power. He did the rounds of the patriots, headed by the Prime Minister Paul Reynaud, Georges Mandel, Otto's closest friend, and a new acquaintance, General Charles de Gaulle, who had entered the reshuffled government as Under-Secretary for Defence. But the defeatists, grouped around Marshal Pétain (now Vice-President of the Council), and the traitors-in-waiting like Pierre Laval, gained in strength with every mile of the German advance. Otto stayed on in Paris with his brother, Karl Ludwig, right down to the eve of the Wehrmacht's seizure of the capital on 14 June. The farewell was conducted in defiant style: a dinner party at the Ritz hosted by the famous American writer and journalist Clare Booth Luce. Otto learned after the war that Erwin Rommel was the next after him to sign the distinguished visitors' book.[9]

The family were reunited again on 16 June, seemingly a world away from Paris. The Empress (travelling as 'Duchesse de Bar') had made three stops with her party on their journey south. The first was at Château Froudrain in Laon, the ancient capital of her Bourbon ancestors in northern France, but that rapidly proved too close for comfort to the German line of advance. From there they pressed on to Bostz, in central France, where her brother, Prince Xavier, had a property. Being there brought back memories of many a peacetime gathering, but there was little time for reminiscence. Again they were warned on the phone by the ever-watchful Mandel to move closer to Bordeaux, where he himself was still trying to function as Interior Minister in Reynaud's last government, itself now little better than a Cabinet on-the-run. The final Habsburg refuge was again a château, this time at Lamonzie-Montastrue, just outside the great sea port on the Gironde. There was in fact a double family reunion. The property belonged to Zita's sister, the Grand Duchess Charlotte of Luxembourg, who was waiting there – guarded by French Moroccan soldiers – for her three children who had been in the Empress's keeping. It was now Sunday 16 June, the last day of the Third Republic.

Bordeaux had twice before played host to the provisional government of France: once in 1871, when, after defeat in the war with Prussia, Paris fell into enemy hands; and, for a briefer spell, in 1914, when the capital was again under the threat of German occupation. But nothing in its history matched the drama and the tragedy of midsummer 1940. Otto and Karl Ludwig plunged straight on into the thick of things within an hour of arriving at Lamonzie. They were seeking what everyone else milling around in the maelstrom was after: travel papers and visas to get them across the Pyrenees to safety. Otto particularly remembered one figure among the hotchpotch of Western diplomats who were managing somehow to function in the mayhem: an aristocrat who rejoiced in the full name of Aristides de Sousa Mendes do Amaral Abranches.

> The Portuguese Consul-General was a real hero, who gave vital help not just to us but to the several thousands of Austrians who were concentrated nearby in the area of Lectoure. He was under orders from Lisbon to issue as few visas as possible and to refuse them entirely to certain categories of refugees, including Jews. He simply defied his instructions and went ahead non-stop! [10]

It was not just the Austrians who benefited from this defiance and not

only the queues of applicants who besieged his consulate on the Quai Louis
XVIII. Sousa Mendes, a conservative Catholic, had no fewer than fourteen
children and he had constructed a special extension to his Ford motor-car
big enough to accommodate the lot of them when travelling. On this
extraordinary vehicle he now made sorties all around the city, stamping
visas in the streets or in his car for anyone with travel papers to put them
in: Jews and non-Jews alike; Germans, Austrians, Czechs, Poles – even Baltic
refugees who had somehow found their way down to this south-western
corner of France to escape the Nazis. Otto von Habsburg and his family
were among the natural beneficiaries (and of the vital transit permits issued
by the Spanish political representative in Bordeaux, Propper y Calejon).
Working night and day, Sousa Mendes was estimated to have handed out
some thirty thousand other visas (one-third of them to Jews) in the three
weeks he had left before the Germans entered Bordeaux to put a stop to
his heroics. As a final gesture of defiance, he took the last batch he had
documented down to the French frontier himself, at the wheel of that
extraordinary vehicle.[11]

Like everyone else milling around in Bordeaux, Otto found the atmosphere frantic and menacing but somehow unreal. This was partly because
the enemy was still invisible so that official life of a sort could still continue.
But it was the way in which that officialdom now functioned which made
it so bizarre. France was crumbling away here and the rival fragments
struggling for power were dispersed in an incongruous fashion throughout
the city. Pierre Laval, the eventual inheritor of office under Hitler, had
found an ally and a co-conspirator in the Mayor, André Marquet. He
allotted his friend the best accommodation in the best hotel (aptly named
the 'Splendide') by simply ejecting the ex-Queen of Portugal from the suite.
Countess Hélène de Pourtales, Reynaud's malevolently anti-British mistress,
was given a double room with bath in the same establishment.

Thus it came about that both the last current Prime Minister of a free
France and his pro-Nazi successor conducted some of their political combat
from separate hotel bedrooms, though Reynaud had a base in the military
headquarters and Laval had an 'office' in the parlour of Marquet's quarters
in the town hall. Mandel made do at nights with a camp bed in the house
of the Prefect of Bordeaux, where Albert Lebrun, the President of the
Republic, was still playing at Head of State. The eighty-four-year-old Marshal
Pétain, who was soon to take over from Reynaud and sign the armistice
with Hitler, was staying at a friend's house in the Boulevard Wilson. But
at one time or another all of them, except the aged Marshal, came together
in the most unlikely setting of all – the grotto-like dining-room of 'Le
Chapon Fin' at No. 5, Rue de Montesquieu.

This was then Bordeaux's finest restaurant, but what Otto went there for – like the other luminaries of the city's political turmoil – was not so much to eat well as to keep up with the gossip and the debates.[12] This centred every night on how the battle was going between the defeatists, headed by Laval, with Pétain in the background, and the patriots, still grouped around Reynaud with Georges Mandel at their heart.[13] The factions and the power-brokers all had their tables. Laval and Marquet would usually eat at a corner table by themselves. Reynaud's followers sat at a larger table, as did Sir Ronald Campbell, the British Ambassador, and Major-General Sir Edward Spears, the chief British military liaison officer, who on Churchill's orders were striving in vain to keep Reynaud in office and France in the war. The latter's mistress, Madam de Pourtales, was a regular visitor, always in male company.

Mandel also turned up at irregular intervals, especially for lunch: his own headquarters was in the Hôtel Montreux (where Campbell had also set up his 'embassy') and its main entrance was dead opposite the Chapon Fin. It was while he was lunching here on 17 June that, for him, the end came. The struggle to maintain the semblance of a free France had ended late the previous evening with an exhausted Paul Reynaud, outnumbered by the defeatist camp, handing over his office to Marshal Pétain. The Marshal had immediately formed a new Cabinet of his followers, all pledged to seek an immediate armistice with Germany. Mandel knew that his political future was now over, but had no immediate fears for his personal safety.

That illusion was broken by a tap on the shoulder from behind just as he had finished the main course of his meal. It was a colonel of the gendarmerie who had come to take him into custody. Mandel kept his composure by politely requesting that he might first finish up the cherry desert which had just been put in front of him. The request was denied and the man who only the day before had been the French Minister of Interior was led away. He was released after a few hours, with Pétain personally apologising for the 'misunderstanding'.[14] But Mandel realised he would not remain at liberty once Germany's grip on the Marshal tightened. Much less would his Habsburg protégés, for the Gestapo's *Haftbefehl* against Otto was about to be embellished by Pétain's *ordre d'arrêt*. Mandel's first act on regaining his liberty later that day was to get a message to the royal exiles urging them to leave immediately for the border.

Otto needed no convincing of the plight they were all in, once those powerful ministerial hands, which had protected them ever since the out-break of war, were manacled. But while the escape convoy was being mustered, he risked one more trip into what was now a Nazi Bordeaux to try and help the rest of the Austrian colony. In hurried calls on both the

Portuguese and Spanish consulates, he secured promises that any Austrians still stranded without visas would be given their permits before the Germans arrived. As regards Spain, he was pleading in particular for his Socialist and Communist enemies – hundreds of whom had taken refuge in southern France after fleeing from the Franco regime which had crushed them in the Civil War.

When he returned to Lamonzie, the convoy was ready to move off; it had grown into a substantial procession of five motor cars and two lorries. The occupants were all travelling on a special *laissez-passer* authorised by Mandel in his last days as Minister of Interior and signed by Rochat, another old ally, on the writing paper of the Ministry of Foreign Affairs. It amounted to a general warrant for the Empress, calling on all civil and military authorities to 'accord to Madame la Duchesse de Bar all the respect due to her rank while travelling to Spain accompanied by her family and her suite'.[15] This looked impressive enough, except for the fact that it had been issued by authorities who were now no longer in power. The agonising question was whether the Pétain regime in Bordeaux would have had enough time to order the French frontier guards to reject these travel papers and, indeed, arrest one of the travellers.

They never found out, for a freakish incident got them safely across on the morning of 18 June. The French officer in command of the border post had just had word of de Gaulle's famous broadcast from London, appealing to all patriotic Frenchmen to come and join his struggle. The lieutenant at the frontier station instantly decided which side he was on and, with a salute, waved the Duchesse de Bar's motorcade through.

Control on the Spanish side was understandably tight and there was a hold-up while their papers were examined and debated. By a second coincidence, one of the officials happened to be a native of the nearby fishing village where the family had passed seven happy years in 1920s. He hailed Zita as 'Our Empress of Lequeitio' and bid her welcome. It was a delightful surprise, but they would eventually have got through anyway. Thanks to the efforts of Señor Propper y Calejon back in Bordeaux, a military guard was already awaiting to escort the royal party to the next train bound for Portugal.[16]

Lisbon should have proved a safe haven for the fugitives. It did not feel safe, however, nor was it in fact. The Third Reich maintained a powerful presence in the capital of this small neutral country and it made that presence felt as soon as the arrival of the royal party became known. As ever, Otto was the main Nazi target. The German embassy promptly presented itself to the Portuguese Foreign Ministry demanding that he should be arrested and handed over to them, according to the provisions of the French armistice.[17] The Foreign Minister referred the problem to President Salazar, who had ruled the country with an iron rod for the past eight years and took all the key decisions.

The problem was a tricky one for the dictator. Only four months before, Salazar had greeted Otto in Lisbon, when the young Archduke was in the privileged position of travelling to the United States as the personal guest of its President. In that context, the Habsburg Pretender was a useful person to know. Now he was a man on the run, and his pursuers were looking ominously like the new masters of Europe. Otto was fully prepared for what happened next:

> Salazar summoned me to say that, of course, there was absolutely no question of him ever surrendering me to the Germans. But he found himself in an awkward situation and so he had to ask me as a friend to get out of the way as soon as possible. I found that quite understandable in the light of the circumstances.[18]

But where to? That was the problem which now had to be thrashed out by the family, who were staying at Dafundo, near the capital, the home of one of their closest Portuguese friends, Count José Saldanha da Gama. Otto was all for London, and proposed to take his brothers Karl Ludwig and Rudolph with him to join up there with Robert. The so-called 'Austrian Office' which had been set up in the British capital was the nearest thing to a political headquarters that the refugee movement possessed. Perhaps this could one day be turned into a proper government in exile. In any case, it seemed the only body capable of issuing a plausible declaration, in the name of all Austrian exiles, of solidarity with the Allied cause. Quite apart from Austrian politics, London was also where all the European action was. King Haakon of Norway had gone there to establish his wartime administration. General de Gaulle, whom Otto knew well and greatly admired, had just raised the flag of Free France from a house in Westminster's Carlton Gardens. The free Poles were flying their colours there too and Otto also knew the leaders of this government-in-exile, including General Sikorski, its Prime Minister, and General Sosnowski, the Chief of Staff of its steadily growing armed forces. He was under no illusions about the perils which Britain faced. But he had a gut feeling that, under Churchill, it would pull through the winter and, after that, anything might happen.

Otto found himself in a minority of one with his ideas. All the others, led by his mother and the influential Count Degenfeld, were daunted by the prospect of having all four of the available Habsburg brothers (the fifth, Felix, was already in Washington) concentrated in a capital which was under direct enemy threat. Nor did they entirely share Otto's confidence in Britain's prospects of survival. The best course, surely, was to make for Washington and take up, through Archduke Felix, the President's offer of asylum which was already on the table. As for the free Poles, they were also training in Canada so contact could be made with them there.[19] These arguments carried the day, not least, as Otto later recalled, because of the logistics of the situation. Air connections between Lisbon and London were virtually non-existent at the time, in contrast to those splendid Pan American flying-boats which made regular flights across the Atlantic. So, in the first week of July 1940, Otto boarded an America-bound Clipper, again to be followed, later in the month, by the rest of the party, headed by his mother.

The Empress was making her second air-flight into history. Compared with the cramped bucket seats of that hired Junkers F13 monoplane which had taken her and her husband to a hazardous landing in western Hungary nearly twenty years before, the comfort and security of the great flying-boat was luxury indeed. The welcome that awaited them was also to prove more durable than the short-lived ecstasy of their doomed restoration bid. But the task which mother and son faced now was almost as formidable. They were seeking to persuade the New World to restore something of the shattered order in the Old: to repair ravages started by an American President in the recent past, continued by a Nazi dictator in the present, and finally threatened by a Soviet tyrant in the near future. Not surprisingly, it was not to be all plain sailing after landing.

13

Across the Water

The two halves of his father's empire had each brought their special head-aches for the crown, sometimes simultaneously. The German-speaking subjects of the Austrian half had no clear profile of their own and therefore no sense of unity. Moreover, Vienna always faced challenges from the Slav peoples it ruled, especially from the Czechs on their dogged march to nationhood. There was no such lack of unity or identity in the Hungarian kingdom. Indeed, for the Emperor, the Magyars had rather too much of both for comfort and took any outside help they could find to promote their cause. Much of that help came, ironically, from Germany, the Monarchy's principal ally.

Now, a generation later, with the components of that old empire severely amputated and the dynasty banished, its young Pretender set about helping what was left of the two halves – from a distance of three thousand miles. He found himself up against the same problems in exile as his father had faced when in power. The most urgent task was the familiar one of persuading the Austrians that they had an identity of their own. This had been hard enough when they all stood on their native soil. To attempt it in the diaspora of exile and to make that effort credible to a somewhat sceptical Washington administration was doubly daunting – and eventually doomed. The campaign was launched by Otto and his brothers along two lines, military and political.[1] Lethal cross-threads ran between them, but they are best taken separately.

It was President Roosevelt who, at his first reunion meeting with Otto in July 1940, had urged the Archduke to raise a volunteer battalion out of the thousands of exiles living in the United States so that the concept of a Free Austria would have some credibility in American eyes. The President was well aware that, in 1938, not a shot had been fired against the German 'invaders'. He was also aware that, with the Ostmark now part and parcel of the Nazi war machine, Hitler's armed forces fighting the Allies included more than a million Austrians. Their divisions performed with no lack of zest, especially in the East, after Hitler foolishly dragged Russia into the war in June 1941. However, when six months later, Japan, with equal rashness, prodded the United States to join in the 'Grand

Alliance', Washington intensified the search for any anti-Nazi assets it could find. The outcome, as far as the Austrian émigrés and exiles were concerned, was the setting up, towards the end of 1942, of the 101st US Infantry Battalion at Camp Attenbury in Indiana. This was the War Department's official designation for what was supposed to be the fighting arm of Free Austria – small in strength but potentially powerful in symbolism.

The project turned out to be a flop and a public relations disaster. Among its first volunteers were the Archdukes Felix and Louis, who joined up as private soldiers. For a few weeks, things seemed to be going well as several hundred Austrian nationals turned up at Camp Attenbury, most of them transferred from other American army units into which they had been posted at various times. In numbers, the planned unit was now at two-thirds strength. Its effective strength was revealed in humiliating fashion on 25 March when senior officers from the War Department – accompanied by some thirty press photographers – arrived for formal drafting in proceedings to launch the 'Free Austria Battalion'. What they witnessed instead was a mass walk-out. Every man was given an individual interview and each asked to confirm his enlistment. The great majority declined and simply made off. By the end of that afternoon, Felix sadly wrote to Otto,[2] the much-advertised unit had sunk from 650 men to a mere ninety. The Jewish exiles, who accounted for the bulk of these 'refuseniks', deserted almost to a man. The 'Austrian Battalion' had, in effect, died on the very day it was mustered. In July of that summer, the War Department in Washington duly pronounced its death sentence and the 101st U.S. Infantry Battalion was officially disbanded.

Otto had conspicuously kept out of the military limelight in America. He was all too aware that the idea of him being the 'Supreme War Lord' (of a vanished dynasty dealing now with a miscellaneous scattering of exiles) had torpedoed whatever slim prospects the 'Austrian Battalion' project had ever had in France. But after the Camp Attenbury fiasco he felt that some symbolic link had to be kept up with the War Department, to suggest that at least the Habsburgs were prepared to fight for the Allied cause. So, with the personal sponsorship of President Roosevelt, an infantry training course was arranged for him at Camp Robinson in Arkansas, after which he was to be passed on to the Adjutant-General's department as an officer candidate. This link seems to have remained symbolic, if only because the Habsburg brothers (based at the Broadmore Hotel in Washington) now concentrated their efforts on the political front. The objective was the same that had been tackled on the other side of the Atlantic: to set up some united forum which would have the semblance of an Austrian government in exile. Otto soon found that the attempt to muster Austria's refugee groups on the same parade ground was child's play compared with the task of persuading them all to gather under one political umbrella.

The main problem was the same in Washington as it had been in Paris: the refusal of the left-wing Socialist faction to join any combination which included their hated right-wing opponents from the Dollfuss-Schuschnigg era. Two things had made a solution look even more remote. The first was the corrosive effect of time and distance. The longer negotiations went on, the more acrimonious they became. The greater the mileage separating the exiles from their homeland grew, the wider the ideological gap between them seemed to stretch. This, of course, is what threatens all émigré politics, where the actors, without any real power, spend their time chewing over the past and arguing about the future. But, above and beyond all that, the right-wing Austrian exiles in general, and the Habsburg clan in particular, now had to face an enemy who was as powerful as he was implacable: Edouard Beneš.

Beneš had been Masaryk's right-hand man in the creation of the Czecho-slovak Republic a generation twenty years before and had succeeded him as President of the new state in 1935. Driven into exile by Hitler, he became the inevitable choice to head the Provisional Czech Government set up in London in 1940. He was also hyperactive in America, buttressed by generous funds derived from gold reserves and other assets transferred to Britain before the Nazis took over in Prague. Apart from money and a political standing which put him head and shoulders above any other émigré leader, Beneš found that the odds were now increasingly on his side. As the massive scale of Russia's suffering in the war became more and more apparent, and with it the growing weight of its contribution to the Allied effort, pro-Soviet tides flowed ever stronger around the Washington administration, and lapped into the White House itself.

Otto's natural allies were in the Catholic camp, but he collected others wherever he could find them. The eventual tally included several influential figures: Cardinal Spellman; Supreme Court Justice Frank Murphy; the Senators Robert Taft and Claude Pepper, and the Congressmen Pete Jarman and Herman P. Eberharter, and Sol Bloom, President of the Foreign Affairs Committee.[3] All were sympathetic to the idea of a conservative Catholic forum set up without the participation of Socialist émigrés and in the teeth of fierce opposition from the Beneš camp. Such a body, the 'Free Austria Movement', had, in fact, sprung into life in New York in 1942. The Habsburgs were careful to keep their names off its office writing-paper, despite the fact that Otto was the only Austrian exile who was a name on Washington's political horizon. Instead, its President was the same Hans Rott who, as the only ex-Minister in exile, had headed the group in Paris.

He was joined on the committee by other right-wing stalwarts who had made their way with Otto across the Atlantic: Martin Fuchs, Franz von Hildebrand and Walter Schuschnigg, the ex-Chancellor's son by his first marriage.[4]

A committee headed by an obscure Minister without Portfolio from Schuschnigg's last Cabinet was no match for the formally constituted Czech Provisional Government, headed by the world-famous Beneš. The Czech statesman's promotion of his own cause carried with it a determination to destroy that of the Habsburgs, with their programme of a post-war conservative-led federation along the banks of the Danube. The Kremlin was equally resolved, for its own purposes, to block this concept and, after Russia's entry into the war, backed a joint Czech-Soviet propaganda campaign run from offices in New York's Rockefeller Centre. They were thought to have found (or bought) sympathetic outlets in up to four hundred newspapers or local radio stations throughout the United States and the collapse of the 'Austrian Battalion' project was due not least to their efforts. Otto managed to drum up some support for his conservative message, especially in the Scripps-Howard and Gannet newspaper chains, but the media battle with Beneš, like the political one, was unequal from the start.

His best card remained, however, the highest one in the whole pack – President Roosevelt himself. The President's personal sympathy for the royal exiles deepened after his meetings with Otto's mother. In September of 1943, the Empress had left her Quebec refuge to revisit America, where she stayed at the luxurious estate in Royalston, Massachusetts, of Calvin Bullock, the same wealthy banker who had played host to the family when they first landed in 1940. Like all who got to know this remarkable royal lady, then or later, the President was impressed by someone who combined so much natural dignity and intelligence with so little bitterness or intrigue. Like her son, she avoided recriminations about the past as well as any talk of restoration in the future.

The fact that the family were known to stand in such favour in the White House helped their campaign to secure some acknowledged status both for the Austrian exiles and for their distant homeland. This was a battle against Washington's bureaucracy as well as the all-pervasive influence of the Beneš camp. The first of two rounds had been won early in 1942, when, with the United States newly entered into the war, most of the Austrians in America had been rounded up, together with those of German or Japanese origin, and despatched to internment camps as enemy aliens. After a long tussle with the Justice Department, they were reassessed and released as 'friendly aliens' and their bank accounts and other assets, which had been frozen in the aftermath of the Pearl Harbor attack, restored to them. Otto had led the campaign, though it was of course backed by every faction in the Austrian colony. As so often in their history, the Austrians had squeezed through by being neither one thing nor another.

The second round in this struggle for separate status came late the following year and here the credit was entirely due to the leader of the Habsburg camp. For him success was especially sweet as it was secured in what might be called a philatelic contest with Beneš and the Czechs. The United States Post Office had launched a special series of stamps for 'Occupied Nations'. When Otto learned that Czechoslovakia (along with Belgium, Denmark, Norway and the others) was to be commemorated, he launched a one-man campaign in the Senate, the administration and, above all, the Ministry of Posts, headed by a sympathetic Frank Walker, to secure a similar tribute for Austria. He was only too aware from personal experience of Austria's shortcomings in the past. He was trying to put all that behind him and create at least the symbolism for a better future.

Again, the sympathy of the White House provided the invaluable background. Though the President does not appear to have been directly involved on this occasion, he was doing all he could to help his royal protégé's efforts to produce even the trappings of an Austrian government in exile. Thus, in June 1943, when the Archduke put forward the idea of having three Austrian Consulates set up and recognised, Roosevelt replied, in a letter of 12 June beginning 'My dear Otto',[5] that he was passing on the suggestion with his blessing to the State Department. More encouragingly, the President went on to say that 'the American people would be happy to see the people of Austria regain their place as an independent nation'.

This people-to-people concept fell deliberately short of declaring governmental recognition. It was, however, enough to make the postage stamp project fall naturally into place and, on 28 November 1943, Austria took her place in the commemorative series. It was perhaps no accident, given the sponsor of idea, that the Habsburg Empire, rather than the Austrian Republic, was chosen as the symbol of national identity. The first day issues carried, alongside the standard five cent American franking, a reproduction of the 1917 ten heller stamp of the Monarchy's military post, with the portrait of Otto's father looking out from the middle. Beneš must have been very put out.

By now, Austria's resurrection had moved beyond the realms of philately. Four weeks before that commemorative stamp was finally issued, its fate had been decided for her – as ever, for good or for ill, by outside forces. On 1 November 1943 the Foreign Ministries of the Grand Alliance,[6] meeting in Moscow to map out the future shape of Europe, issued a joint declaration which was, in effect, the birth certificate of the post-war Austrian state.

After describing Austria (somewhat flatteringly) as 'the first free country to fall victim to Hitlerite aggression', they recorded their wish to see its independence restored. Recognition had to be made for the fact that, as citizens and soldiers of the Third Reich, the Austrians had become the instruments as well as the victims of the Nazi reign of terror. Accordingly, the declaration concluded: 'Austria is reminded, however, that she bears a responsibility for participation in the war on the side of Hitlerite Germany and that, in the final settlement, account will inevitably be taken of her contribution to her liberation.'

Otto would not have quarrelled with a word of this. He knew all about the debt to history which his countrymen ought to pay off and had striven, ever since the outbreak of war, to conjure up some Austrian contribution towards the armed struggle of the Allies – either by promoting even token resistance inside the Ostmark or by the attempt to raise an Austrian military unit in the West. Now the need for the Austrian people to establish their own *bona fides* had been proclaimed by the Grand Alliance, though it is important to recall – in view of the myths and misconceptions concerning this tripartite declaration – exactly how it had come about. The ceaseless lobbying of the Habsburg team had certainly played a part in keeping the concept of Austria's post-war freedom alive. Yet, had they known, it had been actually requested by Stalin, for his own purposes, as far back as December 1941, when Churchill sent Anthony Eden to Moscow for the first political reconnaissance since the Grand Alliance had come about. Stalin proposed that the borders of post-war Poland should expand westwards at Germany's expense but that all the other occupied countries should return to their old frontiers, adding specifically 'Austria to be restored'. Eden replied on Churchill's behalf: 'We are certainly in favour of an independent Austria.'[7]

There have also been muddled accounts over the requirement, laid down in Moscow two years later, for the Austrians to earn their post-war freedom by doing something towards ending the war in the first place. This was not, as has been put about,[8] a demand suddenly slapped on the table by Stalin to make Austria's claim for independent status more difficult to achieve. The text had been evolved during lengthy discussions between British and American officials throughout the summer and early autumn of 1943. There was much debate as to whether, given the fact that in 1938 Austria had rolled over like a puppy dog in the path of the German army, the Anschluss could even be called an annexation. Did it not merely amount to 'occupation'? The war guilt clause had been the trickiest of all to phrase, but also the most essential. In Italy, the lively campaigns of the partisans (whose members were eventually to execute the Duce off their own bat) raised the question of how the seemingly sluggish Austrians could be stirred into similar armed resistance.

The formula worked out was a mixture of carrot and stick: Austria's future independence would be assured provided her people took some decisive steps along that road themselves.[9] All Stalin did when the Western draft was presented to him in Moscow was to tighten its terminology at one or two points: thus, the Austrians were no longer politely 'asked to remember' their part in Hitler's march-in, but bluntly 'reminded of it'. This was hardly an unreasonable demand for a war leader who had seen dozens of Austrian divisions doing deadly battle on his soil.[10]

The real differences between Anglo-American and Soviet perceptions of post-war Austria went far deeper than any tinkering with the war guilt clause. Here the future of the Habsburgs themselves played an important if unspoken role. With the British war leader, the royal exiles were pushing at an open door in their ideas for a post-war Central Europe. The traditionalist and painter of broad-canvas history went even further on the record than they were prepared to go in private. Thus, on 13 December 1942, when the question of an independent Austrian battalion came up for discussion, Winston Churchill declared it to be 'a very good thing ... if it could be managed without too much trouble'. He then went on:

> I am extremely interested in Austria and hope that Vienna may become the capital of a great Confederation of the Danube ... the separation of the Austrians and Southern Germans from the Prussians is essential to the harmonious reconstitution of history.[11]

At this stage, Otto had not yet met Churchill and, though his brother Robert had been pleading the conservative Austrian cause in London, the indefatigable visionary did not need any persuading to indulge in yet another of his historical sweeps. For a while, he carried Roosevelt along with him and, by the summer of 1943, the idea that Austria should become the linchpin of a democratic federation which would include Bavaria, Württemberg and Baden was still agreed Anglo-American policy.[12]

It should be noted that this was far from being a rallying-call for the Habsburgs. Indeed, the inclusion of south German states in the proposed grouping would have virtually ruled out any restoration of the dynasty, except conceivably in some presidential role. Even this possibility was soon to be knocked on the head. To begin with, Roosevelt was turning more and more (under the influence of his pro-Soviet persuaders) to regarding 'Uncle Joe' as an amiable and well-meaning ally. Moreover, it was becoming increasingly clear that the Russian bear was determined to plant his own paws along the Danube banks, and that it was going to be very hard to stop him grabbing one so-called independent Danubian state after another.

In this context, the Moscow Declaration of November 1943 on Austria can be seen a part of a Soviet campaign to bury the Danubian Federation idea. The re-establishment of an independent republic, confined to the borders of 1938, would ensure that post-war Vienna was unlikely to look beyond those borders. The declaration was unexpectedly splendid news for the Austrians. Ironically, it only prejudiced the chances of the Habsburgs, who had lobbied so hard in the wings to support it. That would have troubled Otto less than might have been supposed. Ever since the ominous pact of 1936 between Schuschnigg and Hitler, he had put the struggle for Austrian independence above the short-term interests of the dynasty. So, thanks to the implacable opposition of Stalin (and the growing weight of the Red Army), the Danube Federation project was first sidelined and then abandoned at successive summit gatherings. Churchill could only scowl as he lost the political argument, though, as we shall see, he was to renew it on the military front.

In this last phase, however, all three members of the Grand Alliance and the exiled dynasty were, uniquely, to find themselves of the same mind on one point: the need to draw Horthy's Hungary over to the Allied side. January 1943 was the moment in the war when the Regent realised not only that he had mounted the wrong horse in the race but that his people were paying an unacceptable price for the ride. The realisation that Hitler might well be heading towards defeat had come, of course – for Horthy as for hundreds of thousands of others who had been sitting on fences throughout occupied Europe – with the destruction of the German Sixth Army at Stalingrad at the end of that crucial month. But for Hungary, the searing catastrophe which changed everything had taken place a fortnight before, some four hundred miles northwards on the same Don battle-line.

At Voronesh, the Second Hungarian Army, which was holding a long stretch of the river front without either proper fortified positions or regular supply lines, was smashed to pieces by a Red Army offensive launched on 12 January. Within a week, half of the original force had been wiped out: over 50,000 taken prisoner and some 30,000 killed. It was the most disastrous loss in a single action in Magyar military history. Bitterness was added to grief when it became clear that, at several points in the action, German divisions had sacrificed Hungarian troops to assist their own getaway. For their part, the Germans accused the Second Army of cowardly surrender. After Voronesh, military cooperation between the two unequal allies had become a dead letter. This had an immediate impact on the political front as efforts were intensified to extract Hungary from the Nazi alliance altogether.

The key figure here was Miklós Kállay, Horthy's Prime Minister, who also held the Foreign Office portfolio until July of 1943. He had long been toying with the concept of Budapest steering more of an independent course between the Nazi and Allied camps, and he now set sail for the West, steering for every harbour he could think of. Within the first six weeks of the New Year, his secret emissaries had arrived in Istanbul, Stockholm, Geneva, Rome and Lisbon. All carried the same message for any Western official who would listen: Hungary was ready to change sides if only the Allies could make it possible. It was the Lisbon channel which led straight to Otto, who had several trusty helpers in the Portuguese capital. One was the strongly anti-Nazi Hungarian Minister there, M. Wodianer, who provided the vital communication link. As Otto later recalled it:

Contacts were first established fairly soon after Pearl Harbor with the Hungarian Legation in Lisbon. To begin with, these went through our good friend, José Saldanha da Gama, who eventually came over to the United States to discuss with me and the American administration how we could set up proper negotiations with the Hungarian government. [13]

In Washington, I was working mainly with Mr Tibor Eckhardt, the former President of the Independent Smallholders party in Hungary, who left the country when he saw the direction Horthy was taking in order to build up a Hungarian representation abroad. Eckhardt was a man of great courage and intelligence and, furthermore, an expert on foreign affairs since he had been very active at the League of Nations. I first met him in 1937 and we had remained in close contact ever since. He had, for obvious reasons, no political connections in the United States and I was able to provide him with these. In return, he did much of the actual planning and presentation as to how Hungary could be saved by changing sides.[14]

Horthy, of course, knew in general terms of Kállay's efforts, though the details were often concealed from him. Keeping him at a distance proved as well, for whenever the Regent tried to put his own oar in to the Potomac waters, there was an ugly splash. Otto recalls:

The messages we received in Washington on the Regent's behalf were less concerned with his country's fate than with his own personal prospects should Hungary be received in the Allied camp. He wanted to know, for example, what pension or income he would be given and what offices, honours or decorations he would retain and indeed whether these would be added to. It was all so embarrassing that we decided simply to ignore the requests rather than pass them on.[15]

This was one Danubian leopard which had not changed his spots. It was still the same Niklós Horthy making the same preposterous demands that had so exasperated Otto's father twenty years before when he had tried, in his own royal palace in Budapest, to persuade his perfidious Regent to hand back power.

In view of all the efforts Otto and Eckhardt were making in Washington at White House level, it was somewhat ironical that the nearest thing during 1943 to a breakthrough in these tortuous negotiations with the Allies should have come instead in Istanbul. Moreover, it was the British, not the Americans, who took the initiative. Kállay's main emissary to the Allied missions in the Turkish capital had been a senior Hungarian Foreign official, László Veress, who had spent most of the summer probing, without success, for a real opening. Then, abruptly, Veress was summoned on 8 September to a midnight meeting on the yacht of the British envoy, Sir Hughe Knatchbull-Hugesson which lay anchored in the Sea of Marmora. Sir Hughe presented his credentials (in the form of a telegram of authorisation signed by Eden) and then read out a list of 'preliminary conditions' for official talks with the Hungarian government. The actual document was not handed over; Veress had to take the points down from dictation.

This was hardly a promising omen; anything on offer could later be disclaimed if the need arose. Nonetheless, the two sides had, for the first time, touched hands. It was certainly appropriate that it should have been on a yacht that the question of Hungary jumping ship from the Axis powers was now properly examined. The main points laid down on Eden's behalf were that any agreement formally reached through diplomatic channels should not be made known 'before the Allies reached the frontiers of Hungary', but that, in the meantime, Budapest would do everything it could to help the armies of the Western powers. Measures set out under this heading included a progressive reduction of military and economic cooperation with the Germans; resistance to any attempt by Hitler to take over their country and, indeed, secret preparations for an attack on his forces; the withdrawal of the last remnants of the Second Hungarian Army (now known at home as the 'Dead Army') from Russia; and a pledge to place all resources, including air bases, at the Allies' disposal 'at a given moment'.[16]

There was not much in these terms which Kállay could oppose when Veress delivered them to him in Budapest a week later. However, the Hungarian Prime Minister did jib very strongly at the demand for 'unconditional surrender' in which the whole British package was wrapped up.[17] Agreement was, in fact, never reached on this point of principle. It was therefore left in suspension when the Istanbul draft was finally 'ratified' in October.[18]

These diplomatic formalities were concluded in Lisbon, with Wodianer signing for Kállay, and Sir Ronald Campbell, now his colleague as British Minister to Portugal, franking the document on behalf of the Allies. As we have seen, Lisbon had always been Otto's main channel of communication and persuasion on Danubian affairs, and it is quite possible that his trans-atlantic influence played an indirect part in the Istanbul pact. On 19 August 1943 – only three weeks before Kállay's emissary boarded the British yacht – the first plenary session opened in Quebec of the far-reaching Anglo-American summit conference, code-named 'Quadrant'. As Churchill's own account of the meeting makes clear,[19] the future of Central Europe did not figure as such on the agenda, which was fully taken up with matters such as preparations for the 1944 invasion of Nazi-occupied France, the development of the Italian campaign and a new joint command in South-East Asia; and, of course, 'Tube Alloys', the code-name for the nuclear bomb programme. Compared with these issues, all of them both massive and pressing, post-war politics along the Danube's banks seemed pretty remote stuff. However, Otto was, as usual, busy in the wings of great events. Though his name is not mentioned in the index to the relevant volume of Churchill's memoirs, the Archduke is known to have seen the two great war leaders together and to have been assured by both the President and the Prime Minister that they still supported his hopes for a conservative solution in Central Europe.[20] The meeting in the Sea of Marmora certainly fitted in with those aspirations.

On the other hand, the contrast which surfaced again at Quebec between long-term political visions and immediate military priorities lay at the heart of Otto's problems. He was very strong on the former but quite inexperienced and, indeed, uninformed about the latter. Yet these were times when decisions were dictated from the battlefield rather than from the council chamber.

For that matter, it is worth noting that the only practical results which emerged during 1943 from all Kállay's feelers to the West concerned the nuts and bolts of the actual fighting. Whether in Stockholm, Switzerland, Istanbul or Lisbon, Western emissaries (including a mysterious 'Mr H.' from London) had insisted that what the Allies wanted were deeds rather than words. Some positive signs were needed that Hungary was detaching herself from Hitler's military grip. After the collapse of Italy in July 1943, Kállay nerved himself to show some carefully-measured defiance. Thus, in August, he diverted the bulk of German railway traffic headed for the Balkans away from Budapest, forcing the Wehrmacht to use meandering single-track routes for its supply lines. In the autumn, he went a step further by allowing Allied bombers to fly unmolested over Hungarian territory – provided they did not drop any of their loads en route.[21]

It was on this military front that all the political dreams of Otto, Eckhardt,

Kállay and many another were to flourish or flounder. Everything centred on one prime issue of Allied grand strategy: what was the importance of the Mediterranean theatre of war compared with the Western Front, and above all, the Normandy landings? That debate led to another: could the Mediterranean campaign, whatever its priority, ever be extended to include a lunge northwards towards the Danube Basin?

Needless to say, Churchill was all for the lunge and his fervour only mounted as the struggle reached its climax in the summer of 1944. On the one hand, battle was now engaged in France so that the argument over the distribution of Allied resources had moved off the drawing board to become the urgent order of the day. Meanwhile, in the east, the Red Army was moving steadily closer to Central Europe, dragging its Communist doctrine with its tank tracks. This, Churchill's personal physician noted, seemed almost to be upsetting the mental balance of his famous patient: 'Winston never talks of Hitler these days', he wrote in the last midsummer of the war; 'he is always harping on the dangers of Communism. He dreams of the Red Army spreading like a cancer from one country to another. It has become an obsession and he seems to think of little else.' 22

Given the grim fulfilment of those forebodings, it was a pity that the obsession was not shared more widely in the Western camp. One problem was Churchill's unhappy record in such endeavours. When given an atlas in one hand and a handful of divisional flags in the other, he could never resist drawing great arrows across the map by which military advances would also bring political triumphs. The Gallipoli campaign of 1917 had been one such arrow disastrously buried in the Turkish soil at very short range. The planned march of the White Russian armies from the Crimea all the way up to Bolshevik Moscow in 1921 (a project backed by Churchill almost alone in the Cabinet of the day) eventually flopped to earth because, in this case, the range was simply too long.

Now, here he was at it again, as usual with a graphic label for his plans. Just as the entire Mediterranean campaign (directed from the start by the British) had been a strike at 'the soft underbelly of the Axis', so now its final flourish was tagged as 'a dagger in the enemy's armpit'. What this amounted to in planning terms was to seize Trieste with a sea-borne force of some five or six Allied divisions. These would then head north through the Julian Alps via the strategic Ljubljana gap and then fan out towards the Danube Basin, beating the Red Army to it in both Budapest and Vienna.

Serious doubts could, and were, being aired about the idea on basic operational grounds. The Julian Alps made a stony armpit for any dagger to penetrate, even if the initial capture of Trieste went to plan. For the naval experts the shallow waters and heavy minefields of the Adriatic made even the landings a risky affair. Moreover, help from Tito's partisans could not be taken for granted. At this period Tito was still a fervent Communist comrade of the Russians who would oppose any such campaign; for that matter, he had ambitions of his own in Austria.[23] Above all, was the proposed force powerful enough? A handful of divisions would have had their work cut out to occupy the whole of the central Danubian plain, including its twin capitals of Vienna and Budapest. In the event, the debates within and between the Allied Chiefs of Staff were to be decided for them in advance by the political decisions of their leaders.

At the crucial summit meeting in Teheran in November of 1943, Roosevelt had begun by continuing his support for Churchill's Istrian 'dagger'. But by the end, he had fallen in line with a strategy for 1944 laid down by Stalin, whose effect was to keep that dagger firmly in its sheath. He agreed with Stalin not only that 'Overlord', the Normandy invasion, should remain the absolute priority for the coming summer, but also that its supporting operation should be launched against the beaches of southern France. Due to the shortage of suitable landing craft in the Mediterranean theatre, this was to render any simultaneous amphibious strike against Trieste impossible. For good measure, the Marshal also shot down any and all Anglo-American ideas about a Danubian Federation. The President, to Churchill's dismay, now seemed to give in on that front as well.

Otto and his team had, of course, no inkling of the military plans of the Grand Alliance, nor of the debates which had arisen among their general staffs over implementation. Indeed, it was not to be until well after the war that he learned about the political decision taken at Teheran or at subsequent Allied summits. But what he was well aware of in the closing stages of the war was the extent to which his illustrious friend and helper seemed to be leaning ever more towards a pro-Soviet line. Washington, then as now, was a great rumour mill of hearsay, so the young Archduke based his evidence only on what the President had actually said to him in private.

One such remark touched on the increasing penetration of the White House by left-wing sympathisers and the President's doubts about some of his key advisers. Thus, in September 1944 – at what was to be their last meeting – Otto had handed over a message just received via Lisbon from the Hungarian Prime Minister of the day.[24] The message was personal and highly confidential and the Archduke stressed that it should stay that way. Roosevelt's reply, as he took the document, was: 'I will put this in the one White House safe to which Harry Hopkins has no access'.[25] His young admirer found the remark more disturbing than reassuring. Hopkins had been the President's closest aide throughout the war, the man at his side at all the top-level talks with Churchill and Stalin.

Another, almost equally worrying comment came when Otto was questioning the President about the risks of making so many wartime concessions
to the Russians. 'That will be no problem', came the confident reply. 'When
this war is over, the Russians will be so weak economically, and so dependent
on our aid that we will be able to set our own conditions'. Roosevelt was
already a mortally sick man when he made that prediction. It was just as
well for him that he never lived to see what a total miscalculation it was
to prove.

By the time Otto said his farewells the British plan for an advance on
the Danube seemed already to be dead in the water and, quite unbeknown
to the Archduke, it was his great friend and protector who had fired the
last torpedoes into it. During the summer of 1944, Churchill had had little
difficulty in winning the support of his own generals in the Mediterranean
(the Supreme Allied Commander, Sir Henry Maitland Wilson, and Sir
Harold Alexander, the Commander-in-Chief of the Italian campaign). Wilson had eagerly drawn up battle plans to land six sea-borne divisions in
Trieste from where the hundred-mile thrust up to the Austrian border
would be launched. But August was the last month in which the Russians
– whose main forces were then still some five hundred miles away from
Budapest – could feasibly have been challenged in the race for the Danube.
Despite passionate personal pleas from Prime Minister to President to
have vital tank-landing ships diverted from the southern France operation
to the Adriatic, Roosevelt stood firm behind his own military advisers and
the strategic pledges given to Stalin at Teheran.

The two Western leaders debated the matter more amicably again at their
second Quebec summit (13–16 September).[26] But the moment for decisive
action had passed. Even Churchill was driven to wondering whether, as a
last resort, Alexander might have to settle for 'a dash with his armoured
cars' towards the Danube. It had been agreed, from the very start of all
Hungary's secret contacts with the West, that the country could only jump
free from Hitler's grasp when it had some firm Allied embrace to fall into.
A few squadrons of armoured cars – even if they had made it all the way
to Hungary – hardly fitted that description. Otto returned to Europe sharing
all of Churchill's forebodings about the future, and little of Roosevelt's airy
optimism.[27]

When Otto looked back, much later in life, on the myriad of impressions
and memories from those four wartime years in America, two stood out
in particular. The first concerned a great mistake; the second a great revelation. The mistake, which he judged the biggest of his young life, was to
have frittered away so much of his time, money and energy in the self-
destructive battles of émigré politics instead of concentrating from the start

on the broader diplomatic front. There was much to be learned from this lesson, but the impact of the revelation went far deeper, and it arrived, appropriately, in a flash.

Towards the end of 1941, he arrived in Arizona, where he was due to make a round of speeches. At a press interview at the airport, one of the local journalists asked their distinguished polyglot visitor what he thought of as his home country. Rather to his own astonishment, as well as theirs, he heard himself answering: 'I'm a European.' The reply marked a transformation of his horizons of which he had hitherto been unaware. He once calculated that, in his hectic American travel schedule, he had visited every single state of the Union at least half a dozen times. What had imprinted itself on his subconscious was how, despite their diversity of climate, culture and populations, all were held together by a single continental unity, a common bond which transcended all regional loyalties. Why could this not be the post-war pattern for the Old World, now so grievously divided? And, if so, even the eleven-nation foundations of his own dynasty would need to be absorbed in this broader homeland. That instinctive reaction at an Arizona airport was to remould the rest of his political life. As he commented on it years later: 'I suddenly realised that there was something much bigger and much more important than Austria or Hungary or whatever simply because Europe itself exists and we could only solve its problems by uniting.' [28]

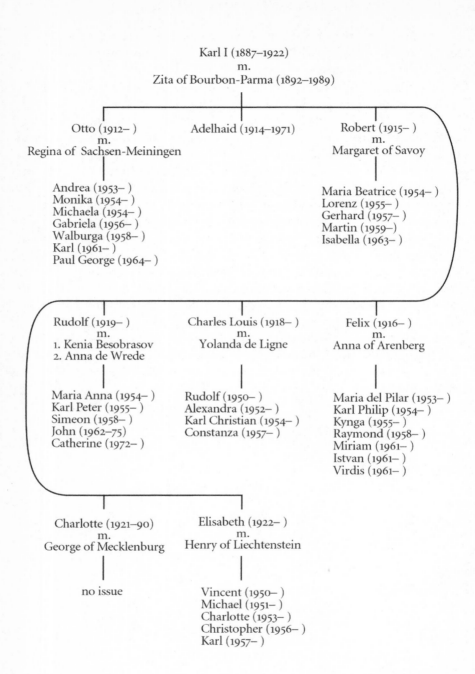

Karl I (1887–1922)
m.
Zita of Bourbon-Parma (1892–1989)

Otto (1912–)
m.
Regina of Sachsen-Meiningen

Andrea (1953–)
Monika (1954–)
Michaela (1954–)
Gabriela (1956–)
Walburga (1958–)
Karl (1961–)
Paul George (1964–)

Adelhaid (1914–1971)

Robert (1915–)
m.
Margaret of Savoy

Maria Beatrice (1954–)
Lorenz (1955–)
Gerhard (1957–)
Martin (1959–)
Isabella (1963–)

Rudolf (1919–)
m.
1. Kenia Besobrasov
2. Anna de Wrede

Maria Anna (1954–)
Karl Peter (1955–)
Simeon (1958–)
John (1962–75)
Catherine (1972–)

Charles Louis (1918–)
m.
Yolanda de Ligne

Rudolf (1950–)
Alexandra (1952–)
Karl Christian (1954–)
Constanza (1957–)

Felix (1916–)
m.
Anna of Arenberg

Maria del Pilar (1953–)
Karl Philip (1954–)
Kynga (1955–)
Raymond (1958–)
Miriam (1961–)
Istvan (1961–)
Virdis (1961–)

Charlotte (1921–90)
m.
George of Mecklenburg

no issue

Elisabeth (1922–)
m.
Henry of Liechtenstein

Vincent (1950–)
Michael (1951–)
Charlotte (1953–)
Christopher (1956–)
Karl (1957–)

Otto von Habsburg's family.

14

Dropping Anchor

A Clipper brought Otto Habsburg three thousand miles closer to his old homelands, even if he had no idea as yet where his own home was to be. But he had also landed a world away from Washington and the White House, which, for the past four years, had been the fulcrum of any political pressure he had been able to exert. While the ever-weakening President Roosevelt was still alive, a long-distance link survived. When, for example, Otto moved from Portugal to a liberated Paris in January 1945, the President gladly extended to him, and his brother Felix, the same privilege they had enjoyed in Lisbon, namely to send their White House correspondence by diplomatic pouch.

By now, it was more than their operational base that had changed. Their target had also been shifted for them by the tide of events. After the Anschluss of March 1938, Austria was lost for the foreseeable future to the Habsburg camp, which moved its sights across to Hungary. Now, in the closing stages of Hitler's war, Hungary in turn had become a lost cause. The first shift had come in the autumn of 1944, only a few days before Otto had flown hopefully back to Europe. The Führer's growing impatience with Horthy's double-dealing finally erupted into action with a German army clamp-down in Budapest, where, on 16 October, the Admiral announced his formal abdication as Regent. As no steps were taken, by him or anyone else, to propose a successor,[1] Hungary no longer had a head of state, either *de facto* or *de jure*. St Stephen's crown itself had been tossed by Hitler into a constitutional limbo. This hardly mattered for, within six months, the Red Army had driven the Germans out of Budapest and Hungary started its slide into the Soviet Empire, just as, six years before, Austria had been swallowed up in the Third Reich.

That same Austria, soon to become *redivivus* as the Second Republic, now took Hungary's place again in Habsburg attentions. Two problems preoccupied Otto in the winter before Austria's independence was formally restored. One was surreal, in the literal sense that it was so removed from reality. In December 1944, more than a year after the Allies had called on the Austrians to earn their freedom by fighting for it, a resistance body was finally set up in Vienna which purported to represent the nation as a whole.

Six more weeks were to pass before the leadership of the Provisional Austrian National Committee could be finalised, [2] bringing right-wing Conservatives, Socialists, Communists (by far the most consistently active among the resistance) all together with some churchmen and army officers. While this process was grinding laboriously away, Otto received overoptimistic secret reports which almost suggested that Hitler's Ostmark was about to erupt like a volcano over the Nazis' heads and bury them in ashes. However surprising this seemed (for the Austrian temperament, as he well knew, is more one of fretful simmering than of boiling over in Magyar or Gallic fashion), Otto was sufficiently concerned to send an alarm call to Roosevelt. Austrian resistance, he told the President, must not be allowed to break out prematurely or another tragedy like the disastrous Warsaw uprising could occur.

The Archduke need not have worried. As with nearly all of the Austrian resistance movements, this one too was undermined by indiscretion, ill-discipline and outright treachery. The Gestapo were onto the Provisional Austrian National Committee almost from the start and on 2 March 1945 they swooped to snuff it out. Only in the Tyrol did a more determined and unified movement survive to make contact with the Allies during the final stages of Germany's collapse. Otto's younger brother, Rudolf, had managed to join this movement, travelling under false French papers. The family could not be accused of simply exhorting from abroad.

Otto's other concern about his homeland in this last winter of the war was one which touched on his favourite domain of Allied politics. Through-out the summer of 1944, a little-known body called the European Advisory Commission had been meeting in London at ambassadorial level to seek agreement over the division of occupation zones in post-war Germany and Austria between the American, Russian and British forces, as well as the mechanisms for joint tripartite control. The initial proposal of the State Department regarding Austria had been to limit the American contribution to one paltry infantry division and – even more bizarrely – to station this force in the capital. This would have left the rest of the country to be divided up between British and Soviet troops, moving in from the south and east respectively. It was not until 8 December that Roosevelt scrapped this absurd scenario in favour of a proper American occupation zone in western Austria to border on the territories their forces were proposing to take over in southern Germany.

The key adviser who brought about this victory for commonsense was the American delegate on the European Advisory Commission, John G. Winant, who had replaced the egregious Joseph Kennedy as Ambassador in London nearly two years before. Winant's argument was irrefutable: unless they matched their Allies by running an occupation zone of their own, the Americans would have scant authority when it came to tripartite decisions thrashed out in Vienna. Indeed, they could be reduced to the status of observers. Now it is true to say that the immensely popular Winant included Archduke Robert among his wide circle of friends. Otto's brother had, over the past four years, built up his own pro-Austrian group with supporters in society, Parliament, business, and even through the help of that remarkable young diplomat Frank Roberts,[3] in the basically hostile Foreign Office. As and when the opportunity occurred, all would have pressed Winant to scrap the State Department's nonsensical blueprint for Austria.

They were, however, pressing at an already open door. The British, who were only allotting one Eighth Army division to Austria, were neither militarily equipped nor politically willing to take on the arduous task of sharing the entire responsibility for the occupation with the Red Army. Even more to the point, the Soviet representative at the London talks, Ambassador Gusev, was himself urging Winant to deliver the full tripartite arrangements whereby the United States would honour its own obligations to the alliance by taking responsibility for its own occupation zone. Such Soviet insistence may have appeared strange to those bureaucrats far removed from the scene in Washington. But Winant, like all who had been dealing with the Russians for months on the spot in London, knew the reason. Tripartite control in Austria was part of a vast scenario already agreed for post-war Europe that guaranteed the Russians, among other things, an 80 per cent control of Bulgaria and Roumania and a strong foothold in Hungary and Yugoslavia. The Russians treated anything formally agreed almost reverentially and to be executed to the letter. They now feared their whole European package might become unravelled if the Americans started fiddling about with the string over Austria – a country which Stalin was anyway confident of bringing, one day, into his ambit.

There was a splendid New Year's gift for the Habsburg brothers in general – and for Otto in particular – when, early in 1945, the liberated France of General de Gaulle was admitted into the framework of the Grand Alliance. Moreover, as a technically equal partner, it was allotted its own post-war occupation zones in both Germany and Austria, thus converting the entire control mechanism into a quadripartite operation. The section carved out for her in Austria, the two westernmost provinces of Tyrol and Vorarlberg, might have been chosen by the Habsburgs themselves. They were not only the most accessible and most lovely parts of the country. They were also, in conservative monarchist terms, the most loyal. More than once in its troubled history, the dynasty had sought refuge in Innsbruck, the Tyrolean capital, which the Empress Maria Theresia had embellished as a favourite residence. Now, nearly two hundred years later, in late April 1945, her young descendant arrived in the town, to plunge into the maelstrom of post-war twentieth-century republican politics.

He was in understandably ecstatic mood. The last time he had seen Innsbruck, nestling in its bowl of mountain peaks, was as a six-year-old child, gazing through the windows of that special train which was carrying his whole family into exile. Since early adulthood he had tried to shape Austria's fate, but always from a distance of hundreds or even thousands of miles. Now he was back again on Austrian soil though, ironically, still facing the same adversary who had confronted his father a generation before. [4] Karl Renner, that infinitely malleable and durable pragmatist, who had moved smoothly from monarchy to republic and from republic into the Third Reich was now busy trying to ride back into power from the top of Red Army tanks.

He had promptly sought the Russians out in Gloggnitz, the village at the foot of the Semmering Pass, where he had spent the war years in deliberate obscurity. As it turned out, he had no need to offer them his services, since the Kremlin was already looking for him. To Stalin, the former Socialist Chancellor was the ideal candidate to lend respectability to another of those so-called National Unity governments planned for all the Danubian countries his forces were overrunning. A group of four Austrian Communist party leaders, who had spent the war in Moscow,[5] arrived in Vienna, on the very day, 3 April 1945, that the search order for Renner was issued to the commander of the Third Ukrainian Army, which had swept into eastern Austria. The prearranged task of this quartet was so to station themselves in Ministries as to exert real power in any post-war Austrian regime.

This prospect rang loud alarm bells for every one of the right-wing Austrian politicians who had survived Hitler's war or his concentration camps and who were now struggling to regroup together on their own. Several of them were in touch with Otto at his 'headquarters' in Innsbruck's Hotel Kreith. Though he could play no direct role in the creation of their new movement, eventually restyled 'People's Party', he was able – and more than willing – to enter the ring over Renner. On 15 April, from Eichbüchl Castle, the splendid residence in Lower Austria now put at his disposal by the Russians, the former Chancellor had penned his famous (or infamous) letter to Stalin. He began by recalling fond memories of his own pre-war meetings with Lenin and Trotsky (the inclusion of the latter was surely a slip). He ended with an outright offer to join with the Austrian Communists 'to work together on an equal brotherly footing to refound the Republic step by step together'.

In retrospect, it was an unnecessary as well as an embarrassing exercise in wheedling. Fraternal cooperation among the left-wingers was precisely what the Russians had in mind, with the step-by-step process leading eventually to a Communist take-over. This was indeed the direction in which Austria seemed to be heading when Renner, now Federal Chancellor again, presented the list of his 'Provisional Government' to the Soviet High Command for their approval. The key portfolios of the Interior Ministry (control over the police) and Education (control over propaganda) were both placed in Communist hands,[6] and the right wing was severely underrepresented, though this was largely due to shortcomings of its own.

Alarm only grew in the right-wing camp, and among the Western powers themselves, when, throughout that midsummer, the Russians denied their allies full access to their zones, and, even more ominously, entry into Vienna itself. On 2 July Otto chipped in, as best he could, with a letter to the White House. Fortunately, its current occupant, Harry S. Truman (who had moved in after Roosevelt's death in April) was well known to him personally: they had been fellow-residents of the Broadmore apartment complex in Washington. Truman had little of Roosevelt's political clout, nor did he share his predecessor's warm friendship with the young Archduke. It was therefore likely that Otto's letter (which combined a plea for American relief aid with a warning about the Communist threat) did no more than add a brick to the wall of Western resistance which was belatedly building up against Russian penetration in Vienna. The timing was certainly fortuitous. Within little more than a fortnight, the last summit of the rapidly disintegrating Grand Alliance convened in Berlin.

Austria barely figured on the agenda, which was taken up almost entirely with the problems of disarmament and four-power control in conquered Germany. But when, towards the end of the fortnight long meeting, the political situation in Vienna cropped up for discussion, both America and, even more strongly, Britain, refused to recognise the validity of the Renner regime. Their sanction was not to be finalised until 20 October – when all the Western Allies were firmly ensconced in the Austrian capital and after Renner had promised, among many other things, to announce the firm date of 25 November for the holding of a free general election.

Looking back on the episode, Otto commented:

I certainly had respect for Renner's intellect for, in my father's time on the throne, he had put forward some excellent ideas about possible federal solutions and so on. But I had absolutely no respect for his character. How could I? Here was someone who had said 'Yes' to Hitler and had been placarded as such up and down Austria in 1938 and then, after Hitler's defeat, had written such a servile letter to Stalin – and it could not have been more servile. How could one place any trust in such a person?

He was a weak man, and, quite apart from that, I had been asked by many Austrians, including some senior political figures of the day, to undertake this appeal. So I took it upon myself to write the letter to Truman. It seemed the best thing to do in the context of what was happening at the time, though, thank God, things turned out differently.[7]

They certainly did. When the votes were counted in that historic poll of 25 November 1945, they showed nearly 50 per cent support for the new right-wing grouping of the People's Party, compared with 44.6 per cent for Renner's Socialists and, running a paltry third, little more than 5 per cent for the Communists. When translated into parliamentary representation, this gave the People's Party a clear lead of eighty-five seats compared with the seventy-six of the Socialists. To the surprise of all,[8] the Communists could only claim four – just enough for the Moscow-trained quartet. What everyone, and especially the Russians, had underestimated, was an extraordinary display of gutsy resistance among both peasants and factory workers alike in the Soviet occupation zone.[9]

But Renner, duly promoted Federal President after he had relinquished the Chancellorship, nonetheless had his final revenge on the Archduke. It was all like an uncanny rerun of the drama at Eckartsau a generation before. Then, as now, a defeated Austria was occupied by the Allied victors. Then, as now, that same Chancellor, Karl Renner, had been struggling to push the Habsburg family out of their homeland. Then, as now, the struggle was lost once a legitimate republican government had been elected and formally recognised. In 1919 that turning-point had come on 15 March; in 1945 it came on 19 December, when Austrian's new coalition government was approved by the Allied Council. On both occasions, the Allies had also tacitly approved the statutes of the republic, which included the same pledge to banish and disinherit the dynasty.

Also on both occasions, an ally had appeared from the Western camp: Colonel Strutt in 1919, who had been so powerful and so resourceful as to bludgeon and blackmail Karl Renner into doing his bidding. The would-be saviour now had a higher rank but less power: the French High Commissioner and Commander-in-Chief of the Western provinces, General Bethouard, who struggled to obstruct the expulsion order. But, in the end, Otto and his brothers, Robert, Karl Ludwig and Rudolf, simply had to go so that, before January 1946 was out, the Socialist press of Vienna could celebrate 'the elimination of the monarchist nest of Innsbruck'.[10]

Otto's appeal to President Truman was to be his last such public political activity for many years to come. Moreover, when he stepped back into private life, he was stepping into a void: he had no legal identity. He later recalled this alarming situation:

> After being compelled to leave Austria, I was in real trouble, for I no longer had any passport or travel papers of any sort at my disposal. Up to then, I had still enjoyed the Belgian diplomatic passport, but this was rescinded by the direct order of Prince Charles, who, in the bitter dispute between himself and his brother, the former King Leopold III over the succession, had got himself appointed Regent. I had shown support for Leopold's cause which meant that, for the time being, I had backed the wrong horse.[11] I was also in trouble because I had confided in the then Belgian Minister of State, M. Theunis, in the belief that he was on my side. In fact, he was in the other camp, to whom he passed on all my plans.
>
> The situation was only resolved when my friend, General de Bénouville, who had been one of the leaders of the Gaullist resistance, got in touch with another war-time target of the Gestapo, M. Witasse. He was now Minister of State in the principality of Monaco, and persuaded the ruler to give me a Monegasque passport so that I could at least travel.[12]

The newly-minted citizen of Monaco faced another novelty: for the first time in his life, the thirty-four-year-old Archduke had to earn his living in normal professional style. During the war, and especially during his stay in America, politics had entered his bloodstream and was to stay there for the rest of his days. This seemed to rule out any career in industry or commerce. Instead, he chose the media and became a journalist, an author and a lecturer. It was an uncertain freelance existence, but at least it meant that he could continue to get his conservative messages across to readers and listeners all over the world.

The global foundations were laid by an extensive tour he made with his brother Robert in 1948: the Near East, Pakistan, India, Vietnam, China, the Philippines and other islands of the Pacific. To Asian audiences, he spoke of Europe and the West. All the while, he was collecting material for lectures later on in America, where his listeners were interested above all in China. These Americans tours became the most demanding and most exhausting part of his professional life. They were also, by far, the most rewarding. Indeed, by the 1950s, they had brought him moderate prosperity as well as the satisfaction of paying off all the debts he had accumulated during his asylum years in the United States. These were settled down to the last cent. His American creditors, he recalled, had been very considerate in their patience.

The prospect of financial stability meant that he could seriously contemplate the most important step in his, or indeed anybody's, personal life: marriage and the founding of a family. It was high time. As the 1950s came round, Otto was thirty-eight years old and two of his siblings had already made their way to the altar: his youngest sister Elisabeth, who was married to Prince Heinrich of Liechtenstein in September 1949, and his brother Karl Ludwig, whose wedding to Princess Yolanda de Ligne took place in January 1950. There was no obvious partner in sight for the head of the Habsburg dynasty among the former ruling families of Catholic Europe, but in 1950 one appeared on the scene out of the blue, conjured up by, of all things, a war in Asia.

This was the year when the conflict between the Communist and non-Communist halves of Korea erupted along the Thirty-Eighth Parallel and the shock waves began to reverberate throughout Europe. Nowhere was the agitation greater than in the camps set up in Germany by the Allies for Hungarian and other refugees from Soviet-dominated Central Europe. Some of these were so close to the East-West dividing line that the inmates could see the Red Army's control towers along the border. Panic had broken out among them that a Korean-style armed conflict could start up here too, and bring them again under Soviet rule.

> General Henyey, the Foreign Minister of the pro-Allied Lakotos government, who had been liberated from a German concentration camp, had taken control of the Hungarian emigrants problem. He visited me in Paris asking me to come to Germany and speak to the Hungarians in the camps to reassure them that they were safe. I, of course, agreed and made a tour all along the Czech and Austrian border. It was in the summer of 1950 at a camp refugee centre in Munich that I met Regina for the first time. She was working there as a nurse with one of the Catholic charities. She was a refugee herself. Her father, Duke Georg of Sachsen-Meiningen, whose estates were just inside the Soviet occupation zone, had been taken prisoner by the Red Army and had died in captivity.[13]

The physical chemistry between the pair was immediate for it sprang from that most powerful of impulses, the attraction of opposites. Regina, with her blonde hair, blue eyes and regular features, looked, at first glance, like the typical Germanic beauty. Regina was, however, no prototype: there was too much individuality about her face for that. The dark-haired Otto, though equally attractive, was more difficult to classify. That was hardly surprising for there were French and Portuguese strains in his immediate ancestry, alongside the Austrian blood of his father. At all events, as he later recalled, 'things moved quite briskly' after that first meeting. The couple were engaged within six months, and their wedding followed on 10 May of the following year.

That day marked, first and foremost, the union of a couple, compatible in both looks and lineage, who were also deeply in love. But the ceremony itself had been choreographed, down to the last detail, to celebrate a once-mighty dynasty that still had resonance, even though now powerless and in exile. It was, in fact, the most impressive public display of Habsburg pride and pomp to be staged anywhere since the wedding of the groom's parents in another Europe forty years before. In 1951, the dynasty only had its history to call upon, but there was more than enough of that.

The chosen setting was an evocation in itself. They were married in the chapel of Les Cordeliers in Nancy. The city was the one-time capital of the dukedom of Lorraine, the tiny kingdom of medieval Lotharingia which had been fused with the Habsburg dynasty in 1738, after the marriage of the future Empress Maria Theresia to its ruler, Duke Franz Stephan. The church was in fact the family chapel of the ducal palace, and many of Otto's ancestors lay buried there. He would have preferred a wedding in Austria, but it was to be another fifteen years before – after a tedious and sometimes sordid process of negotiation – he was finally allowed to return to his homeland. Though republican Austria was notable for its absence among the throng of guests who attended, the homeland was well represented in symbols.

Regina's white lace veil had once been worn by one of the daughters of the great sovereign Maria Theresia.[14] The bride's magnificent diamond diadem was the same one – a wedding gift from the Emperor Franz Josef – which her mother-in-law had worn at her Schwarzau wedding in 1911. The stems of myrtle in the bridal bouquet had been picked from the park of Schönbrunn Palace, and the pair knelt on brocade cushions filled with Austrian soil. At the altar was that most venerated of religious symbols, the statue of the Magna Mater Austriae, the dynasty's patroness, whose resting place was the great Styrian pilgrimage church of Mariazell. The Capuchin monk who had brought it joined with no fewer than forty other priests from Austria and Hungary in the ceremony, which was conducted by the Bishop of Nancy, Monseigneur Lalier. It was a display rooted in the past, but one which suggested that all those roots had not yet withered. The honeymoon was, by contrast, low key. Its first station was at the little Basque fishing village of Lequeitio, where Otto had spent the most peaceful years of his childhood.

They now faced the main preoccupation of any freshly-married couple: the search for a home where a family could be brought up. The only preconditions were a site fairly close to the Central European homelands and a house of manageable proportions which would provide a secure and tranquil base. They started the search from France – at first in a small apartment in Paris and then to a house near Rambouillet, just outside the capital. As Otto plunged straight away into his lectures and newspaper work, it was Regina who conducted most of the search, and it was she who finally found the solution. The villa at No. 15 Hindenburgstrasse in the small Bavarian village of Pöcking certainly met the geographical requirements. Surrounded by a small park with a short winding drive, it also provided the peace and quiet required. But, as she later recalled: 'It was in a simply awful state when we took over. It had previously been split up into separate apartments and needed an enormous amount of work to convert back into a one-family house'.[15]

The great advantage for the couple was that enough money happened to be available at the time, both for the purchase and the substantial rebuilding costs. The capital came mainly from those substantial American lecture fees and a stroke of luck had augmented their value.

> At that time, the German mark was still at a fairly low rate and funds in the country could not be exported. The American film industry had amassed a great deal of money through the distribution of their films to eager post-war audiences and were very interested in getting rid of their blocked accounts. I was therefore able to buy up some of those foreign marks at a very favourable special rate against my dollars.[16]

The Kaiservilla or Villa Austria (as it soon came to be called) proved a happy and very durable selection. Both inside and out, it resembled the *grand bourgeois* home of some prosperous Bavarian businessman. Only the faces and signatures inside the silver photo frames on the grand piano in the unpretentious drawing-room and some of the oil portraits on the walls revealed a more august occupant. But they did nothing to change the homely atmosphere of the place, an ideal setting in which to rear a family. That family duly grew at regular intervals and without complications over the next ten years, though there was growing concern to begin with over the balance between the sexes. Five daughters appeared, one after the other, in the space of the first five years,[17] and the disturbing prospect had to be faced that the House of Habsburg, like the House of Orange, might turn back into the female dynasty of Maria Theresia. Then, to great relief, the first son (christened Karl after his grandfather) was born in 1961, to be followed by a brother, Paul Georg, three years later. That meant that there were now two male successors to the headship of the house and what remained of its claims. The arrival of these two boys did more than change the sleeping arrangements and the look of the dining table at the Villa Austria. It meant that Otto could now take the plunge away from any personal dynastic ambitions and exchange them for political ones.

The shift had been going on gradually in his mind for several years. It had been quickened by the exhausting argument with successive governments in Vienna as to when, and under what conditions, the republic's bar of 1919 would at last be lifted, to allow him to set foot again in his homeland. He started proceedings after the four-power occupation of Austria finally came to an end in May of 1955 and the Second Republic gained its full sovereignty. Despite the efforts of the then Chancellor, Julius Raab (a pragmatic right-winger), to relax or even abolish the anti-Habsburg laws of 1919, these were formally reaffirmed in article 10, paragraph 2 of the State Treaty.[18] The key measure of those old laws, dated 3 April 1919 and published a week later, deserves quoting in full:

> In the interests of the Republic's safety, the former wearer of the crown and all other members of the House of Habsburg-Lothringen are banned from entering the land unless they specifically renounce their membership of this House and all its associated claims of sovereignty and declare themselves loyal citizens of the Republic.

Otto's first offer, put forward on 21 February 1958 was confined to 'recognising the current laws of the Republic' and declaring his loyalty to it. This was rejected by the government in Vienna, which still strove for Renner's full ounce of Habsburg flesh by the dismantling of the family, as well as the dynasty. Three years later, after the birth of his first male heir,[19] Otto gave in and prepared another declaration which amounted to acceptance in full for his own person of the 1919 formula.

He knew there would be opposition from his mother. She, after all, had actually been crowned an Apostolic Majesty and had promised her husband on his death-bed to bring up their first-born in every way as the future Emperor. He had therefore prepared the ground by discussing with her, and other members of the family, the errors of what they called 'Chambordism'.[20] All were agreed that monarchies should not cling to old symbols just for the sake of them but had to move with the times. The question was how soon and how far. The idea of disowning the family as the price to cross the border into their homeland stuck in the throats of both his mother and his more conservative brothers.[21] But Otto nonetheless managed to persuade the matriarch that what he was doing only made sense.

> There was indeed a debate with her about it, but this was nothing compared with the painful conflict going on inside me. All right, I had said to myself, if I want to act on the European stage – and I had clearly seen that European path ahead of me since the Second World War – then I could not afford to get myself in a position of conflict as Pretender to the throne of any of those European countries which would have made it difficult for me to achieve my aims. So that is why I took the step I did, for purely practical reasons. But I must confess it wasn't easy for me, not because I harboured any illusions but because of the sheer infamy of what was being demanded. I mean, to insist that one had to

resign from one's own family, that was such a crazy idea which could only have come from the brain of some demented so and so.[22]

It did, indeed, spring from dementia in the sense that blind hatred which had festered during decades of political defeat had warped judgement. For this venom was what all along – in exile and now at home – had made Austria's left-wing fanatics so virulent compared with their comrades elsewhere in Europe. Republics had sent dynasties packing in Bourbon France, Hohenzollern Germany, Braganza Portugal and the Italy of the House of Savoy. But only in Austria had a group of fanatics emerged, dubbed the 'Habsburg Hasser', the haters of the dynasty.

Otto did possess an Austrian passport, something which could not be denied to a person born of Austrian parents at the Villa Wartholz on the Semmering Pass. But it was a bizarre, and possibly unique document, for it authorised the bearer to travel anywhere in the world, except, by specific exclusion, to his own homeland. It was this exclusion which the exiled Archduke had sought to overturn by his unqualified pledge of renunciation. On 24 May 1963, the Austrian Constitutional Court ruled in his favour but the Socialists in a coalition cabinet continued to block the issue, despite the reservations of moderate left-wingers like the Socialist Foreign Minister Bruno Kreisky, who worked away in private to bring the curtain down on this long pantomime of squabbling between Parliament, government and the law courts. Strong personal as well as ideological factors came into play here.

Bruno Kreisky had spent the war years in Stockholm, where he had married a Swedish wife, founding a family in a setting far removed from that cauldron of émigré rivalries in America. Kreisky had remained a pragmatic and moderate left-winger, despite the fact that, as a leader of the pre-war Socialist youth movement, he had been interned under the Dollfuss and Schuschnigg regimes. Above all, he had a sense of history.[23] As a four-year-old child, he had been taken by his father to watch the funeral cortège of Franz Joseph wind its way through the streets of Vienna and had seen the small figure of the new Crown Prince, almost the same age as himself, walking just behind the coffin. Kreisky's family upbringing continued to be one of respect for the Monarchy, something which was a fact not lost on that Crown Prince as a banished Pretender:

> Kreisky was a man of broad vision as well as high intelligence. One could always, sooner or later, reach an understanding with someone like that, as opposed to these blinkered little provincial politicians, of whom there were far too many about.
>
> He was one of the Czech Jewish community of Brünn, and these Brünner Jews

– who had been politically prominent since the time of the Thirty Years War – were something special: very important to the economy but also politically very enlightened.[24]

But it was not until 1 June 1966, when a right-wing government had come into power that the exclusion clause was finally expunged from the Archduke's passport so that 'Dr Otto Habsburg' was able to step on Austrian soil legally for the first time in almost half a century. His initial trip went only as far as Innsbruck to visit the grave of that pillar of the dynasty, Archduke Eugène. Frequent visits to Vienna followed, and on one of them came the symbolic face-to-face encounter with Kreisky, by now Chancellor of a Socialist majority government. This low-key greeting marked the moment when the muddle-headed little republic finally came to terms with its imperial past. The bridge had been formed by a simple handshake.

This wearisome and time-consuming wrangle over citizenship had come at a period when Otto was already at full stretch. To begin with there was the constant need to earn money to sustain the family, which was growing steadily throughout the 1950s and early 1960s. Those profitable American lecture tours continued to provide the bulk of his income but at the cost of long periods of separation from his wife and children. There were times when he had to spend two to three months away from them, sometimes twice within the space of a year. These absences threw a heavy burden on the shoulders of his wife, but she carried the load willingly and well. What could have been a troubled upbringing for the children was, for the most part, a carefree one.

She was, in her own words, the *Ruhepol* or steadying influence in the family and this reflected another harmony of contrasts between the couple. Otto was always the restless workaholic, ever on the move because – quite apart from his absolute dedication to politics – he always found it so difficult to sit still. She, on the other hand, was the high-born housewife, who never meddled in his political affairs and nurtured no ambitions for herself. The marriage thus replicated the equally harmonious relationship between Otto's parents, though as its reverse image. In that match, the Empress Zita had been the dynamic partner, often, as with those doomed restoration bids, driving the more easy-going Emperor into action. It was a role which would never have fitted the unobtrusive Regina; and, happily, she never aspired to it.

The other thing which during these early years absorbed so much of Otto's energy was the endless search for an ideological platform. As he possessed neither a private fortune nor the slightest of executive powers, he had to rely on persuasive influence, and to exert that he needed a forum.

The Pan-European Movement, whose presidency he eventually took over from its founder, Richard Coudenhove-Kalergi, while still in America, was to prove the most durable of these arenas of public persuasion. Another, and very little known one, went under the initials CEDI (Centre of European Documentation and Information).[25] He later described how this mysterious body ('very right-wing' in his words) had sprung into life:

> It was all the result of a conversation I had at the Eucharistic Congress of 1952 in Barcelona with the then Christian Democrat Foreign Minister of Spain, Alberto Martin-Artajo and Alfredo Sanchez-Bella, the President of the Spanish Cultural Institute. We agreed to start up an international movement which fixed as its primary aim to get Spain into the European Union. Under my presidency, its activities widened. For example, it played a role in supporting General de Gaulle especially during the critical period of the uprising in Algeria, which brought him back to power in 1959.[26]

However, once Spain was safely ensconced in the Strasbourg Parliament, CEDI was allowed to evaporate by the same invisible means of private consultation which had conjured it up.

There was something of the conjuror's art about the way in which Otto's next platform rose up. It was the most powerful he was ever to know, and one he was to relish. By a process both unexpected and inevitable, he was to become a full-time professional politician, and this on a stage he could only have dreamt of.

15

'Mr Europe'

It was not long after he had settled into Pöcking that the drift into politics began. It was not a question of the bear being tempted by honey. Otto needed no luring. After four years in America, where he had witnessed, if only from the wings of the stage, the drama of world affairs, the air of politics was in his lungs and he could breathe nothing else. To begin with, he again had to play the role of the eager and sometimes influential by-stander. The right-wing Catholic Christian Socialist Party of Bavaria was his natural ideological home. Its chief, the dynamic if controversial Prime Minister of Bavaria Franz Josef Strauss, was his natural patron (the fact that this butcher's son from Munich had been baptised, back in the days of empire, with the names of Otto's illustrious ancestor, seemed to make the match preordained).

As an Austrian, however, Otto could not join Strauss's party. What he could do was work closely with some of its influential members, such as Prince Konstantin and Heinrich Aigner. He linked them as closely as possible with his pan-European Union (as ever the trusty servant of his ideas) and gradually became an unofficial foreign policy adviser to Strauss. Again, the ideal forum for this was found. The CSU, like most German political parties, ran its own international conference centre – in this case a one-time royal shooting lodge in the forests of Wildbad Kreuth. To this idyllic place, run on sumptuous lines, guests were welcomed from all over the world.[1] Otto was the ideal person to run such an establishment for Strauss, and this he did in polished style in the early 1970s. But he remained an outsider, with only one foot dangling over the wall of Bavarian politics.

Then came the surprise move which was to put him with both feet across a much broader wall. As he recalled it:

> One day early in 1978, Dr Aigner, who had sat for Bavaria for many years in the non-elected European Parliament, called on me with the proposal that I should run for a seat myself at the forthcoming direct elections. I was, he said, absolutely predestined for it. My reaction was that it simply wasn't possible. I was an Austrian, technically a foreigner despite my long residence in Bavaria, and I was not prepared to give up that citizenship. To do what he suggested, however much it appealed to me, would mean I would have to become a German subject instead.

His reply was: 'Well, if I can find a way around that, will you do it?' I agreed, of course, but added that, whatever the answer was, Franz Josef Strauss would have to support it.[2]

The answer, with which Strauss heartily agreed, was to arrange for Otto dual citizenship, German as well as Austrian. Here the most arcane of connections came to his aid. Dr Otto Habsburg happened to be a member of the Académie Française (to which he had been elected on several counts) and for some reason this qualified him for German citizenship, even if he held another passport. Like his stewardship of Wildbad Kreuth, the arrangement could have been fashioned with the Archduke in mind.

There was, of course, the shadow of the Third Reich to be reckoned with. As we have seen, the best and bravest of the Austrian monarchist movement, along with thousands of other anti-Nazi suspects, had been seized by the Gestapo and had suffered or died in Hitler's prisons and concentration camps. How would the survivors and their families feel about the heir to the Habsburg claims becoming a German, even though it was by now nearly twenty-five years after the end of the war? One way of countering such resentment was to recall Otto's proven record of helping thousands of Jews during the Hitler terror, as, for example, at Bordeaux during the fall of France. This point was made by Strauss himself, when the Prime Minister rose to defend Otto's case in the Bavarian Parliament.

Another justification went back much further in history: his ancestors had, for centuries, been the titular sovereigns of the ancient Holy Roman Reich of the German Nation, of which Hitler's twentieth-century copy had been but a wicked travesty. The plain fact was that Otto had so much symbolic headgear in his cupboard that something suitable could always be pulled out for him to put on: on this occasion, the plumed hat of the Académie Française followed by the image of Charlemagne's crown.

It was, however, not only in Munich that the matter was contested. The Socialist faction of the Federal Parliament in Bonn took up the protest cry, encouraged by some of their left-wing colleagues in Vienna. Even among the Christian Socialists of Bavaria there were some rumbles of discontent at the idea of an outsider competing with them for one of the coveted Strasbourg seats. But, in the end, Otto's greatest tussle for nomination was with the calendar. Even after the dual nationality problem was settled, this newly-appointed German citizen was advised that he had to receive his papers at least twelve months before the European direct elections took place. He squeaked home. It turned out to be a year plus one day.

The Habsburg family bandwagon – with daughter Walburga and both sons to the fore – hurtled gleefully, if at times chaotically, onto the electioneering scene. Throughout his life, their father had been in the wings of politics, sometimes with influence, sometimes not. Now his children were helping him to a post which, though never powerful, was both public and official (as well as well-remunerated and even satisfactorily pension-able). The key to their campaign was the Habsburg technique of using one forum to promote another. In this case, it was the Pan European Movement (PEM) which became the platform to lift its President up to a higher stage. Munich was, in any case, its headquarters and the fourteen thousand people who, on 12 May 1979, filled the city's Olympia Hall for a pro-Otto meeting represented the greatest demonstration the movement had ever organised.

But Otto was himself the most effective architect of his victory. He turned out, possibly to his own surprise, to be a star at the political hustings. Hitherto, the lectures and speeches he had given in his life (in any one of six languages; without text; and timed to the minute to last half an hour) had been formal affairs, addressed in the main to formal audiences. He now discovered that he could adapt the tone, the content and the length to the hurly-burly of any on-the-spot canvassing opportunity which cropped up. He also, as though he were a veteran performer, fell into the knack of the electoral gimmick. At one appearance in the beer tent of a remote Bavarian village, the local brass band had been welcoming him with a thunderous cacophony of German tunes.

Suddenly as a special tribute to the visitor, it broke into the Radetsky March. This is one of the greatest of all military marches, composed by Johann Strauss the Elder to honour the Austrian general who, in 1848, had scored a rare victory for the Monarchy in the Northern Italy campaigns. The moment he heard the first cheerfully rousing sound of brass, Otto jumped up, seized the baton and 'conducted' himself. Despite the fact that, like all non-musicians, he did it in precisely the wrong manner – jerking the baton down for the beat instead of up – the bandsmen, looking stolidly ahead, got through it, to applause which shook the canvas roof. Again, old connections joined hands intertwined. The candidate in a German election of the late twentieth century had drawn on memories of the vanished Austrian Monarchy in the mid nineteenth to help his cause.[3]

Those connections surfaced again when, on 17 July 1979, Otto took his place as the member for Upper Bavaria in the first directly elected European Parliament, then of nine member states. The President of Honour was the eighty-six-year-old Louise Weiss, a veteran of bridge-building attempts between France and Germany back in the 1920s. She not only singled out Otto by name as leader of the Pan-European Movement. She also invoked the memory of his great ancestor, Charlemagne, as the ruler of the (admittedly doomed) united Europe of his day. No new member could have asked for a better introduction.

Otto von Habsburg sat in the Strasbourg Parliament for the next twenty years. He had become the 'Father of the House' long before, on 7 May 1999, he rose to make his last speech. Not surprisingly, he stayed at his seat for as long as circumstances allowed, for it had provided him with the greatest political platform of his life. It should be stressed that he never regarded it, and never treated it, as a personal springboard. For him, Strasbourg was not an arena for personal ambition but the forum for promoting those aims and ideals he had cherished long before entering the Parliament. Any year by year record of his time there would therefore be superfluous, as well as tedious. The principal thrusts were twofold and never changed.

The first prong was to help unite all the right-wing Christian Democratic members of any nationality into one group, with its own secretariat, budget and its own broadly-agreed programme. This emerged as the 'Partie Populaire Européene' or PPE, which was eventually joined by the British and Danish conservatives to form the most powerful centre-right faction of the Parliament. The variety of the other political groupings, many with internal splits, gave everyone the opportunity to form ad hoc tactical alliances to push through programmes agreed across ideological divides. Thus, though Otto never wavered in his conviction that the Christian faith was, in his words, 'the soul of Europe' (he was to leave the scene before the appearance of any Moslem state),[4] he took delight in roping in Socialists and even Communists where a common specific aim could be established.

Otto's most influential role at Strasbourg was established from 1981 onwards, after he was elected as his group's spokesman on the Political Affairs Committee of the Parliament. This was its senior committee and dealt essentially with the foreign policy of the European Union. It is important to stress that it did not itself lay down this foreign policy. Slow to form and shaky in operation at the best of times, this was decided by the Council of Foreign Ministers at their regular or emergency summits. Yet again, Otto's role within the committee on which he sat was that of the lobbyist and persuader. He and his colleagues probed the Council with questions. They put forward their own resolutions – condemning the Soviet invasion of Afghanistan, for example; supporting Britain over the Falklands War; criticising the American 'Star Wars' military space programme; or simply calling for peace in Northern Ireland.

Neither the Russian, nor the British, nor the American governments would have changed their policies as a result, while the problems of the island of Ireland remained still seemingly intractable. Indeed, in the Cold

War era, the big powers took even less notice of the Strasbourg Parliament over any key issue than they did of the United Nations General Assembly. Nor did the elected Parliament's standing among Western public opinion in these early years help its cause. It was widely regarded as an ineffectual talk-shop, with retired or failed politicians doing most of the talking, while profiting in the process from handsome salaries and pensions. Added to that came the generous perks of travel, subsistence and secretarial allowances made even more generous at the European taxpayer's expense whenever they were abused.[5] There was little that any individual member – even one like Otto, who played strictly by the rules throughout the two decades of his tenure – could do to alter that public perception. All he could, and did, do was to join the struggle to cut down abuse and waste, a campaign led by his old friend and sponsor, Heinrich Aigner, in his capacity as Chairman of the Budget Control Committee.

But if the European Parliament failed to strike many sparks of popular enthusiasm in the West, it was a very different story in Central and Eastern Europe – above all during the long years of Soviet Communist hegemony. As long as the Iron Curtain endured, the captive peoples behind it saw Strasbourg as a beacon, however dim and distant, on the horizon of a better future. This brings us to the second, and the main permanent, thrust of Otto's parliamentary career: to bring all these peoples, and especially the nations of the old Habsburg Empire, under the shelter of the same European roof. Hence the saga of the 'empty chair' which he launched and saw through to the end. As he later recalled:

> From the very beginning, my efforts in the Foreign Affairs Committee were concentrated on enlargement. It was not an easy task since at first the majority opinion of the committee was to accept the idea that the line which had been drawn across Europe at the Yalta summit of 1945 should remain the permanent division of the continent. In fact, at the outset, there were only four members of that committee who were determined to change that mentality and declare the Yalta borders unacceptable. These four were the British Conservative Adam Fergusson, the Danish Liberal Niels Haagerup, a French Gaullist Gérard Israel and, finally, myself. The battle was really joined over a proposal I had made that, whenever general European topics were being debated, there should be an empty chair reserved in Parliament to mark those nations missing from our community. There was quite an ugly struggle over the issue, of which the brunt was borne by Adam Fergusson, as rapporteur of my proposal. Thanks largely to his dynamism and determination, the motion was finally carried, if only by a narrow majority and after two years of debate.[6]

Otto would doubtless have liked a special chair with a special designation. He had to be content with something less distinctive: one of the numerous seats which anyway yawned empty, sometimes in long rows, during the Strasbourg proceedings. Yet it was a symbol of sorts. The essential victory was the disclaiming of the Yalta pact by the Parliament's senior committee.

His interest stretched to all countries which had been, or still were, under Russian domination. He had first met anti-Soviet émigré movements from the Baltic countries during his wartime years in America and had learnt to respect them 'because they were real patriots, unlike some of the other émigré spokesmen'. From the first, he continued to sponsor their cause in the European Parliament and duly became rapporteur on Baltic issues.[7] But his most significant work in that capacity was closer to his old homeland and, in particular, what remained for him the heart of that homeland, Hungary.

On 26 April 1990 the Foreign Affairs Committee appointed 'Mr Habsburg' as rapporteur on the political situation in Hungary. Two years later he was re-appointed, this time to prepare an association agreement between what was then the European Economic Community and the post-Communist Hungarian government. As a six-year-old Crown Prince, he had watched, through the windows of Budapest's royal palace, his father being crowned sovereign of the ancient Magyar kingdom. Now, more than seventy years later, he found himself guiding the republican rump of that kingdom on the first stage of its journey back into the Christian West. That was the future vision. The current reality was a long tramp through the undergrowth of the Brussels bureaucracy. The proposed association had to be approved by the Committees on Agriculture, Fisheries and Rural Development; Social Affairs; Employment and Working Environment; Economic, Monetary Affairs and Industrial Policy; Energy, Research and Technology; Environ- ment Public Health and Consumer Protection; Culture, Youth, Education and the Media; External Economic Relations; and finally, that for Transport and Tourism.

Before the agreement could be ratified by Parliament, each of these bodies had to accept Otto Habsburg's submissions of sponsorship.[8] These admitted Hungary's shortcomings such as inflation, foreign debt, concealed unem- ployment, an overcomplex electoral law and the reluctance of both the trades unions and the professional organisations to come to terms with the post-Communist era. The grave problem was also noted of the large numbers of ethnic Hungarians who, thanks to the peace treaties of the First World War, were still living as minorities in neighbouring countries. Some were 'not being treated satisfactorily' (Slovakia and Roumania, the chief culprits in Magyar eyes, were not however singled out by name). Despite all this, the submissions argued that Hungary was now set on the path of democracy and stability and therefore deserved helping along the road to

Strasbourg. Indeed, the Hungarian nation – presented as second to none in its enthusiasm for the EEC – could lead by example. The final statement concluded: 'Hungary has a good chance of continuing to play a pioneering role in the passage of Central Europe to freedom and democracy. In this task, it deserves the support of the European Community and the democratic world as a whole.'[9]

On 16 September 1992, less than two months after these papers had gone the rounds, that support was officially given, inasmuch as the European Parliament gave its consent to the association agreement. The rapporteur knew that the end of the road – Hungary's admission as a full member of the European Community – probably lay more than a decade ahead.

There is a coda to this pro-Hungary campaign. It provided yet another example of the Habsburg talent for linking their platforms together. In his 'Explanatory Statement' of 17 July 1992 to the European Parliament, Otto was at pains to stress the significance of the so-called 'Sopron Picnic', staged on the Austro-Hungarian border three years earlier, as a stage in Hungary's march towards democratisation. The organiser of this event, he pointed out, had been his own Pan-European Movement. If this linkage was typical of his technique, the way in which the affair had been conjured up was a classic example of that spontaneous improvisation by which the Habsburg family ran the movement they led. Looking back on it twenty-three years later, Otto recalled:

> I honestly do not know whose idea it was. It started this way. We had a meeting during my first visits to Hungary in the summer of 1989 at the University of Debrecen which my father had cultivated in his time. They had invited me, together with local democratic political groups, to decide how best to start a dialogue about liberalisation with the Communist regime which was still in power in Budapest. After a rousing gathering in the university, the local democratic leaders, together with some of the professors, joined me and my younger son, George, and daughter Walburga at the restaurant of the city's famous hotel, the 'Irany Bika', or Golden Bull. We were searching for a way to dramatise this extraordinary upheaval in public opinion, something which would demonstrate that frontiers of the Iron Curtain now no longer existed. Then someone came up with the idea of staging a Pan-European picnic at Sopron, along the barbed wire border. It was either George or Walburga but neither of them knows for certain, as it surfaced in the midst of a lively discussion.
>
> At all events, it was taken up by Szabó Lukács of the local Democratic Forum who started to organise it, with enthusiastic help from the people of Sopron.[10]

Otto himself did not turn up when the mass picnic was staged on 19 August 1989, many of the Pan-European members equipped with wire-cutters for their own ceremony of dismantling. He felt that his presence might give too high a political profile to what was intended to look like a spontaneous demonstration. Moreover, he could not forget that eastern Hungary had once been the graveyard of his father's restoration plans. Walburga, who was in Budapest at the time to learn the language (a task which was straining even her considerable linguistic talents), deputised very effectively for her father.

As her own account of the event made clear,[11] the picnic demonstrators were not in any way responsible for the collapse of the Iron Curtain, either here or at any other point in its hideous eight hundred mile stretch. The implosion of Soviet Communism throughout Eastern Europe was pulling the barbed wire down with it. What was left of one of those regimes in Budapest had already agreed with the Austrian and German authorities not only the day, but the precise hour, 2.30 in the afternoon of 19 August, when the border crossing at Sopron would be opened up.[12] The German government was involved because the grounds of its Embassy in Budapest were by now packed with hundreds of East Germans who had camped there on an escape route to the West. During the previous fortnight, their food and water from the Embassy had been distributed, together with small maps showing the way to Sopron. When the gates were opened, a total of 661 East Germans swarmed through to join the picnic. It was, Walburga said, 'like watching birds escaping from a cage, embracing freedom as though it were the first dawn of spring'. She and her youthful fellow Pan-Europeans had lived up to their name. They were, however, obliged to witness the welcome which Western governments initially extended to these migrants damping down dramatically, once the 'escaping birds' increased from single flocks to uncontrollable swarms which filled the sky.

By then Hungary had been virtually displaced by Croatia as the focus of Otto's concerns and activities. The disintegration of Communist Yugoslavia had been sparked by the Croat declaration of independence, a challenge which the Belgrade regime sought to repress by a massive and murderous invasion. Now, as in his father's time, Serbia had emerged as the declared foe. Otto threw everything he had into a barnstorming campaign to gain recognition for the fledgling Croatian state, which had once been the most loyal of all the crown lands of his father's empire. He spoke at meeting after meeting of Croatian pre-independence migrants in his own Bavarian power-base; visited Zagreb, the Croatian capital, while Serb troops were still in the town; and delivered speech after speech on behalf of the Croat cause at the European Parliament.

He found that, even within his own centre-right group, historic ties were initially lined up against one another. Thus some British conservative members were pro-Serb because they had once fought with, or supported, the

Mikhailovic partisans in the Second World War. The Greeks, by a longer tradition, tended also to be pro-Serb. On the other hand, the Italian members of the group were solidly in support of the Catholic Croat nation, which had been backed by the Vatican even during its wartime descent into the least salubrious of Fascist puppet states. Otto rode over all this, acting on the guiding principle, inherited from his father, that he had to keep faith with the peoples, irrespective of whatever their leaders had done. There is a film recording of one of these Strasbourg speeches where he declares, in ringing tones in the German language: 'Ja, ich bin ein Croat!' ('Yes, I am a Croat!'). Though he had never held a Croatian passport, the claim had a certain historical validity. King of Croatia was one of the titles he had inherited as a nine-year-old child in exile.

In the event, it was Germany who led the European charge of diplomatic support. The Federal Republic declared its recognition of an independent Croat state on 19 December 1991, a move followed by all the other members of the European community which acted unanimously on 15 January 1992. Meanwhile, Otto had been taking steps to widen Croatia's acceptance far beyond Europe's frontiers. In an extraordinary personal initiative – taken without the official knowledge, let alone approval, of any governmental or parliamentary body, he set off for Morocco to convert King Hassan and, through him, the Arab world, to the cause. The King, with whom he was on close terms, duly received him on the night of 15/16 April 1992. Otto recalls:

> It did not take much persuasion to get the King, who was a remarkable person and deeply interested in European affairs, to see the importance of this step.[13] As usual, he made up his mind rapidly and decided on immediate action. He then called in Filali, his Foreign Minister, and instructed him not only to issue Morocco's recognition but to approach other Arab countries to join in.[14] This meant that our talks lasted deep into the night and I remember that, when I left, there in the anteroom, was the Palestinian leader Yasser Arafat, who had been kept waiting for hours for his audience.
>
> After this I had many contacts with the Croats and actually witnessed two of the major military confrontations of the war between Serb and Croat forces: the liberation of Eastern Slavonia and of the Kraijina. In both cases, I took the opportunity to talk with the defeated Serbs and assured them they would be treated reasonably. My Serbo-Croat, which I spoke fluently as a child, was very rusty but German helped because so many of them had worked for a year or two at the Mercedes plants in Baden-Württemberg.[15]

Whatever the outcome of Otto's front-line reassurances, back in the Belgrade of Slobodan Milosevic, he had long since become Serbia's detested enemy for his tireless and effective support of the Croats. Indeed, he even received a death threat from Arkan, Serbia's notorious paramilitary killer, who was himself to be assassinated in January of 2000. In a personal letter, Arkan reminded Otto of what had happened to his great uncle, the Archduke Franz Ferdinand, in Sarajevo back in June 1914. If the great nephew stepped foot in the city today, Arkan warned, he would suffer the same fate. Otto's reaction was to visit Sarajevo as soon as he could. Nothing happened, apart from some clapping, as he walked around the streets.

16

Balance Sheet

Though the peoples once behind the Iron Curtain – and especially those which had been part of the Habsburg Monarchy – were Otto's constant concern, he spread his parliamentary wings far wider, often roaming well outside political horizons. Indeed, the complete list of his motions for resolution, oral and written questions submitted, and above all, the texts of the many speeches he delivered during his twenty-year stint at Strasbourg,[1] show a man eager to pluck at any topic where wrong needed to be righted or even an unnecessary irritant to life removed.

The motions he helped to table ranged from major issues such as human rights abuse in China and the Soviet Union, the combating of terrorism, the war in Afghanistan, conflict in the Persian Gulf, the Kashmir dispute, and East-West arms control talks, to a bewildering assortment of lesser, if also worthy, matters. Thus, with other sponsors, he is found pleading for European relief to help Third World countries stricken by famine or floods, and there are even motions concerning such mundane matters as the price fixing of books or the plea for 'a topical and urgent debate to encourage the sale of butter within the Community'. But his own dynastic backyard of Central and Eastern Europe never stayed for long out of the picture. A whole series of motions for debate concerned the treatment by Roumania of its subjects in Transylvania, which held the largest of the Magyar populations lopped off from the Hungarian motherland after the First World War. And, inevitably once the Yugoslav state fragmented in bloody conflict, there came motion after motion for urgent debates on the crisis there. Ironically, in view of what he had hoped to achieve via King Hassan, one was to request immediate action by the Parliament 'on the offensive launched against Srebenica' in which eight thousand Moslems were slaughtered. Like many other motions of concern, this was but an arrow fired into the air. The long roll of the questions, written or oral, tabled under his name also range from weighty international issues such as aid for apartheid victims to relative trivia. The latter, which figure largely under this list are remarkable for their variety. He showed interest in the situation of foreign tourist guides; in the standardisation of clothing and shoe sizes; in subsidies for fighting bulls (linked, obviously, with his pro-Spanish sympathies); in au pair visas; in the protection of veal calves, and also of cormorants and herons.[2] There was a whole series of protests about excessive hand luggage carried aboard aeroplanes, an irritant but also, in his view, a serious safety hazard. (Nothing seems to have been done on the matter despite repeated complaints from a man who virtually lived in planes.)

It was in his speeches to plenary sessions of the Parliament that the quality of the man came out. To begin with, he could deliver them, with equal fluency, in no fewer than seven languages: English, French, German, Hungarian, Italian, Spanish and Portuguese.[3] This meant that, in addition to being able to lobby the majority of his parliamentary colleagues in their own tongues, he could also switch language, wherever appropriate, during the crisis of a debate. Nor were the dead languages a closed book. In one discussion over a legal issue a colleague tried to make his point by using halting and rudimentary Latin. Otto replied in the same tongue, fluently and flawlessly. Nobody ever tried to upstage him again on linguistics.

Reading through the reams of speeches he delivered over the years, one is struck not only by their compact precision but by their outspokenness. A vivid example (if on a relatively minor affair) concerned the uproar created by a book written by one of the European Commissioners, a Danish lady named Ritt Bjerregaard. The book revealed confidential matters about the internal workings of the Commission and criticised by name several European politicians. It had enjoyed a huge *succès de scandale* when it appeared in Denmark, reportedly selling half a million copies in a week before being withdrawn in the face of a court action. What, Otto von Habsburg had demanded to know in the debate of 14 November 1995, did the Commission intend to do about it, to prevent 'any repetition of these scandalous events'? When the British Vice-President of the Commission, Sir Leon Brittan, attempted to bury the issue on the grounds that the work had been withdrawn, the member for Upper Bavaria made it quite clear that it was the author, rather than the book, he was complaining about. He went on:

> Mrs Bjerregaard has a murky past. Let us be frank. She had problems as a Minister because she spent too much money. She had problems as a party chairman for the same reason – a taste for gambling and money. Then she was sent to us because they obviously wanted to get rid of her at home. How can we be expected to accept such a Commissioner? Would it not be better to put to her that she should resign?[4]

Whether or not the lady followed this advice is not so significant as the manner in which it was delivered. Otto was certainly not vindictive by nature and there was anyway no reason to believe that the delinquent official had picked any quarrel with him. What had infuriated him was that the

Commission as a whole, and with it the European Community, and his own membership of it, had been demeaned. Still, it was very strong language and it is doubtful whether any other member of the Parliament would have had the self-confidence needed to use it.

He was equally unequivocal on other issues, great or small. A debate was held in November 1991 on 'freedom of movement for employees and transfer fees for professional footballers'. All manner of arcane legal arguments were advanced by speakers to suggest that such freedom was guaranteed as citizens' rights to all workers under article 48, paragraph 3, sub (a) of the EEC Treaty which should not be flouted. When Otto rose he left such technicalities aside and widened the entire scope of the discussion in his usual uncompromising style:

> We are touching on a real problem here, and it's not just football. Professional sport is very big business today and it operates in a legal vacuum where all sorts of things happen in an uncontrolled nineteenth-century kind of way. It is high time something was done about it. It's exactly the same in boxing, all-in wrestling and tennis. It's a really dirty scene here.
>
> When, in tennis, for example, I see children of sixteen, seventeen, eighteen, reaching the peak of their careers before the age of twenty and then being tossed on the scrap heap – burnt out – I have to say that society is responsible here and particularly the European Community which seeks to create a social order in Europe. It should lay down professional rules for professional sport to put an end to these extremes and exploitations ... because otherwise there will be a terrible scandal which will damage us all.[5]

In fact, there was nothing that the European Parliament – or anyone else for that matter – could do about teenage sporting prodigies being reared by calculating parents or sponsors like force-fed young geese expected to lay clutches of golden eggs for them. If anything, Otto Habsburg's 'really dirty scene' in the commercial exploitation of sport and its players got even dirtier as the years went by. But his appeal remained a good example of an instinctive feeling for the broad issues of moral responsibility as opposed to the narrow margins of regulations.

As we have seen, it was during his exile in America that he first declared himself to be a European (before even being an Austrian or a Hungarian); yet, as 'Mr Europe' he was always proud of his American links and ready to draw on American experience. Thus his main contribution to a debate on evolving a Community action plan for combating drugs was that the Commission should follow the approach practised in the United States, from where he had just returned. This was to shape the legal system to make drug trafficking more difficult within the consumer countries, as opposed to concentrating, as the Community seemed to be doing, on controlling drug shipments from outside. However, whenever a case arose of outright competition between American and European interests, there could be no doubt where he would plant his flag.

A prime example was the controversy in 1986 over whether Britain should equip herself with American Sikorsky helicopters or furnish her armed forces with more of the native Westland product. The debate had split the Conservative government of the day apart, with the Prime Minister, Margaret Thatcher (a devout Atlanticist as well as a Eurosceptic) going for the American product, and her deputy, Michael Heseltine (a Europhile down to the soles of his boots) holding out for the British model. Heseltine lost and walked out of the Cabinet in protest, but not before he had found some significant allies at Strasbourg. Otto Habsburg was one of the foremost and, as so often, he sought to get at the answer by widening the context:

> I would just like to point out that whereas, fifteen years ago, the Americans had 100 per cent of the civil aircraft market, the Airbus has now enabled us to regain first place. We can do the same thing in the helicopter field if the political resolve is there ... only a Europe which can stand on its own two feet can also be a friend to the United States. A Europe that was a type of American technological protectorate would be riddled with inferiority complexes and would continually challenge and criticise the Americans ... It is in our interests as Europeans that this advanced technology helicopter industry should not pass out of European hands ...[6]

That particular battle was not won, nor were many others in which he had joined. Indeed, a note of frustration runs through these twenty years. The sensation of excitement at standing on the broadest political platform of his life never died away, but it is dampened by the realisation that it is only that: a public forum for argument and declamation with the decisions being taken elsewhere, and, all too often, ignoring its pleas. This particularly applied to the armed conflicts which erupted during his final years at Strasbourg. Thus, on 13 February 1995, he uttered a rather desperate *cri de coeur* over the Russian invasion of Chechnya, by then two months old. This was not a war, he declared, but genocide, and it was 'a disgrace' that the West had been so reticent about it. Would the President of the Parliament at least 'make an immediate statement' on the matter?[7] The expression of concern was duly made, and had not the slightest effect. The Western powers were too concerned with buttressing the stability of the post-Communist regime in Moscow, however repugnant some of its measures were. Otto got a 'thank you' from the Chechnyans in the form of an honorary citizenship, but the Russian tanks rolled on.

When war broke out much closer to home, in the chaos of Yugoslavia's collapse, such concern understandably turns to anguish at what he saw as the prejudice of the outside world in favour of those ancient enemies of his house, the Serbs. 'For the nth time, we are adopting resolutions on Bosnia, or Bosnia and Croatia', he complained at one point.

> It is a sign of Western Europe's weakness and inability for so long to create order because it simply doesn't dare to speak out the plain truth. There can be no peace in this area so long as a balance is not established and so long as the arms embargo against Croatia and Bosnia is maintained. After all, the Serbs have no reason at all to make peace. They can import all the arms they want. The Croats and Bosnians cannot. The Serbs ... will remain the stronger side so long as this situation continues.[8]

Two months later, he returned to the charge, declaring the way in which the European Union had behaved over the form Yugoslavia was nothing short of 'scandalous'. One problem, he said, was that it lacked any proper intelligence organisation of its own and so was unable to make independent judgements. 'We need an analysis centre, not only for Parliament, but for all the institutions of our Union ... only with such a centre can we operate the kind of future-oriented diplomacy that is so absolutely essential to us.'[9]

He had many other concerns about the internal running of the Parliament to which he was so proud to belong. The most basic was the fact that the vast majority of its members treated attendance as a four-day-a-week job. They would depart, using their lavishly calculated travel allowances, on Thursdays and not show themselves again until some time the following Monday. The result was that, at the end of the working week, the building resembled an empty shell. This infuriated Otto, not merely because (unlike the average member) he was a workaholic (and proud of it) but because of a genuine feeling that he and his colleagues had a moral duty to do the job for which they were so well paid. Accordingly he persuaded a few kindred spirits to form the so-called 'Friday Club'. This was an ad hoc gathering of members of any party or political persuasion, who only had one thing in common: willingness to do the five-day week for which they had been appointed. The turn-out, Otto recalls, ranged from a mere handful to as many as forty or fifty. The main parliamentary machine – for which the mere existence of these sessions was a tacit rebuke – took its revenge by trying to trivialise them. The result was yet more frustration for the prime mover of the idea. There came this outburst from Otto at their meeting of 3 April 1995:

> Mr President, I want to protest yet again, *as I do at every session* about the increasingly second-class status of Friday ... We must finally make it clear that

Friday is a working day like any other. That is why we have been sent here –
not that we can go home on Thursday! [10]

He returned to the charge when a small band of only eleven members took
their seats at 9.00 a.m. on Friday, 27 October 1995, with a Mrs Pery in the
chair:

Madame President, I should like to draw your attention to the way our agendas
are currently organised. Today's agenda is practically empty ... I regard this as
a mean of starving Strasbourg of sustenance, of destroying our Friday part-sessions
and dealing with interesting items elsewhere.[11]

As usual, his protests 'were noted'. As usual, nothing came of them. What
must have set his teeth even more on edge at this particular gathering was
that part of the time for their meagre agenda was taken up by arguing over
which parliamentary group was most to blame for the rows of empty seats
stretching around the chamber. As every group had voted in principle for
the Friday meetings, it was an invidious exercise. Otto at least had the
satisfaction of noting that his own PPE group produced the best showing
on that morning – three out of the eleven present.

He always made the most of the situation by using these sessions for
informal discussions on any subject to which any gathering on any particular
Friday seemed tailored. These ranged from modest subjects such as fishing
rights to major issues such as the introduction of a European passport, of
which Otto was a leading champion. Because of the contrasts among those
present, these discussions were often stimulating as well as useful and served
to widen his already broad range of personal contacts. But the blocking
tactics used against him only increased the uneasy feeling that the European
Union had become something of a torpid giant which would resist any
challenge to its settled and privileged ways.

The crux of this was how to tackle the Commission's gross mismanagement of its own affairs. Otto had served on Budgetary Control Committees
from 1982 down to 1994 and had seen and heard more than enough to raise
his eyebrows. But the evidence of outright wrongdoing was largely anecdotal
until disgusted 'whistle-blowers', who had served in the Commission,
emerged to give first-hand accounts of fraud, nepotism and corruption in
its ranks. The scandals could no longer be swept under the carpet. The
outcome, on 14 January 1999, was the European Parliament's historic
(by its lethargic standards) motion of censure and vote of no confidence
in the Commission as a whole, coupled with the rejection of its budget.
The legislature had finally assaulted the hitherto impregnable executive.

The bureaucracy reacted with a mixture of denial, obfuscation and, above
all, delay. Under that last heading came the appointment of a body mystically

entitled 'The Wise Men', to examine the allegations. [12] Their two reports, delivered in March and September of 1999, postponed matters until the autumn but their final verdict was damning. The Commission had no choice but to resign *en bloc*. Several commissioners whose departments, like they themselves, had escaped criticism, were to be reappointed. Others, identified and culpable, disappeared forever from the Brussels scene they had disgraced. The most notable of those shown shrilly protesting to the door was the French Commissioner Edith Cresson, whose catalogue of alleged misdeeds was long and varied.

By the time this long-running crisis was resolved, the Father of the House had at last become an ex-MEP. Moreover, his elder son Karl, the next head of the dynasty, had also lost the mandate gained in 1995 as the member for Salzburg of the right-wing Austrian People's Party. There could have been no greater contrast than the manner of their departure, unless it was the contrast between the two men themselves. Otto left to the farewell plaudits of his Bavarian Christian Socialist colleagues and the warm praise of the President of the Parliament he had served so long and so well. His son simply melted away, rejected by his own party which had intrigued against him and with a cloud of malicious though unproven financial irregularities buzzing over his head.

Otto's departure was voluntary, prompted by the rarest of setbacks in a long life blessed with seemingly inexhaustible vitality. In the winter of 1998 he went down with a severe attack of pneumonia which, with its attendant complications, kept him out of action for weeks. After his recovery, he decided to give up that action altogether, at least as regards his cherished Strasbourg stage. If he could no longer take his health for granted, then he could no longer guarantee properly to serve the party which had selected him and the electorate who had voted for him. Resignation, after his current mandate expired in June 1999, was the obvious honourable outcome. He went ahead with it despite every indication from his Bavarian Christian Socialists that they were prepared to put him up for a record fifth successive mandate. That would have kept him at Strasbourg until the summer of 2004, when he would be in his ninety-third year.

That calculation cannot have escaped Otto; though he never admitted it publicly, he was, for the first time in his life, bending the knee to Father Time. This comes out in some of the private letters he wrote to friends about his decision. Thus, in one of them,[13] written when his batteries were obviously fully charged again, he was full of plans to help, as a private citizen, in various European election campaigns. But, as for the decision not to stand again himself, 'this, after all, is relatively logical for somebody aged eighty-six'.

The same note is struck by the penultimate speech he delivered to Parliament on 16 April 1999. Significantly, the debate was on ageism, or the plight of senior citizens in the twenty-first century. His contribution began on a very personal note which drew general applause:

> Mr President, I am speaking here from a unique position as the only member of this House who was born before the First World War and who, moreover, was elected to this Parliament long after reaching pensionable age. Since then, I have enjoyed twenty wonderful years of life and work here.

The rest of his speech was a long plea for the 'rights of the elderly' to be respected. They should be allowed, even encouraged, to work on beyond retirement age. This need not prevent young people from getting work and, in any case, 'there is sometimes an unduly strong inclination to indulge in a certain glorification of youth'. Many pensioners, on the other hand, 'bring the benefits of a lifetime of experience to their work. The elderly must have freedom of choice, which would actually help towards controlling the shifting demographic pyramid of today. The priority must be "to safeguard their freedom".' He sat down to a further round of applause which, unsurprisingly, came from all parts of the chamber.

By the time he made this speech, Otto was confronting, head on, a shattering tremor which had struck the political pyramid of his own family. There had been advance rumblings of trouble ahead. The Habsburgs had launched an intensified right-wing offensive of their own after the collapse of the Berlin Wall. This had opened up gleams of hope for the dynasty as well as a new era of freedom for the millions who had lived for more than forty years under Communist rule. That Sopron Iron Curtain picnic, staged by their faithful foot-soldiers in the Pan-European Union, was the highlight of the campaign. What the family did not, at first, perceive was the political and ideological backlash this had produced, above all in the Austrian left-wing camp.

There was a feeling, not confined to the hard core of the 'Habsburg Haters', that the former ruling family were getting altogether too big for their polished boots and ought to be taken down a peg or two before they started trampling over hallowed republican territory.[14] This feeling deepened when, five years after that Iron Curtain coup, Karl joined his father at the Strasbourg Parliament. The spectacle of the son and grandson of the last Austrian Emperor standing side by side (and they rarely separated) at the Assembly sessions seemed to personify the perceived monarchist menace. But Otto himself was invulnerable. His prestige was second to none among the 616 members of the House; his personal integrity could not be challenged on any score. That made Karl Habsburg the only target to be shot at and, unhappily, he seemed at times to invite the arrows.

The fact he was always more vulnerable than his famous father had as much to do with his generation as with his make-up. Even had television existed in Otto's youth, his mother would have seen to it that he avoided, like the plague, its chat shows and news quizzes, which Karl agreed to host in Vienna for months on end. Furthermore, had that matriarch, and the rigid standards of her caste, still been flourishing when Karl decided he wanted to marry Fräulein Francesca von Thyssen, it is unlikely that the wedding would ever have taken place. That the young woman's family had unfortunate wartime associations in Nazi Germany (or that she herself had once led a distinctively racy life) would not have counted so much as the fact that the next head of the Habsburg clan had chosen for his bride the daughter of a mere Hungarian Baron, and a recently ennobled one at that. The fact that the bride could be expected to be extremely rich or even that the couple had fallen genuinely in love (as was the case) would not weigh, in the old scales of balance, half as heavily as that glaring discrepancy of blood.

The 1990s were, however, not the 1960s in the prevailing social standards of any family, even that of a once-great dynasty. Otto accepted the situation with good grace, though there is little doubt that the wedding did Karl (and indeed his father) no good in those monarchist circles still rooted with all ten toes in the past.[15] Baron von Thyssen's own life-style and the degrading and ruinously expensive litigation over the disposal of his vast fortune went on to perturb far wider audiences than that of the ultra-loyalists. These were social setbacks which Karl and his wife, who were happily raising their family, had done nothing to provoke and could do little to counter. But, politically, Karl and his friends helped to dig his own grave.

In the winter of 1998, it was already clear that his Austrian People's Party (where he had made many enemies, mainly by refusing in Strasbourg to obey its diktats issued from Vienna) was determined to bury him. By Christmas, they had been handed the shovel: an outcry over alleged mismanagement of money raised for the relief charity World Vision. Sums totalling some £30,000 were said to have been diverted, first into the coffers of the Pan-European Union and then, in reduced volume, into the campaigning fund of Karl himself.

There was no evidence that he had been personally involved in the affair and he denied even having any knowledge of it, a denial which was never rebutted. The sums involved were also in dispute. Nonetheless, the picture was not a pretty one. The two main figures involved, a married couple, were both long-standing friends and colleagues of Karl, and their positions at the time automatically exposed them to suspicion. Wolfgang Krones was the General Secretary of the Austrian Pan-European Union while his wife

Tina had been head of the World Vision movement. Both were held in police custody for questioning, though in the end no trial resulted. The legal outcome and indeed the true share of guilt were irrelevant for Karl's cause. Thanks to an intensive media campaign, inspired both by his ideological opponents on the left and the rivals in his own right-wing camp, he was besmirched by mere association in the affair. The withdrawal of his European mandate soon became a foregone conclusion.

The way in which he ended his parliamentary career in Strasbourg was, however, as debatable as his choice of friends had been in Vienna. When it came to the great showdown vote over corruption, the orders from his People's Party leadership were to support the Commission whose misdeeds they appeared to favour. Instead, alone among his group, he joined the extreme right-wing members of the Austrian Freedom Party who, like his father's Christian Socialists, were voting solidly for rejection. To have simply abstained would have made Karl's point in full. To team up on any issue with the movement led by Austria's neo-Nazi Jorg Haider was to make an invidious exit from the political scene. It only served to fuel further damaging rumours that, in order to cling on at all costs to his parliamentary seat, he was angling in desperation for a Freedom Party mandate.

How desperate that search had become was demonstrated in the 1999 national elections to the new European Parliament where the campaigning started in Austria in the spring. There was a newcomer to the otherwise familiar party lists. The so-called 'Christian Social Alliance' was presented as an independent idealistic and strongly Catholic alternative to a degenerate People's Party. Its organiser and spokesman was a forty-one-year-old aristocrat, Count Carl Albert Waldstein, whose wealth (from family estates restituted by the Czechs) far exceeded his political nous. It soon became clear that the prime objective of his venture was the more prosaic matter of getting Karl Habsburg, as the party's prime candidate, returned to Brussels on a new ticket.

To achieve this, the Alliance would have needed to secure some 160,000 votes or 4.5 per cent of the electorate. However, when the urns were emptied on 13 June 1999, only 42,438 Austrians had declared for the young Archduke, representing barely 1.5 per cent of the 5,850,000 voters. His father and mother, whose public support had never wavered throughout the 'World Vision' affair (whatever was said within the family conclaves), had turned out to help the campaign. That was a matter of loyalty and honour. But Otto's political antennae were too finely tuned for him not to have realised that he was backing a hopeless outsider in this particular race. Soon afterwards, the Alliance duly abandoned all hope of becoming a regular feature on the landscape and simply melted away into the mists from which it had emerged. As a political force inside his own country, Karl vanished with it. As far ahead as the eye could see, there would be no place for him on the parliamentary benches of either Strasbourg or Vienna, and there was nowhere else for him to look.

For the father, this was a heavy personal blow. He would have rather that the blow had landed on his own head. It had turned the intended climax of his long career – handing over the parliamentary baton to his eldest son – into something of a sour disappointment. Was it a subconscious exercise by way of compensation for both of them that, as he left his beloved Strasbourg, it was with the thought that the Parliament and indeed the Union were now no longer enough by themselves to fill his vision for the future?

17

Royal Endgame

If the departure from Strasbourg had been a sober, even sombre, affair for the Habsburg family, they soon had something truly joyous to look forward to. May 2001 marked Otto and Regina's golden wedding anniversary and lengthy planning had gone on as to how the event should be marked. It was, first and foremost, a personal affair: a thanksgiving for the fifty years of harmony and happiness of a union which had by then produced twenty grandchildren by the two sons and five daughters of the marriage. But, inevitably, it was also a projection of the dynasty itself: of the role it still sought to play in European affairs and the merit of the traditional Christian values it cherished even for today's world. All this came out strongly in the first and most significant of the three celebrations held, that staged on 10 May at Nancy, capital of the Dukes of Lorraine, where, exactly half a century before, the couple had been married.

'Staged' is not too strong a word, for every detail seemed to emphasise the family's relevance as well as its obvious resonance. The latter was reflected in the guest list. This embraced not merely the Catholic royalty of Europe and those regular standard-bearers of monarchism such as the Tyrolean riflemen, but also included the Mayor of Nancy, André Rossinot, who, indeed, was more host than guest. After the public mass in the chapel of Les Cordeliers, where the wedding had taken place in 1951, it was he who gave the official reception on behalf of the municipality. It was here that the Habsburgs' steady contribution to Europe's well-being, even when in exile, was underlined.

The town hall was decorated to symbolise this continuity. The floral decorations were all in red and white (once the dynasty's colours, but those still flown by the Austrian Republic). From the balcony trailed the fifteen-starred banner of the European Union, whose Parliament Otto had served for twenty years. He had fought successively 'against the Nazi barbarism and the Stalinist red order' long before entering that Parliament, the Mayor pointed out in a speech of welcome. After entering Strasbourg, Otto von Habsburg had been 'deeply involved in the construction of a dynamic Europe stretching beyond his own family and historic roots'. It was a tribute to someone who had never lost touch with the present, however long and deep the shadow of the past. The large crowd assembled in Stanislav Square beneath the Town Hall balcony seemed happy to cheer both. Otto confined himself to stressing that he remained 'a faithful son of Lorraine'.[1]

Other celebrations followed in Austria and Hungary, the rump states of what had once been the sprawling halves of the Habsburg Monarchy. The happiest of these was at Mariazell, the Styrian pilgrimage church which held such sacred meaning for the dynasty, and that dynasty was very much in evidence throughout the carefully orchestrated proceedings. The streets of the little town were crammed with uniforms of the vanished Monarchy: Hungarian hussars with their cloaks and high boots, sailors in the garb of the old Imperial Navy and, inevitably, once again, those colourful stage props of nostalgia, the riflemen of Tyrol. In all, traditional uniforms from seven lands of the old empire were on show: Bohemia, Moravia, Galicia, Friaul and South Tyrol, as well as Austria and Hungary. Had it not been for the police motorcycles of the Austrian Republic, Mariazell might have been caught in a time warp that day. The procession even included a vintage Gräf and Stift automobile that had once belonged to Austria's last Emperor, while, at the mass inside the vast twin-spired church, the couple leant on the long prayer-cushion which that monarch had used. However, those police motor-cycles were not the only contribution which the post-war Austrian Republic had made. Bofors guns from a Vienna artillery regiment fired a twenty-one gun salute; a brass band from Wels played the old imperial anthem; and even the republic itself was officially represented, albeit at the modest level of Dr Riess-Passer, a female Vice-Chancellor.[2] It was not a good day for the Austrian left wing that had for so long succeeded in keeping Otto out of his homeland.

In Hungary, the celebrations also brought past and present together, though here the link was more poignant. The setting chosen was the old imperial castle of Gödöllö, on the outskirts of the capital. For many years, it had been the favourite retreat within the Monarchy of the Empress Elisabeth, Franz Josef's restless and melancholy wife. But that was not the memory that stirred in Otto on 24 May 2001, when he and his wife received the long queue of well-wishers at the head of the ceremonial staircase,[3] restored, like the rest of the building, to its original beauty. The last time he had been within these walls was more than eighty years before, as a scared toddler Crown Prince, awaiting rescue from a Budapest aflame with revolution. It was to the relative security of his beleaguered family in Vienna he had been whisked away then and, in a strictly non-political speech, it was only of family that he spoke now. It was, he told the guests, the very foundation of life, and the resurgence of a nation could only happen with the flourishing of family values. This was low-key talk from the man who,

when he first revisited post-Communist Budapest, had heard shouts of
'Éljén a Király!' ('Long live the King!') from the crowds outside the cathedral
where he had once watched his father being crowned. Nonetheless, a circle
in his life had now been happily closed, and, with it, the last such public
hurrah the family could count upon.

Otto von Habsburg was not the only exiled royal to be welcomed inside
one of his old palaces again during that summer. In Belgrade, the Yugoslav
Crown Prince Alexander, born as a refugee in war-time London,[4] was
actually handed back in July 2001 both of the former royal palaces of
the capital as permanent residences for himself and his family.[5] Though
restored to his people and his palaces, Prince Alexander was still a long
way, if ever, from being restored to his throne. It was an issue he prudently
side-stepped.

Closer along that path was the most spectacular royal returnee of that
summer, Crown Prince Simeon of Bulgaria. He had founded his own party,
the 'National Movement for Simeon II', which swept to power in the
Bulgarian general elections, inducing him, after long deliberation, to take
over as Prime Minister. That was gamble enough. Even more hazardous
was the precondition he had set before proposing any referendum on the
return of the monarchy itself. This was nothing less than to restore, within
the strange time-frame of eight hundred days, the economy of his near-
bankrupt homeland, a country paralysed by mismanagement and corruption
on a scale which outstripped even Balkan norms. Otto had known Simeon
well for over thirty years and greatly admired him for maintaining his
Bulgarian identity throughout his career as a New York banker. He had
been urging his friend into political activity long before the summer of
2001, but had to admit that the course Simeon finally decided on was a
very high-risk strategy.

Asked about the significance for his own family of Simeon's return, Otto
replied simply: 'No, it will not affect our position though we are happy
that, if Bulgaria goes the right way, maybe other nations will follow.'[6] As
he knew better than anyone, it was all a question of scale. The vast historic
palaces of Vienna and Budapest had been the seats of long-established
emperors, not recently imported German kinglets, like the Saxe-Coburg-
Gothas of Sofia. There was little prospect of them being filled again by
anything but the tourists who flocked to see Austria-Hungary's past. Vienna
had never been a coronation city, and was now settled in its republican
guise. Karl, the only feasible candidate to lead a conservative-monarchist
movement within the framework of that republic, had disappeared with
embarrassing finality from its political scene.

Budapest was historically very much a Habsburg coronation capital. Otto had, however, realised from the first years of the post-war era that the most his family could realistically hope for was not the kingship but the presidency of the country – and that only on the basis of a popular vote. There were times, during his early visits to post-Communist Hungary, when he was indeed treated almost as though he were a head of state in waiting.[7] But though the welcome always remained, the euphoric mood ebbed, in true Magyar fashion. By the time the republic set its sights on membership of the European Union, it had no wish to compromise its candidacy by controversial political experiments. By then, in any case, Otto was growing too old for any such long-term ventures.

So what, looking back on it all, was the balance sheet of his life as he stepped down from public office? Those twenty years at Strasbourg had been the coping-stone of his political career, and he was happy to see some of the initiatives he had taken there – such as the introduction of a common passport – come to fruition.[8] Yet he remained apprehensive that the European Union might be marching too fast too soon towards fusion on a broader front:

> I personally have always opposed any idea of writing a European constitution. I felt this was premature and would remain so for a long time to come. I was therefore close to de Gaulle's thinking, and to his call for *l'Europe des patries* ... The fatherlands are indeed the first national power base. As things progress, they will certainly find other forms (and federation is, after all, only a confederation which works). But from the very beginning, on the basis of my own experience, Europe to me was something which must grow like a tree and not simply be put there like an American skyscraper!
>
> Furthermore, in my work with Robert Schuman soon after the war on his vision for Europe, I had learnt that the greatest error you could make was to take the second step before the first. When we were discussing his initial idea for a common coal and steel community I begged him to aim at something more ambitious from the start. I still thank the Lord that he did not listen to me![9]

Otto's ideas for the expansion of the European Union follow the same step-by-step path. Quite apart from the absorption of the smaller Central and East European states already queuing up for membership, the structure will, in his view, never be complete without the inclusion of Russia.[10] But this expansion beyond the Urals would only come with a precondition. For him, Russia is the last of those colonial empires which history has discarded. If it sought membership it would first have to give freedom to peoples such as the Chechnyans whom it has held captive.

Indeed, towards the end of his time at Strasbourg he floated the idea that, even if the Union ultimately extended all the way from the Atlantic to the Pacific, it should still look and go further. His very last speech to that Parliament, delivered on 7 May 1999, contained this passage:

> The fact is that we can no longer afford to operate just within the European Union: we must also take Europe out into a world that is, whether we like it or not, becoming increasingly globalised and in which partnerships in the Far East are also of vital importance to us ... The Asians are, after all, our natural partners.[11]

The speech ended with a plea for the projection of European culture throughout the world. It was a strange swan song from which some notes, such as the old primacies of economic and political union, seemed to have been supplanted.

It came as no surprise that, even before his farewell speech was made, the Pan-European Movement, that venerable and trusty instrument of his mission, had adapted itself to the new course. In what can only be described as carefully synchronised empathy, it had changed its name to 'Pan-European International', as though the question of union had already been dealt with by higher powers. Moreover, it had broadened its scope and altered its main thrust in precisely the manner Otto had prescribed. By changing itself into a 'Non-Governmental Organisation', it had entered that jungle of NGOs which swirls around the entire globe with its tangle of charitable, medical, scientific, economic and religious strands. This gave it not merely a recognisable, if fuzzy, status, but the opportunity to spread its own contacts wider by attendance at international gatherings. Politics now being taboo, it henceforth concentrated on the projection of Europe's cultural values – precisely the formula Otto proposed.[12] Moreover, it took its message to Asia, the area he had singled out for European partnerships. Flying the cultural banner, it sought to open a branch in Tokyo,[13] and – for some unfathomable reason – was even cultivated by the Cuban population of Florida.

The supreme advantage conferred by this transformation was the promise of longevity. European culture could be promoted long after European unity had been achieved. However, the move away from politics carried with it a move away from the Habsburg label. Otto continued to serve as International President of the organisation as he had done for nearly thirty years (surely a record in such matters). But it will be recalled that when Pan-Europe staged its most transparently political display (the Iron Curtain mass picnic) he prudently stayed away so as to avoid any dynastic label being stuck on the occasion.

His very capable daughter Walburga, who had long been the executive driving force behind the movement, displayed similar prudence. She only officially assumed the role and title of its general secretary after her marriage to a Swedish aristocrat (of Scottish descent), Count Douglas. This avoided the name Walburga von Habsburg immediately following that of Otto von Habsburg on the movement's promotional literature.[14] The family, though timeless, had moved with the times.

It is ironic to reflect that Otto's leadership of the Pan-European Movement is unlikely to figure largely, if at all, in the history books. These will principally be concerned with the name of its founder and first President, Count Richard Coudenhove-Kalergi, for his was the vision and his was the initiative, launched when that vision seemed wildly utopian. In a way, this is symbolic of Otto's whole life. He never possessed a private fortune, so there was no hospital wing or charity or university foundation raised by his money, to carry his name. Nor did he ever hold ministerial office, so there is no international treaty which bears his signature.

The one great public battle he fought on the world scene was his struggle to save his Austrian homeland from Hitler's embrace. Yet this was doomed almost from the start by the wobbly self-belief of his countrymen and the equally wobbly will of the European powers in the face of the Nazi threat. The battle he fought during the ensuing war – to save Hungary, the other half of the old Monarchy, from the Red Army – was fought in private and in secret from Washington. It also ended in failure, largely due to a similar lack of unity and resolution among the Western democracies. He lived to see the implosion of the Soviet Danubian empire which that Red Army had carved out. Yet he could play no part in the key measures which helped bring about that collapse, such as the creation of the NATO alliance, which put a military ring-fence around Russian expansion, or the nuclear arms race which did so much to bankrupt the Soviet economy.

The picture was similar with his writings. Though he produced more than a dozen books, he did not seek to be, and never laid claim to be, a significant figure in twentieth-century literature. There were three respectable biographies, all of them about the greatest of his own Habsburg ancestors, and thus serving as another projection of the dynasty. Apart from these, his books repeated, and often reproduced, the themes and texts of the thousands of newspaper articles, lectures, interviews and media appearances he had made over the years. The message was the same, and hammered home time and time again: the importance of a strong, free and self-reliant Europe (he tended to omit the word democratic);[15] the key roles of Christianity and traditional values as the basis for Western society; and, of course, until the Communist tyranny started to self-destruct, the need to combat it with all and any means at hand and to repair the split it had driven right down the European continent.

He took the same message – occasionally tailoring it for his interlocutory

– to all the heads of state and government he had known and talked with in over half a century of post-war travels. When asked to provide some sort of a list of these from memory, he gave up after naming more than sixty. These ranged from Chiang-Kai Chek, Chou en Lai, Pandit Nehru, Abdul Nasser and the Emperor Hirohito in the earlier years, down to Ronald Reagan, Mikhail Gorbachev, Boris Yeltsin and Helmuth Kohl in more recent times. As a Foreign Affairs group spokesman in Strasbourg, he met all the leaders of the fifteen member states as a matter of course, but in many cases his contacts stretched back much further. Those in Paris had begun with the pre-war Prime Minister and staunch enemy of Hitler, Edouard Herriot, while in Ankara he had met with all of Turkey's Prime Ministers since the war. Yet no declaration was ever issued; no minutes were ever taken (at least on his side); and barely a single photograph exists to record all these private encounters.[16] There is thus, in all this, no single lunge of his which transformed the shape of events. His political endeavour was rather one long series of pleas and nudges for the conservative and European cause. The end effect is impossible to write off but equally impossible to quantify.

To his delight and surprise (and rather to his wife's dismay) retirement from public politics brought no enforced tranquillity into his private life. The candidate countries for EU membership with whom he had special links, such as Hungary, Poland and the Czech Republic, all sought his advice and help on how to ensure and speed up their admission. On top of this came invitations to party gatherings at home, international congresses abroad, and the still lively demand for media interviews. As a result, much of his life continued to be spent in aeroplanes. Regina, who had been looking forward to a quieter and more domestic final phase to their marriage, accepted the situation philosophically as she had always done. She knew that the adrenalin simply had to go on flowing in her husband's blood stream – if he were to survive at all, let alone feel fulfilled.

In 1972, when a newly-elected member of the European Parliament, he was interviewed about his aims and ambitions. Asked what political job he would most like to hold, he replied 'Foreign Minister'. The nearest he came to that was as the foreign affairs spokesman for his party group at Strasbourg. Asked what he most desired from life, he gave the unusual answer: 'To be actively engaged even in old age'. That request was to be granted in full.

Notes

Notes to Chapter 1: A Shaky Heritage

1. He was right. Even as late as 1912, there were only 1275 motor-cars registered in Vienna, while the two provinces of Bukowina and Dalmatia had less than a hundred between them.

2. Here he would have been thinking of Italy as by far the weakest among the five major states of the old European order, with Germany, Britain and France as the three strongest.

3. Robert Musil, *The Man without Qualities*, i, pp. 32–33.

4. Thomas Masaryk, the Czech nationalist leader, who eventually became President of the Czechoslovak Republic.

5. Only foreign affairs, the military and financial policy were reserved as imperial concerns to be thrashed out jointly in Vienna, with acrimonious reviews every ten years.

6. Quoted in the *Neue Freie Presse*, 1 January 1900.

7. In 1875, he persuaded nineteen fellow students at the traditionalist Imperial Academy of Arts to walk out *en bloc* and form their own Modernist group.

8. According to the census of 1910, the last to be taken of the Monarchy, less than ten million of this Western half were German-speakers, compared with a combined total of some 18,500,000 of the others.

9. Its latest reincarnation was in the play 'The Blue Room', produced in 1999, almost a century after it had been written.

10. Johann Strauss, who had died in the summer of 1899, was entered in chronological order and without further ado. A separate notice was, however, given to the death of a lesser but equally popular composer, Karl Millöcker, who had left it to the very last hours of New Year's Eve to join the 'Waltz King', as though he were running to catch up with the cortége. It was noted that, as Franz von Suppé had died five years before, all of Vienna's three light music composers had now vanished. The new century, it seemed, was no longer for operetta, which had been such a part of the old escapism.

11. On 10 September 1898, his beautiful but restlessly neurotic wife, the Empress Elisabeth, was stabbed to death on the shores of Lake Geneva – by a deranged Italian anarchist.

12. He had only reluctantly agreed, in March 1908, that the pageant should take place, setting a frantic task for the organisers.

13. By the time he was speaking the six European powers were already ranged

against each other in two groups of three: Italy had joined Germany and Austria to form the Triple Alliance; France, Russia and England were linked together in the so-called Triple Entente.

14. A seventy-two hour notice of the decision had been distributed to the major European capitals but the King's copy had been late in arriving. Even those powers advised at the last minute were not invited to any consultation.

15. It is possible that the Emperor was not yet fully in the picture. The annexation was only approved by his Cabinet on 19 August.

16. Ironically, he had an even greater urge to polish his social image, having been born as a lowly member of the Mongolian Kalmuck tribe.

Notes to Chapter 2: The Perfect Match

1. As the elder son of the Heir Apparent (later George V), the Duke was in direct line to succeed. Quite what the dynasty had escaped was shown by the horrifying speculation that he could have been Jack the Ripper himself, the never-discovered murderer of London prostitutes in the 1880s.

2. The marriage produced only one child, a daughter, christened Elisabeth after the Empress.

3. The agreement of Hungary's leaders to the pact was especially important. Morganatic marriage was not forbidden by ancient Magyar law so, theoretically, Sophie could be accepted as Queen of Hungary while never becoming Empress of the Dual Monarchy.

4. It had been previously owned down the years by the Lobkowitz family, then by the Medicis, a trio of German dukes, the King of Bavaria and lastly, the Grand Duke of Tuscany. Based on this castle had also been the 'duchy of Reichstadt', the short-lived 'state' created by Napoleon for his ill-fated son.

5. The Emperor had created her Princess of Hohenberg, an ancient Habsburg title, as a wedding gift. Eight years later he had raised her to the rank of duchess, partly as a result of her husband's ceaseless pressure, but mainly perhaps as a reward for her exemplary behaviour and character.

6. Duke Robert's first wife, Maria Pia of Bourbon-Naples, had died in childbirth in 1882. She had born him twelve children in thirteen years, three of whom perished soon after birth, doubtless as a result of the blood relationship between the parents. The Duke's twelve children by his second wife, of whom Zita was the fifth, all lived into middle or extreme old age.

7. The most that were alive at the same time.

8. 'Nicht geschossen ist auch gefehlt', a motto she often came out with in her many talks with the author.

9. The Emperor was the godfather. But, as he was absent in Budapest, it was the infant's uncle, Franz Ferdinand, who stood in for him.

10. *Neue Freie Presse*, 20 November 1912.

Notes to Chapter 3: Collapse: A Child's Eye View

1. Memorandum to author, 4 August 1999, which is the source for all other direct quotes in this chapter.
2. Had the crowd known it, the mere fact that they were marching side by side was due to an unexpectedly brusque decision by the new Emperor. When told that, according to protocol, he must walk alone behind the coffin, followed by the Archdukes and then, behind them, his wife and heir, he told his courtiers 'It is I who decide on protocol', and rearranged the cortège accordingly.
3. Technically, the ceremony could have been held within six months. But the Monarchy was in the middle of a war and vital economic laws needed promulgating in Budapest, which Karl could only do after he had taken the coronation oath.
4. A Coburg by birth, he had been elected as the new King of Bulgaria after the country had been thrown into a pantomime limbo by the flight of the previous monarch, Alexander of Battenburg, also a minor German princeling. In 1908, Ferdinand outraged his fellow monarchs by proclaiming himself Tsar of his tiny kingdom.
5. Adelhaid in 1914, followed by Robert (1915), Felix (1916) and Karl Ludwig (1918).
6. Austria had entered the war as the partner of Germany, with whom she had been militarily allied since 1879. After months of fence-sitting, Bulgaria and Turkey were persuaded to join the Central Powers in 1915.
7. One of its attractions for the children was the small lake in the park, where boat trips could be made in summertime. Meanwhile, audiences and sometimes Crown Council meetings were being held inside.
8. Known as Bratislava to the Slovaks, and Poszony, their ancient seat of kings, to the Hungarians.
9. He had tried in vain in 1917 to dissuade the German High Command from infiltrating Lenin back from his Swiss exile into Russia to plunge the country into unpredictable anarchy.
10. The émigrés had shrewdly raised a 'Czech Legion' to fight for the Allied cause in Russia, thus converting the émigré movement into a miniature military partner.
11. Notably in the so-called 'Sixtus Affair' of March 1917 in which Karl, through the intermediary of his French brother-in-law, had tried to negotiate a separate peace move with the Western powers.
12. With typical effrontery he had first intended to seek protection in Austria, but Karl intercepted his royal escape train and sent it firmly on to Germany.
13. Having sworn to maintain the integrity of the lands of St Stephen's crown, Karl felt unable to extend his decree to Hungary.
14. Károlyi, who had given proof of his liberal convictions before the war by distributing nearly all of his vast estates among the peasantry, underestimated

the genie he was letting out of the bottle. On 31 October 1918, he became Prime Minister of what was still technically a royalist government. A fortnight later, he became President of Hungary's first 'People's Republic'. Three months after that, the Communists briefly seized power.

15. And for ever after until her death in 1973, after fifty-five years uninterrupted service in exile.

16. How the Prince managed to be on leave at this critical juncture in the Monarchy's military plight is something of a mystery.

17. They learned later that Red Guards had come looking for them in Gödöllö a few hours after their flight.

18. The Hungarian troops involved were actually obeying an order from the ex-colonel Bela Linder, made Minister of War in Count Károlyi's ramshackle new regime. He achieved a certain ludicrous fame by declaring, on taking office, 'I never want to see another soldier'.

19. At first, their commander claimed that there was no point in his soldiers staying because the Emperor was no longer present to be protected. When Karl showed himself, there was a shrug and the unit departed just the same.

20. It is worth noting, in view of what has been written about the lack of identity among the inhabitants of 'Cisleithania', that they chose now to call themselves German Austrians – a term which was later banned by the victorious Allies, who forced them into being plain Austrians.

21. The only practical help Karl got at the time was from Vienna's police chief Johannes Schober, who sent a small protective detachment out to the palace. He was later to become a right-wing Chancellor of the Republic.

22. The original German word – *Scheissfamilie* – was even stronger.

Notes to Chapter 4: Exile at Home: Eckartsau

1. When asked, during the revolution in Budapest, what should be done about the crown, one of its keepers, Count Ambrózy, had been told by Károlyi: 'Take it to a bank or put it in your pocket. I don't care.'

2. The loyal Vienna police president, Dr Schober, had risked his political neck by sending a detachment of ten policemen, armed with carbines and revolvers, to guard them.

3. It was established that the 1918–19 outbreak, the worst of the century, claimed at least twenty million lives, more than all the victims of the Great War itself.

4. Renner's smooth transition to republicanism was only the first of many acts of political pliability in his career. He was later to support Hitler's take-over of the republic and then the Soviet take-over which supplanted the Nazi regime – all to save his skin and enhance his prospects.

5. The messenger was Zita's brother, Prince Sixtus, who had been lobbying in Paris and then in London on the Emperor's behalf.

6. The first two officers to arrive at Eckartsau had been Colonel Sir Thomas Cunninghame, head of the British Military Mission in Vienna, and Colonel

Summerhayes of the Royal Army Medical Corps, who was introduced and left in temporary charge.

7. Eckartsau had formerly been one of the Archduke's many hunting lodges whose herd contributed to the tally of 3000 stag which fell to his rifle before he fell himself to the assassin's revolver.

8. London had decided to play safe in its final designation of an envoy. To have the royal family looked after by any member of the British Military Mission in Vienna was deemed unworkable in view of the fact that this was now the capital of a republic. The British commander in the Allied Army of the Orient was accordingly instructed to nominate an officer and Strutt was the immediate choice.

9. The Empress had deliberately struck it off the palace menu, soon after the accession, as a wartime austerity measure.

10. Memorandum of 4 August 1999. (The complaint against the British government presumably referred to its failure to provide financial support for the Emperor during his final exile in Madeira.)

11. With a total misreading of the powers King George possessed, Karl had appealed to him to send an Anglo-French force to the Danube Basin to contain the upsurge of Bolshevism there and to promote the creation of a Danubian federation under the leadership of the Habsburg dynasty. Not surprisingly, there had been no reply.

12. Renner's threefold demand for abdication made a nonsense of later assertions that the Emperor had already renounced his claims with the November Manifesto.

13. They were from a detachment of the Honourably Artillery Company on duty at the pass.

Notes to Chapter 5: Swiss Dramas

1. The Archduke was dominated by his formidable wife, Isabella. She forever smarted under the disappointment of not marrying off her daughter, Maria Christina, to the ill-fated Archduke Franz Ferdinand and thus – until Sarajevo – making her an Empress-in-waiting. St Stephen's crown now seemed the best consolation prize for the family.

2. And not only Germany. Briand knew that the Italian government was planning to marry the half-witted son of Archduke Josef to Princess Jolanda of Italy and thus establish a dynastic foothold in Budapest.

3. Sixtus's fertile imagination had even suggested a method of travel which would not need a passport. This was to cross into Austria by clambering up the pathless mountains of the Lower Engardine. Strutt tried it out but found it was hard going for him, an experienced climber, and out of the question, therefore, for the delicate Emperor.

4. The Emperor's brother and close ally, Archduke Max, had expressed similar fears when he had first learned of the plan at the end of February.

5. Count Teleki had gone on ahead from Szombathely, promising to 'prepare the ground'. In fact, he had prepared nothing, and later claimed that he never reached Budapest in time because his car had broken down (or, even more improbably, had 'got lost').

6. A full description of the encounter was dictated by Karl to his wife immediately after his return. It was published in Berlin in 1925 under the title *Aus Kaiser Karls Nachlass* for limited private distribution.

7. Especially Czechoslovakia and Yugoslavia, two artificial creations set up under the peace treaties by carving up the cadaver of the Habsburg Monarchy.

8. One alternate plan which Horthy had suggested was for Karl to march his tiny loyalist army westward and replant the double-headed eagle in republican Vienna; a hare-brained idea indeed but one which created the illusion there was something to talk about.

9. Formally, all three (England, France and Italy) were opposed to any restoration bid. Indeed, they had just reaffirmed their declaration of 1 February 1920 which had warned against the threat to European stability of any attempt to put a Habsburg back on the throne.

10. After the embarrassing failure of the Easter restoration bid, the Swiss authorities had begun by pressing Karl to seek another country for asylum. But the Habsburg crown – even without its sceptre – proved too heavy to deposit in a hurry. England and Sweden refused outright; Holland was evasive; and Spain could not make up its mind. Eventually Karl was allowed to take a one year lease of the pleasant little castle of Hertenstein near Luzern.

11. For a full description of the disastrous 'October Bid' and the royal couple's subsequent fate, see Gordon Brook-Shepherd, *The Last Habsburg*, pp. 276–314. These chapters were based on the Empress Zita's own account and diaries, as given to the author.

12. The reason for the hurry was that an extra battalion of troops had been sent to western Hungary while the plebiscite over the future of the Sopron area was being conducted. As its commander, Major Ostenburg, was a friend and political ally of Lehár's, this represented reinforcement for the loyalist cause. But Horthy had now ordered it to return to Budapest by 23 October.

13. See Public Records Office, C20162/180/21 and C21686/180/21. These telegrams were based on the Paris Peace Conference resolution of 3 April 1921 (after the abortive Easter bid) and reflected pressure from the 'Successor States' – above all Czechoslovakia – to safeguard their territories which had been carved out of the old Habsburg Empire.

14. The officers of this Budapest garrison regiment had originally declared for the King, a sign of how finely-balanced the issue was. In his first telegrams on the crisis (PRO, C20177/180/21 and C20178/180/21, for example), Hohler had reported the Regent to be nervous and uncertain of himself.

15. Already on 24 October, when Karl seemed to be facing defeat, the French Prime Minister, as he had always warned, withdrew his supporting hand from his secret protégé. M. Briand was, in fact, Chairman of the Paris Ambassadors'

Conference, which had been debating the crisis for the past five days, and he now sent a telegram to Budapest to secure the King's 'removal from Hungary'.

16. By an odd coincidence, it was a Maitland who had commanded the *Bellerophon* to which the French Emperor surrendered in 1815.

17. Not until seventy years later was Otto – now a respected European political figure, though no longer the Pretender – able to see for himself at Buda-Örs a reconstruction of his father's fateful skirmish there.

18. *Documents on British Foreign Policy*, xxii, no. 569.

19. They had been allowed to take a few hours 'exeat' to see their mother in the Paracelsus nunnery, but had to be back in Wartegg that same day.

Notes to Chapter 6: 'Your Majesty'

1. Its first recorded owner was Charles the Bold of Burgundy, who carried it with him as a talisman into battle. It passed to the Medicis in Florence and then to the house of Lorraine, who brought it into the Habsburg treasury when the Empress Maria Theresia married Duke Robert in 1736.

2. Steiner had first entered the service of the Habsburgs before the war, when the Archduke Franz Ferdinand had employed him in the administration of the vast Este estates he had inherited.

3. Zita's brother, Prince Xavier of Bourbon Parma, finally ran Steiner to earth in Wiesbaden. He assured the Prince that the jewels were now safely deposited in a Frankfurt bank and promised to hand them over the following morning. He decamped with his family overnight – leaving no forwarding address.

4. The whole episode is recounted in *DBFP*, xxii, nos 528, 540 and 595.

5. What the troubled girl did not know was that, on 13 February, Karl had been driven to approaching the Entente powers, via his administrator in Vienna, Baron Schager, with a plea for funds. After consulting with the 'Successor States', the Paris Conference sent a polite reply to Madeira acknowledging the difficulty but demanding a detailed statement of all the Emperor's assets before a sum could be agreed. It was a lawyer's paradise for delay – as had doubtless been the intention.

6. Translated from the German original of a letter which is reproduced in Karl Werkmann, *Der Tote auf Madeira* (Munich, 1923).

7. This, and all the quotes which follow about Madeira are from two memoranda to the author, 4 August 1999 and 15 February 2000.

8. As with other Hungarian names, the Christian name has been put first, though its proper place is after the family name.

9. Translated from *Die Presse*, 2 April 1921.

10. Translated from the *Arbeiter Zeitung* of 2 April 1921.

11. A period of fourteen days of mourning, during which no entertainment of any sort was allowed, was indeed being observed in Hungary while in Budapest all the shops were closed and draped in black on the day of the funeral.

12. The story is told in PRO, FO 371, file 7623.

13. Though the palace had been left unoccupied, its owner, Count Torregrossa, declared he wanted it back and obliged the royal family to spend the winter in the nearby resort of San Sebastian. At this, the municipality of Lequeitio set up a special fund-raising committee to buy the building and present it to Zita rent-free for as long as she needed it. The place was razed to the ground in the bitter fighting of the Spanish Civil War.

14. The accounts which follow come largely from Otto von Habsburg's memorandum to the author of 4 August 1999 and an earlier letter of 30 August 1990.

15. Both having vied with the Emperor Karl for the crown of Hungary.

16. A decision later reversed by Otto von Habsburg as head of the family as part of a general attempt to bury the past.

17. Letter from Otto von Habsburg to the author, 4 August 1999.

18. The name by which she was always known. She was born Princess Victoria Eugénie, daughter of the widowed Princess Beatrice of Battenburg, the youngest sister of King Edward VII.

19. The household now comprised Count Henry Degenfeld, who had joined them in Lequeitio and who was to serve for many years as Otto's right-hand man; Baron Gudenus and his wife; Countess Mensdorff; and the Benedictine priest, Father Weber. There was also a secretary for correspondence, a governess, a chauffeur and several Austrian or Hungarian servants. The funds to pay for this came mainly from the Hungarian crown estate at Ráckeve, helped by voluntary contributions from some of the leading families of the old Monarchy.

Notes to Chapter 7: The Conundrum of the Crown

1. From a long memorandum to the author, 8 October 1999.

2. Looking back years later, Otto von Habsburg became convinced that the victory was far from inevitable. A coalition of the Conservatives, the Centre Party, the Social Democrats and the dissident Nazis under Gregor Strasser could have thwarted Hitler; so would an electoral system not based on proportional representation. All such calculations were, in the event, superfluous.

3. They had been incorporated, since the famous Compromise of 1867, into the Hungarian half of the Dual Monarchy.

4. By an irony, the man who fired the fatal shots, Otto Planetta, had once served in the same regiment of the Tyrolean Rifles of which his victim had become a much-decorated officer during the Great War.

5. The story of these Italian moves is set out in HA, cassette no. 24, file nos 814 and 536.

6. One of the family's favourite titles for incognito travels. They had, after all, over a hundred to choose from.

7. The exchange of letters is in the Royal Archives, GV PS 36107, reproduced by gracious permission of Her Majesty the Queen.

8. Memorandum from Otto von Habsburg to the author, 10 August 1999.

9. Otto von Habsburg in conversation with the author, Pöcking, 18 September 1992.

10. The royal family treasured this and other similar deeds which they took with them on every stage of their exile.

11. Four months later, on 8 April 1932, Mayor Kaltenhauser presented himself with his council at Hams Castle 'to appear as peasants before His Majesty'.

12. Memorandum from Otto von Habsburg to the author, 25 July 2000.

13. Memorandum from Otto von Habsburg to the author, 25 July 2000.

14. Until the July 1934 upheaval, he had been serving in the government as Minister of Education.

15. As an army captain, Gömbös had thrown together that ragged emergency force which had driven the royalist troops from the outskirts of Budapest in October 1921, thus saving Horthy's skin. Later, he led the movement of the 'Free Electors', campaigning for an open vote on the kingship.

16. The pretext for the 'unofficial' visit was to give a lecture on political economy. Interestingly, it was the German Industrial Society of Prague which had invited him.

17. The social and cultural ties from the former common empire had never vanished. The Czechs still penetrated every layer of Vienna's society, from tradesmen and domestic servants at the bottom to senior civil servants at the top.

18. As *mutatis mutandis*, was Austria for Czechoslovakia. Beneš had observed, significantly, to his visitor that the Anschluss was a Czech problem as well as an Austrian one.

19. Dollfuss had shown what publicity could achieve against Hitler in January 1934, when he threatened the German government that, unless their subversive activities in Austria ceased 'with immediate effect', he would bring the matter before the League of Nations. Berlin reacted by denying that there was any conflict between the two countries and Dollfuss made sure that his démarche and the German response were published throughout the world press.

Notes to Chapter 8: Meltdown in Vienna

1. And nearly its destruction in the brief but bloody street war of February 1934, when the forces of the Socialist Schutzbund (later banned and driven underground) did battle with government troops.

2. So had Schuschnigg's much smaller Tyrolean force, which he now, with deep regret, was obliged to disband. Its name, 'The Storm Bands of the Eastern March', revealed the innate Germanism of its leader. The 'Ostmark' had been the border province of Charlemagne's Frankish empire in the ninth century. It was soon to be the name by which Hitler would rechristen Austria.

3. Starhemberg delivered a glum report on conversations about a possible restoration he had held with a variety of public figures in London. All were

opposed to it, using the familiar Foreign Office mantra of 'preserving stability'. Memorandum of Otto von Habsburg to the author, 16 January 2001.

4. HA, cassette 25, file no. 375.

5. All pleas for the Emperor's body to be interred in the Habsburg vaults had run into the sands of bureaucracy and politics. At the time of writing, his remains still lie in the little church above Funchal where he was buried in 1922. One of several impediments to a move is said to be Madeira's reluctance to part with this rare mark of a place in history.

6. HA, cassette 25, file no. 375.

7. On 10 October 1935, Italy's action was condemned, almost unanimously, by a plenary session of the League of Nations. Austria teamed up with Hungary and Albania to cast the only dissenting votes.

8. Pfügl's report is in a memorandum of Otto von Habsburg to the author, 8 October 1999.

9. The hapless Dr Kurt Rieth, the German Minister to Austria at the time, had compromised himself and his government by trying to negotiate a safe-conduct for the rebels. He was summarily recalled to Berlin.

10. The Austrian Chancellor had become even more withdrawn after the tragedy of his wife's death in a car crash in 1935.

11. Hitler had sought his nomination as a Special Ambassador directly responsible to himself. This was technically not possible as Austria, a minor power, had nothing but Legations in Vienna. However, Papen soon achieved informal recognition.

12. Then, as now, almost opposite that of the British mission.

13. The main conduits were the monarchist leader Baron Wiesner, of the Foreign Office, and the head of the Chancellor's Press Office, Edmund Weber, who functioned as a courier rather than an adviser.

14. His treason trial in post-war Vienna, which the author was able to attend, symbolised the guilt, or otherwise, of the Austrian people in the Nazi period. Fittingly, the answer was ambivalent. The accused was acquitted, but denied compensation for his time under arrest.

15. A situation finalised three months later by the creation of the so-called 'Berlin-Rome Axis'.

16. The original of this Papen memorandum to Hitler is given in Schuschnigg's *Im Kampf gegen Hitler* (Vienna, 1969), p. 192.

17. From memorandum from Otto von Habsburg to the author, 25 July 2000.

18. The account which follows of the contacts between the Pretender and the Chancellor is based on Otto von Habsburg's memorandum to the author of 20 July 2000, expanded in conversation at Pöcking on 18 November 2000. There is also unique documentary evidence in the family archives.

19. FA, cassette no. 33, file 805.

20. Otto von Habsburg later commented wryly to the author (letter of 25 July 2000) that, at the time, he was convinced that any nation which fell victim to Hitler's aggression would only be eventually re-established if it had

defended itself – a belief which, in Austria's case, he admitted had turned out wrong.

21. Otto von Habsburg's memorandum to the author, 25 July 2000.

22. The exchange is recorded in Documents on German Foreign Policy, series D, i, no. 215.

Notes to Chapter 9: Fatal Encounter

1. The record of the meeting, which survived the war in Nazi archives, was drawn up by one Colonel Hossbach, who was the rapporteur of the conference. All the commanders of Hitler's armed forces, including Marshal Göring, were in attendance.

2. Both reports quoted in HA, cassette 30, file 173. (Lengthy review of the situation drawn up personally by the Pretender in Hams Castle, dated 6 March 1938.)

3. In the end, he never made it. Josef Bürckel, Hitler's former Gauleiter in the Saarland, formally took charge in Vienna in the Führer's name six weeks after the Anschluss.

4. By testimonies both at the War Trials in Nuremberg and the Schmidt treason trial in Vienna.

5. The messenger Seyss chose was a certain Dr Kajetan Muhlmann: by profession an art critic, by allegiances a moderate Nazi, and by nature an incurable political busybody. He reached Berchtesgaden at 7.00 a.m. in the morning of the great day and poured out his story to Hitler's aides, including the Foreign Minister, Ribbentrop.

6. The fullest account was the one he gave verbally himself after regaining Austrian soil and was reproduced in both his *Requiem in Rot-Weiss-Rot* and *Im Kampf gegen Hitler* (Vienna, 1969). The fact that he was quite open about his own inadequacies speaks for its accuracy. The general drift was anyway confirmed by the testimony of several defendants at Nuremberg.

7. Hitler had just completed a wide-ranging purge of the conservative top echelons in both the military command and the Foreign Service, replacing them with radicals or, as in Keitel's case, totally subservient figures.

8. Given by the 'messenger boy', Dr Mühlmann, in the Schmidt treason trial.

9. Thus the doughty General Zehner was allowed to continue as War Minister, though his Chief of Staff, General Jansa (who had devised a strategy whereby the Austrian army could hold up a full-scale German invasion for a week) was to be pensioned off. Similarly, though Schuschnigg was to be allowed to keep his Press Chief, Eduard Ludwig, he had to take on board a notorious crypto-Nazi, Dr Wilhelm Wolf.

10. An attempt by the French to deliver a strongly-worded Anglo-French joint protest in Berlin over the Berchtesgaden affair came to nothing when Anthony Eden chose this moment to resign as Foreign Secretary as a gesture against appeasement in general.

Notes to Chapter 10: Takeover by Telephone

1. Memorandum from Otto von Habsburg to the author, 25 July 2000.
2. Set out in HA, cassette 32, file no. 172.
3. HA, cassette 30, file 173.
4. The signed original of the final draft of the letter and Schuschnigg's response are both in HA, cassette 30, file 173.
5. In an exchange of letters between Schuschnigg and the author in February 1962, preceded by meetings in Salzburg and New York in September 1960.
6. This, despite his pledge at Einsiedln twelve months before to resolve it in the year ahead.
7. HA, cassette 32, file no. 172.
8. HA, cassette 30, file no. 173.
9. The Berlin propaganda machine was alarmed by this implicitly anti-Nazi display and urged the press authorities in Vienna to play it down. To avoid provoking Hitler prematurely, they obliged.
10. After Berchtesgaden, contacts had been stepped up between Vienna's conservative Mayor Richard Schmitz and Friedrich Hillegeist, head of the still illegal 'Free Trades Unions'. On 7 March, the leaders of all the banned left-wing movements had agreed, with virtual unanimity, to back Schuschnigg.
11. Kurt von Schuschnigg, *Im Kampf gegen Hitler* (Vienna, 1969), pp. 292 et seq.
12. The word he used here was *Volk* which also had a strong racial connotation.
13. Text reproduced in *Schmidt Trial Protocols*, pp. 576–77.
14. In the event, Britain and France delivered separate notes to Berlin on the evening of 11 March (not a joint action, as France had wanted). They protested 'most emphatically against the use of coercion backed by force against an independent state', but, beyond vague warnings of possible trouble ahead, left it at that.
15. Suicide in his prison cell at Nuremberg in 1946 while on 'death row' awaiting execution for war crimes.
16. His complete testimony on this in *International Military Tribunal*, ix, pp. 333 et. seq.
17. He was one of the candidates sounded out by President Miklas to take over from Schuschnigg. The General had replied that he was 'only a soldier'. Dr Skubl, Vienna's loyal security chief, had likewise declared his was 'merely a policeman'. The third person approached, the former right-wing Chancellor, Dr Otto Ender, responded with disarming frankness that he had had enough of politics.
18. The Archduke's account of these events is taken partly from memoranda and talks in August 1990, when the author was preparing a German-language television programme on his life, and partly from discussion in Pöcking on 18 November 2000.
19. The Royal Belgium Flying Club, of which all his brothers had become members, would have provided the machine.
20. As the author once gently pointed out to this wonderful royal matriarch, this

dictum ignores the fact that the hunter can often shoot and miss, or even worse, merely wound his prey.

21. He went on seeking that basis right to the end. His last contact with a free Austria was a telephone call to the East Tyrol between 1 and 2 a.m. on the morning of 13 March. He was hoping to build a last minute 'Alpine Fortress' of resistance which he was prepared to join. Memorandum of Otto von Habsburg, 30 August 1990.
22. Otto von Habsburg to the author, Pöcking, 18 November 2000.

Notes to Chapter 11: Homecoming

1. All schools had been closed for the day and several thousand Hitler Youth children had been assembled in the square.
2. Austrian engineers had drawn up plans to flood the Inn Valley as a first-line of defence. Now, at all the crossings, Austrian customs officials obligingly helped to dismantle the border posts (sometimes doing it ahead of the advancing troops.)
3. Göring, who was acting as head of government in the Führer's absence, gave this improbable explanation to the lamentably impressionable British envoy, Sir Nevile Henderson.
4. Göring's account of these events of 12 March is given in his Nuremberg testimony, IMT ix, pp. 505 et seq., and by testimony in *Schmidt Trial Protocols*, p. 201.
5. It may be noted in passing that the city preserved its fervent loyalty until the last gasp of the Führer and his regime. At the end of April 1945, with Vienna already fallen to the Red Army and the final collapse of the Reich only days away, Colonel-General Rendulic, Hitler's last-ditch commander in Ostmark, received sixty-five brand new Tiger and Panther tanks which had just rolled off the Linz production lines.
6. Seyss-Inquart had been promised an unspecified role for the future and for the next six months, vainly struggled to have himself nominated as the Ostmark's cultural minister. Hitler ultimately appointed him Nazi Commissioner for the Netherlands and it was for his activities there that he was tried and executed as a war criminal at Nuremberg.
7. Known in Austria as 'Adabeis', short of 'Auch dabeis', or 'Also theres'.
8. Figure given in *Red-White-Red: Justice for Austria* (Vienna, 1946), part 1.
9. The author was, during the immediate post-war period, a General Staff officer with the British High Commission in Vienna and thus able to witness events at first hand with full access to Allied intelligence findings.
10. All those named survived. Though Wiesner, broken in health, died soon after the war, the others were able to resume their official or political careers, Figl becoming the first Chancellor of the new republic.
11. He gives a precise diary of events in *Im Kampf gegen Hitler*, pp. 377–78.
12. Testimony in *Schmidt Trial Protocols*, p. 220.

13. Some thirty Austrian Army officers regarded as politically suspect ended up during the war, like their Chancellor, in concentration camps. However, of the Austrian officers absorbed into the Wehrmacht, more than 200 rose to the rank of general, while Austrian soldiers collected no fewer than 326 highest decorations, the Knight's Cross – more than forty for service in the Waffen SS.
14. Loose file in HA.
15. Carried in the Vienna *Tagblatt* of 3 April 1938.
16. This topped even the 99.8 per cent vote of approval for the Führer's foreign policy registered two years earlier, after his successful reoccupation of the Rhineland.

Notes to Chapter 12: New Horizons

1. Text in HA, cassette no. 21, file 361.
2. Bauer had died in Paris in July 1938.
3. Pope Gregory XIII inaugurated it in 1573 to commemorate the great naval victory of Lepanto two years earlier over the Ottoman navy. The ships of the 'Holy League' which made up the Christian fleet were commanded by Don John of Austria.
4. Letter from Otto von Habsburg to the author, 26 February 2001.
5. One of the first Catholic resistance movements, started up by a Karl Roman Scholz, a twenty-six-year-old priest from the abbey of Klosterneuburg in the Vienna hills, was soon penetrated by a Nazi agent. The Gestapo swooped on it, and two other associated groups, in July of 1940. Scholz was one of eleven among the 127 accused to receive the death penalty. The sentences were not carried out until the summer of 1944. As he was brought to the guillotine in Vienna's Central Prison, Scholz cried out: 'For Christ and Austria!'
6. He had been paralysed from the waist down by poliomyelitis since 1921 and was to die in office on 12 March 1945, just before the final Allied victory against Hitler was secured.
7. Otto von Habsburg in a talk with the author at Pöcking, 18 September 1992.
8. Memorandum from Otto von Habsburg to the author, 24 January 2001.
9. Otto von Habsburg described his last days in Paris in a letter to the author of 23 April 2001.
10. From memorandum by Otto von Habsburg to the author, 24 January 2001.
11. De Sousa Mendes had to wait a long time for recognition. Not until 1994 was a bust erected to his memory by the Bordeaux town authorities, who, like the rest of France, had to be dragged into recognition of their war record. The diplomat, who had died penniless in a Franciscan poorhouse in Lisbon in 1954, was not formally rehabilitated (of treason charges) by his own government until 1988. See José-Alain Fralon, *Le juste de Bordeaux* (Paris, 1998).
12. And still is, sixty years later, with its house specialities of *Foie gras de canard* and *Pigeonnau en bécasse.*
13. Otto von Habsburg recalled, in a letter dated 23 April 2001, how he talked to

nearly all of them, as well as Admiral Darlan, who as commander of the French fleet was a key figure in this tug-of-war.

14. His arrest had been the work of a junior member of the new government, the rabidly anti-Jewish Raphael Alibert. He was later rearrested, to be murdered by Pétain's militia in 1944.

15. The original is in HA, cassette no. 29, file no. 642.

16. The frontier incidents were first related to the author in a talk with Otto von Habsburg on 30 June 1990, and further described in a memorandum of 24 January 2001.

17. The Pétain administration had pledged to hand over to the Germans all persons on the Gestapo's wanted list. Otto von Habsburg's name was near the top.

18. From Otto von Habsburg's memorandum to the author, 24 January 2001.

19. Karl Ludwig and Rudolph had already volunteered for service as officer-cadets in the free Polish Army. Otto followed suit, with the proviso that, if need be, he could be released from duty to discharge urgent political tasks. In fact, he was never called up.

Notes to Chapter 13: Across the Water

1. There were eventually four of them at work together. Felix had been with Otto from the start. The two younger brothers, Karl Ludwig and Rudolf, had come back from Canada to join them once they had completed their studies at the Laval University in Quebec. The Empress had moved there (into very spartan quarters) in October 1940, once she heard that two professors from Louvain were now on the teaching staff.

2. HA, New York Trunk no. 2, file 222, letter of 26 March 1943.

3. From letter from Otto von Habsburg to the author, 23 April 2001.

4. Also included, but only for a time, was Ferdinand Czernin, son of the self-seeking Foreign Minister who had intrigued against Otto's father in the later stages of the war and had been dismissed by what the Emperor regarded as outright betrayal. The son was after revenge and was a corrosive influence in the committee, which eventually parted company from him.

5. A German translation of the letter is provided by Feigl, op. cit. p. 101. Though the English original can only be an authentic document from the Roosevelt archives, it is not identified by any source or reference number.

6. Cordell Hull for the United States; Anthony Eden for Great Britain; and Vyacheslav Molotov for the Soviet Union.

7. The full exchange is given in Eden's memoirs, *The Reckoning*, pp. 289–90 (official protocol of meeting of 16 December).

8. Eric Feigl, *Protokoll eines politischen Lebens* (Vienna, 1987), p. 106, is the worst offender in this *canard*.

9. In the event, the Austrians were to grab the carrot and dodge the stick.

10. Crack Austrian alpine divisions, raised in the Tyrol, were still playing a prominent role in the terrible siege of Leningrad, which was to cost more than a

million Russian lives. Three of the twenty German Army divisions wiped out in Stalingrad at the beginning of 1943 had been raised on Austrian soil and consisted 80 per cent of *Ostmärker*.

11. Minute of Prime Minister to Foreign Secretary, given on p. 810 of appendix C of Winston Churchill, *The Second World War*, volume iv.

12. Set out in a British Foreign Office paper of 11 July 1943 on 'The Future of Austria', which was accepted by the State Department in Washington.

13. It was, in fact, in March of 1943. Saldanha had brought a message for Otto von Habsburg on behalf of Kállay and the Hungarian legitimist leader, Count Sigray, raising the possibility of Hungary joining a conservative Danubian Federation after the war, perhaps under some form of Habsburg patronage. The message was passed to the White House. See C. A. McCartney, *The Habsburg Empire* (London, 1968), p. 143.

14. Memorandum from Otto von Habsburg to the author, 1 December 2000.

15. Conversation with the author at Pöcking, 18 November 2000. It should be noted that, by now, the Regent only had himself to think of. The dead of his beloved son, István, in a mysterious air crash on the Eastern front in August of 1942 had put an end to his father's dream of a 'Horthy dynasty'. The Regent's other son, Miklós, was a lightweight.

16. Text in Macartney, *The Habsburg Empire*, p. 185.

17. This unfortunate, self-defeating formula had been produced by Roosevelt, without previous consultation with Churchill, at their conference in Casablanca in January of 1943.

18. In fact, the issue never arose, for the end of the story saw Hungary being simply flattened first by the Wehrmacht and then by the Red Army.

19. Churchill, *The Second World War*, v, pp. 72 et seq.

20. Otto von Habsburg also (letter to the author of 1 December 2000) had had lunch with Churchill and Eden together. He described the 'visible deep discrepancy' between them on the Danubian question. When Churchill was present, Eden followed his line on a post-war Central European federation. As soon as 'the old gentleman' left the room, Eden returned to his hostile line.

21. After the capture of the large Italian air base of Foggia at the end of September, Allied aircraft came within range of targets in Central Europe.

22. Diaries of Lord Moran, entry for 21 August 1944.

23. The absorption of the Slovene fringe of Carinthia – with as much of the rest of that southern province as he could swallow – into his own Yugoslav state. This ambition nearly led to a head-on clash with British troops in the spring of 1945.

24. Now General Lakatos. Kállay had been forced to resign in March of that year at the insistence of the Germans, who were mounting their military takeover.

25. Otto von Habsburg in conversation with the author, Pöcking, 18 November 2000.

26. Desultory new plans for the Istrian landing were drawn up by Wilson in

November, with a target date of February 1945. By then, Budapest was already in the Red Army's hands.

27. It was not until the end of October that he was able to make the crossing. The transatlantic air-links were booked solid for weeks ahead and it was only after a personal appeal to his good friend at the White House, the President's secretary, Miss Grace Tully, that he was given a priority seat on a Clipper. Like so many of the Archduke's supporters, Miss Tully was an ardent Catholic.

28. A theme first mentioned to the author in discussions at Pöcking on 18 September 1992 and developed on numerous occasions since.

Notes to Chapter 14: Dropping Anchor

1. Horthy was taken prisoner to Bavaria and replaced by the odious Nazi puppet Ferencz Szálasi, who was, however, sworn in only as Minister-Regent.

2. The initials of the German title of the 'Provisional Austrian National Committee'.

3. Later to become Sir Frank Roberts and post-war British Ambassador to Belgrade, NATO, Moscow and Bonn.

4. His base was Innsbruck's Hotel Kreith, owned by the Andreatta family, who had been his supporters since pre-war times.

5. Ernst Fischer, Franz Honner, Johann Koplenig and Friedl Fürnberg.

6. Comrades Honner and Fischer respectively. Renner, ever the pragmatist, had secured Russian assent to the appointment of two moderate Socialists as State Secretaries under both Ministers. Theirs was, however, essentially a watching brief.

7. Otto von Habsburg in a day-long discussion with the author, Pöcking, 19 September 1992.

8. Including the author, who was by then installed with the British High Commission in Schönbrunn Palace and occupied, among other duties, as secretary of the top-secret Joint Intelligence Committee. This august body, with a wealth of Allied source material at its disposal, had forecast anything up to twenty-five seats for the Communists.

9. Franz Olah, the Austrian Trade Union leader, had been a key figure in this resistance. A less laudable factor had been the solid anti-Communist vote of Austria's ex-Nazis. Though some 670,000 had been barred from the polls, around a million of their families and friends were eligible to vote.

10. Evidently, another prominent Habsburg sympathiser had been the Security Direction (i.e. police chief) of Tyrol, Dr Winkler, for he was immediately replaced.

11. The position was to be reversed when, in 1951, Leopold's son Baudoin was crowned King of the Belgians.

12. Letter from Otto von Habsburg to the author, 1 December 2000.

13. Letter from Otto von Habsburg to the author, 1 November,, 2000.

14. The famous Pragmatic Sanction had been exacted in 1713 specifically to alter

the ancient Salic Law of male succession and enable Maria Theresia, the only child of the Emperor Karl VI, to mount the throne.

15. Archduchess Regina to the author, Pöcking, 18 November 2000.

16. From Otto von Habsburg's letter to the author, 24 January 2001.

17. Andrea in 1953; Monika and Michaela (both in 1954); Gabriela in 1956; and Walburga in 1958.

18. This was due to combined pressure from the Austrian Socialists and pan-Germans, supported in the background by the Soviet Union, one of the occupying powers.

19. He had calculated – rightly as it turned out – that the ban would not be extended to any of his children.

20. A reference to his Bourbon uncle, the Comte de Chambord, who had rejected Republic overtures to reassume the crown unless his own family flag of the three lilies, and not the French tricoleur, would fly for the restoration.

21. The Archdukes Felix and Karl Ludwig refused to the end to sign the renunciation pledge and, in March 1996, successfully forced the government to abandon it by simply arriving, unannounced, in Vienna.

22. Otto von Habsburg, in conversation with the author, Pöcking, 18 October 1992.

23. More than once, he told the author, who became a personal friend, that he regarded himself as the bridge between Austria's past and present.

24. Otto von Habsburg, in conversation with the author, Pöcking, 18 September 1992.

25. The 'Centre of European Documentation and Information'.

26. Letter from Otto von Habsburg to the author, 8 October 1999.

Notes to Chapter 15: 'Mr Europe'

1. Including the author who, in the 1970s, attended one such gathering as part of a Conservative Party group, the first to venture on such unfamiliar ground. (Also attending was a Chinese Communist delegation, who were investigating Strauss as a possible helpmate against the Soviet Union!)

2. Conversation with the author at Pöcking, 18 September 1982.

3. This incident was witnessed by the author who, fulfilling a long-standing promise, followed Otto von Habsburg for a few days on this first election campaign.

4. Other factions also shifted like a moving sea bed over the years. Thus, by the 1990s, the Socialists had become the Party of Socialist Europeans, or PSE; twenty-nine Italian members had formed their own Forza Europa, or FE; and the French Gaullists, the Greens, the Liberals and the Radicals all had their own factions.

5. The bureaucrats of the Brussels Commission suffered under similar popular suspicions, which were confirmed in alarming fashion when serious cases of nepotism and blatant corruption were unveiled in the late 1990s.

6. Otto von Habsburg to the author, 1 December 2000.

7. Later on, he was to champion the cause of Chechnya in its struggle for independence against Russia. His efforts led him to be nominated by the Chechnyan Parliament an 'honorary citizen' of the battered country.
8. European Parliament Session Documents, A3–193/90 and A3–0257/92.
9. Ibid.
10. Letter from Otto von Habsburg to the author, 5 July 2001.
11. Passed on to the author, with the memento of a three-inch rusty fragment cut from the barbed wire at the Sopron crossing. She sent similar souvenirs to several other of her friends.
12. In preparation for the now inevitable dismantling of the entire border wire, the Budapest authorities had already prepared their face-saving exercise. The 'fortifications' were in a bad state of disrepair and the government had no available funds to replace them.
13. One argument Otto von Habsburg used was that Arab recognition would help protect the Moslems caught up in the conflict. The massacre of seven thousand of them at Srebrenica showed this to be a vain hope.
14. The official Croatian records show that Moroccan recognition was declared ten days later, on 27 April 1992. Other Arab states followed at irregular intervals over the next two years, but Egypt had beaten Morocco to it. Together with Israel, she announced her recognition on 16 April 1992, the very day of Otto von Habsburg's talks.
15. From a long memorandum by Otto von Habsburg to the author of 1 December 2000.

Notes to Chapter 16: Balance Sheet

1. Made available to the author *in toto*, thanks to the excellent archive retrieval service of the European Parliament.
2. He took the view, which would have been welcomed by fishermen of all types, commercial or sporting, that these birds had become overprotected, and were thus endangering fish stocks.
3. In all but the last-named, his mastery was written as well as spoken.
4. European Parliament Debates, 14 November 1995, no. 4, 47036.
5. European Parliament Debates, no. 3, 411/104.
6. European Parliament Debates, 16 January 1986, no. 2, 334/189.
7. European Parliamentary Debates, no. 4, 457/3.
8. Speech of 6 April 1995, European Parliament Debates, no. 4, 461/194.
9. Speech of 13 June 1995, European Parliament Debates, no. 4, 464/76.
10. European Parliamentary Debates, no. 4, 461/4 (author's italics).
11. European Parliamentary Debates, no. 4, 469/204.
12. A woman, Inga-Britt Ahlenius, the Swedish Auditor-General, was eventually drafted in to avoid any impression of anti-feminism. Her credentials as an independent judge were impeccable.
13. Otto von Habsburg to the author, 26 February 1999.

14. One of the first to warn Otto of the danger was his ardent supporter, the Austrian industrialist Heinrich Turnauer.

15. The author was at a private dinner party, given in Vienna soon after the wedding. He was seated between two ladies of irreproachable character and lineage, each of whom had been given the coveted Star Cross Order, which was in the keeping of the wife of the head of the House of Habsburg. 'How can the Emperor [Otto] do this to us?' they bemoaned. 'After Regina, she will be the head of our Order!' Another world indeed.

Notes to Chapter 17: Royal Endgame

1. The ceremony is described at length in *Le Figaro* of 11 May 2001.

2. She more than made up for her junior rank with her stirring speech. 'Otto von Habsburg', she declared, 'has done more on Austria's behalf than some of its 150 per cent Republicans.'

3. They included a former President of free Hungary, Árpád Göncz, and a onetime member of the current government, Peter Harrach, the Minister for Social and Family Affairs. As at Nancy and Mariazell, official representation had been tailored to republican dimensions.

4. Winston Churchill, then British Prime Minister, had declared a suite at London's Claridge's Hotel to be Yugoslav territory for the day of his birth.

5. The recent occupant of one of them, the so-called White Palace, was the disgraced former President of Yugoslavia, Slobodan Milosevic. He had exchanged their chandeliers for the light bulb of his prison cell in The Hague, where he was awaiting trial as a war criminal.

6. Letter from Otto von Habsburg to the author, 1 July 2001.

7. The author remembers one such occasion in the winter of 1992 when he and his wife were among those attending a special memorial service for the King Emperor Karl at the abbey of Tihany, the scene of his confinement by the Entente powers after the failure of the second restoration bid. The last person to arrive at the crowded church was Otto von Habsburg – in an official car escorted by six motorcycle policemen.

8. The 'Friday Club', however, with which he had been most closely associated, melted away soon after he did and Strasbourg returned, with relief, to a four-day week.

9. From a long memorandum by Otto von Habsburg to the author, 1 December 2000. He cited the project, launched very early on, for a European army as a prime example of premature planning.

10. A reversal of his earlier thinking, which regarded Russia as 'too Asiatic' for membership.

11. Debates of the European Parliament, no. 4, 539/355.

12. His very last words to the Strasbourg Parliament had been: 'We are a cultural continent and we should remember that this is the most abiding feature which Europe possesses'.

13. At the time this was written, 'Pan-European International' counted probably no more than 15,000 members, but they nonetheless covered some forty organisations operating in twenty-seven countries.

14. Her brother, the ill-starred Karl von Habsburg, still, however, featured as the movement's President for Austria.

15. Typical examples were *Entscheidung für Europa* ('Decision Time for Europe') (1958); and *Europa – Grossmacht oder Schlachtfeld* ('Europe – Great Power or Battlefield') (1965).

16. One of the reasons why he had always fought shy of writing his own auto-biography was the impossibility of recalling – even from his formidable memory – what had been discussed only on condition it should never be published.

Bibliography

The next thirty pages could be filled with a list of the works, in various languages, that I have at some time read on European history in the twentieth century – which is the framework of Otto von Habsburg's life and times. Indeed, a page would be needed if I counted up all the books, articles, documentaries and contributions to joint studies I have produced myself over the past fifty years. Little of this is necessary in the present context.

The historian or specialised reader can find all the references he needs in any major history of the period. Thus, C. A. Macartney's *The Habsburg Empire* (London, 1968) lists some 700 mostly familiar works in what is described as 'only a highly selective short list'. The German scholar will find a similar description given to the 900 titles which the late Friedrich Heer cites in his monumental *Der Kampf um die Österreichische Identität* (Vienna, 1981). All that I propose to mention here are a few general works of reference and, of greater interest, studies which contain new source material covering the consecutive sections of the story, especially when they concern Otto himself. To make access easier for the general reader, I have wherever possible chosen English translations or original English language works. These are small in number compared with the mass of German material available, but several are recent.

Thus, on *fin de siècle* Vienna there is *The Garden and the Workshop* by Peter Hannák (Princeton, 1998); *Vienna 1900*, edited by Edward Timms (Edinburgh, 1990); *The Viennese Enlightenment*, edited by Mark Francis (London, 1985); and a very perceptive work, *The Austrian Mind*, by William Johnston (California University Press, 1972). These give insights into, for example, the Viennese obsession with death at the turn of the century, a subject that I had only the space to touch upon.

The first full account in English of the collapse of the Habsburg Monarchy and the royal family's first years in exile is given in Gordon Brook-Shepherd, *The Last Habsburg* (London, 1968), which drew not only on private archives but on the reminiscences and diaries of the late Empress Zita. For the failed restoration attempts and the Emperor's last years in exile, two works by Karl Werkmann, *Der Tote auf Madeira* (Munich, 1923) and *Aus Kaiser Karls Nachlass* (Berlin, 1925), are of special interest. The latter is based on testimony given by the Emperor himself before his premature death in April 1922. An account of the period drawing on Hungarian source material is given in *Ein Königsdrama im Schatten Hitlers* by Emilio Vasari (Vienna, 1968).

The story of young Otto's upbringing in Spanish and Belgian exile is given, in his mother's words, in Gordon Brook-Shepherd, *The Last Empress* (London, 1991). The political turmoil in his Austrian homeland at the time sprang from deep ideological conflicts, which have been reflected in most of the works written afterwards about the twenty-year life of the First Austrian Republic. The socialist camp predominates in autobiographies: notably Otto Bauer in *The Austrian Revolution* (Vienna, 1923); Oskar Helmer in *50 Jahre erlebte Geschichte* (Vienna, 1957); Adolf Schärf in *Österreichs Erneuerung* (Vienna, 1955); and Julius Deutsch, in *Ein weiter Weg* (Zürich, 1960).

The right-wing or 'patriotic' side of the argument is presented in the exculpatory works of the republic's last ill-fated Chancellor, Kurt von Schuschnigg, notably *Im Kampf gegen Hitler* (Vienna, 1969). There is also my own *The Austrian Odyssey* (London, 1957) and *The Anschluss* (London, 1963). Martin Fuchs, one of Otto's closest allies, wrote a valuable account of the republic's final years in *Un pacte avec Hitler* (Paris, 1938).

There have been several attempts by Austrian academics to produce objective accounts of the First Republic's life, such as Walter Goldinger's *Geschichte der Republik Österreich* (Munich, 1962) and Heinrich Benedikt's work, with the same title (Vienna, 1954). But it is hardly possible to treat such controversial subject matter with a bland non-controversial approach. More readable, and very well documented, are *Der Staat der keiner wollte* (Vienna, 1962) by the Austrian journalist Hellmuth Andics, and *50 Jahre unseres Lebens* (Vienna, 1968) by the same author. As with the proceeding works, there are no English translations.

From his exile in America, Otto tried constantly to discover what was going on in his annexed homeland and to stimulate resistance to Hitler. The truth could only be pieced together afterwards in a number of studies, including Richard Grunberger's *Das zwölfjährige Reich* (Vienna, 1972) and the 600-page *Wien vom Anschluss zum Krieg* by Gerhard Botz (Vienna, 1980). Neither exists in translation but one of the very best studies on Austria under Nazi rule is in English: Radomir Luza's *Austro-German Relations in the Anschluss Era* (Princeton, 1975). Its footnotes alone are a goldmine of information.

As to the resistance on which Otto had placed some hope, this proved to be negligible in the context of the Allied struggle against Hitler. The brave if ineffective attempts that were made are described by Otto Molden in *Der*

Ruf des Gewissens (Vienna, 1958) and by his brother Fritz Molden in *Fires in the Night* (London, 1989).

There is little or nothing, beyond the relevant chapters in the present work, on Otto's activity in wartime American exile. Eric Feigl, in his *Protokoll eines politischen Lebens* (Vienna, 1987), produces some interesting documents from President Roosevelt's own archives, though without any information or analysis concerning the royal exile's fascinating friendship with the republican democratic leader. Winston Churchill was Otto's main hope in trying to install some form of post-war conservative federation in the Danube Basin (the next best thing to Habsburg restoration). Volumes 5 and 6 of Churchill's own memoirs (London, 1952 and 1954) show how this hope was gradually extinguished as Stalin's influence came to dominate Allied councils.

The best guide to Otto's twenty-year term as a member of the European Parliament are the hundreds of his own speeches, submissions, reports and interventions, of which the full texts are all available in the excellent archives of that institution. He was the first to protest against the artificial East-West division which had split the post-war continent, psychologically as well as physically. Like everyone else, however, he had to await the sudden implosion of Soviet Communism before the rift could be mended.

Index